Scholars, Scoundrels, and the Sphinx

Figure 1. The Sphinx

Albumen print
Photographer: G. Lékékian & Co.
Frank H. McClung Museum, 3/655
Gift of Marcia S. Young, 1992

The divine Great Sphinx, the embodiment of pharaonic power, fixes his gaze on eternity. Artisans carved the monument in the form of a lion about two hundred and forty feet long out of a living limestone knoll on the Gizeh plateau. The recumbent figure has the body of a lion with the head of a pharaoh. Probably representing King Khafre, one of the builders of the three great pyramids at Gizeh, the sphinx wears the royal *nemes*, or striped head cloth. Traces of the now-missing royal cobra that once centered over his brow can be seen. At some time the head was badly damaged. It has been said that Napoleon's troops took potshots at the face in the late Eighteenth Century. Fragments of a former royal beard were found in the sand. In its glory days the statue may have been coated with gesso and brightly painted.

Scholars, Scoundrels, and the Sphinx:

A Photographic and Archaeological Adventure up the Nile

BY
Elaine Altman Evans

Frank H. McClung Museum
The University of Tennessee

This catalogue is published in conjunction with the exhibition *Scholars, Scoundrels, and the Sphinx: A Photographic and Archaeological Adventure up the Nile.*

Frank H. McClung Museum
The University of Tennessee
January 29–July 30, 2000

Curator
Elaine Altman Evans

Occasional Paper Number 14

Published by
Frank H. McClung Museum
The University of Tennessee
1327 Circle Park Drive
Knoxville, Tennessee 37996-3200
Telephone : (865) 974-2144

Design and production assistance provided by Creative Services, University Relations, the University of Tennessee (job # 5056):
Charles T. Thomas, Designer; Kathryn Aycock, Production Editor; Penny Brooks, Production Coordinator; Robert Hillhouse, Local Photographer

COVER PHOTOGRAPHS (identification and information): FRONT COVER, UPPER LEFT: Figure 4–15, see page 56. FRONT COVER, UPPER RIGHT: Figure 7–3, see page 83. FRONT COVER, BOTTOM: Figure 5–5, see page 63. BACK COVER: Figure 5–8, see page 67.

Publication Authorization Number: R01-0130-48-001-01

2,000 copies printed by Ambrose Printing Co., Nashville, Tenn., July 2000.

ISBN 1-880174-04-9

Table of Contents

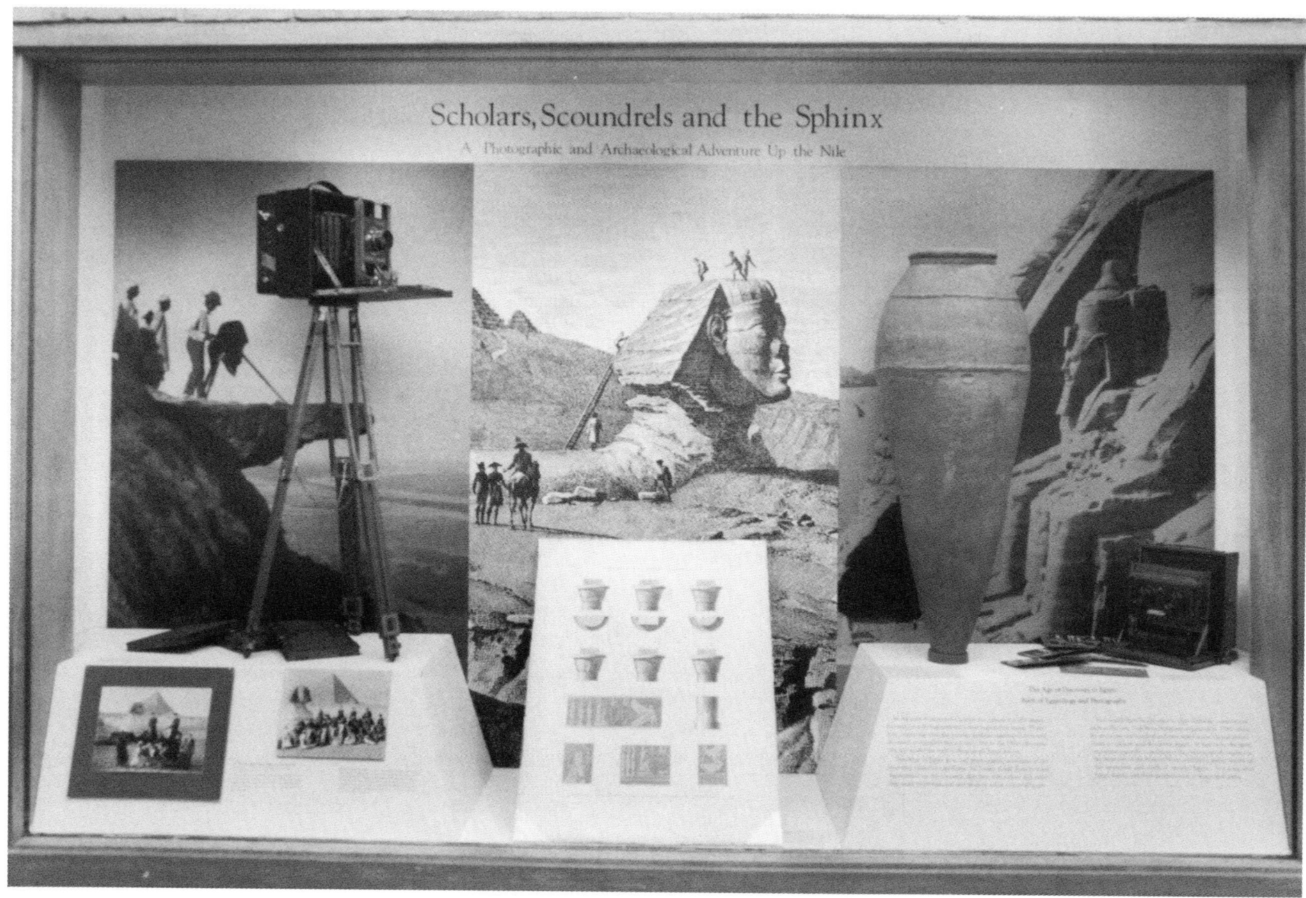

Figure 2. Entrance Case to the Exhibition *(Scholars, Scoundrels, and the Sphinx: A Photographic and Archaeological Adventure up the Nile)*

BACKGROUND BLOWUPS, LEFT TO RIGHT: • Photograph by Lindsey Foote Hall of Harry Burton on an outcropping above the Valley of the Kings, Thebes, 1920s. Courtesy of University Archives, University of Oregon Library System, Eugene. • Engraving of Napoleon's soldiers at Gizeh, 1798-1801. From *La Description de l'Égypte*, 1821. • Photograph by J. Pascal Sébah of the facade of the mortuary temple of Rameses II at Abu Simbel, circa 1870-1890. McClung Museum Photographic Archives: 1996.10.27. Gift of Friends of Egyptology, 1996. *CENTER, LEFT TO RIGHT:* • "Century" Field View Camera and Glass Plate Holders, made in Rochester, New York, 1907, are similar to those used in Egypt. Anonymous Lender. • Light Red Earthenware Jar, Dynasty I, excavated by W.M. Flinders Petrie in 1899 at Abydos. Courtesy The University of Pennsylvania Museum: E 6942. • "Royal Ruby Stereocamera," Thornton-Picard, Altrinchram, England, 1896. The camera has a "time and Instant" shutter, a "Busch Detective Applanat, No. 2" lens, and a 4-1/2" x 6-1/2" field of view. Anonymous Lender. *BOTTOM, LEFT TO RIGHT:* • Photograph of Mr. And Mrs. Louis B. Audigier of Knoxville at the Great Sphinx at Gizeh, 1913. McClung Museum Photographic Archives: A1: 161 C136 IP. Gift of Mr. and Mrs. Louis Bailey Audigier, 1934. • Phoebe Hearst and Egyptologist George A. Reisner pose with friends at Gizeh, circa 1903. Courtesy Phoebe Hearst Museum of Anthropology, University of California at Berkeley. • Original Engraving of capital details and bas-reliefs at Temple of Khnum at Esneh from *La Description de l'Égypte*, 1821. McClung Museum Photographic Archives: 1997.5.31. Gift of Friends of Egyptology, 1997.

Foreword

Interest in ancient Egypt is timeless. As I write this, there are five major exhibitions in the United States; magazines pick up on every discovery; and the Learning and Discovery Channels are filled with wonderful programs on the subject. *Scholars, Scoundrels, and the Sphinx: A Photographic and Archaeological Adventure up the Nile* is indeed current and it addresses an eager audience.

In 1984 Curator Elaine A. Evans brought Egypt to the McClung Museum with a small exhibition titled "Burial Practices in Ancient Egypt." The popularity of this installation led to the formation of the Friends of Egyptology, who, through trips to Egypt and exhibitions, raised funds for the occasional purchase of Egyptian antiquities. It also stimulated the installation of a permanent gallery in 1992—*Ancient Egypt: The Eternal Voice*. The purchase of one hundred forty items from the Toledo Museum of Art and the long-term loan of a number of objects from major museums around the country provided the nucleus of a wonderful overview of ancient Egyptian history and culture. The exhibition continues to be pivotal in the Museum's educational programming, with forty-nine percent of last year's school groups selecting docent-led instruction in the gallery.

As we begin the new millennium, it is both fitting and humbling to revisit a civilization that began more than five thousand years ago. What we know today about ancient Egypt has much of its basis in the discoveries and scholarship of the Nineteenth and early Twentieth Centuries. Elaine Evans is to be commended for bringing together both photographs and objects that tell that story.

Exhibitions are fundamental to the Museum's mission of advancing understanding and appreciation of the earth and its people. This catalogue is an important part of the exhibit process, as it affords the visitor an opportunity to take home a portion of the experience and to explore further the story of the emergence of Egyptology.

Jefferson Chapman, Ph.D.
Director
Frank H. McClung Museum

Acknowledgments

A special thanks is extended to several people who so kindly gave of their time in making the exhibition and catalogue possible. I am particularly indebted to those institutions that granted the loan of and helped me in the selection of objects for the exhibition. The efforts of David Silverman and Denise Doxey (University of Pennsylvania Museum) and Alexandro Pezzati (University Museum Archives) are greatly appreciated, as are the interest and assistance of William Peck and Penelope Slough (Department of Ancient Art, Detroit Institute of Arts) and Gloria Greis (Peabody Museum of Archaeology and Ethnology, Harvard University) on numerous occasions.

A word of recognition for their special help in expediting the loan arrangements is extended to Joan Knudsen (Phoebe Hearst Museum of Anthropology, University of California at Berkeley), Genevieve Fisher (Peabody Museum of Archaeology and Ethnology, Harvard University), Xiuguin Zhou (University of Pennsylvania), and Deborah Harding (Carnegie Museum of Natural History, Pittsburgh).

Those members of organizations who contributed or provided photographic copy prints used in the exhibition and catalogue or granted access to my study of early original print collections are also gratefully acknowledged: C. E. S. Gavin and Elizabeth Carella (Archives of Historical Documentation, Brighton, Massachusetts); from the Metropolitan Museum of Art I would like to thank Dorothea Arnold (Egyptian Department), Paul Caro (Education, Film and Media Department) for arranging the loan of a live-coverage video of the Tutankhamen discovery produced by the Trustees of the British Museum, Mary Doherty (Photographs and Slide Library), and Nora Kennedy (Paper Conservation Department); from the Library of Congress, Verna Curtis and Mary Ison (Photographs, Prints, and Photographic Division) and Margaret Kieckhefer (Photo Duplication Division); Linda Long and Wil Harmon (University of Oregon Archives); John Larsen and Anne Yanaway (Oriental Institute Museum Archives, University of Chicago); Charles Kline (Photographic Archives, University of Pennsylvania Museum); Sylvia Inwood (Photograph Department, Detroit Institute of Arts); Kathleen Bailey (Interlibrary Loan, University of Tennessee); Barbara Takiguchi (Programs, Phoebe Hearst Museum of Anthropology); and Nasrin Rohani (Photographic Archives, Peabody Museum of Archaeology and Ethnology). My sincere appreciation also goes to Jeff Spurr (Aga Khan Program, Harvard University), who assisted me in examining the photographic collection housed in the Fine Arts Library. I am also greatly indebted to John W. Pye of Brockton, Massachusetts, for his generosity in alerting me to the rare, original photographs in his collection and making them available for purchase.

If it had not been for the dedicated attention of the University of Tennessee's Kathryn Aycock, Chuck Thomas, and Penny Brooks (Creative Services) and Robert Hillhouse (Photography Center)—who provided their expertise and talent in editing, layout, design, and photographic images—the completion of this publication would not have been possible. A great debt is owed to Amy Hill, my Student Assistant at McClung Museum, who with cheerful willingness completed the meanest as well as the fun tasks so important to the project. A hearty thank you to Mary and Kenneth Carpenter of Knoxville, who donated their time and expertise in identifying the various technical processes used in the original photographs, and to Robert Toal, who so ably assisted in the dating of the postcards.

Finally, a very special note of appreciation and gratitude to all the staff members of the McClung Museum. A hearty thank you to Jefferson Chapman, the director, for his support and encouragement. Complements to Steve Long and Charles Hurst of the Museum's Exhibition Department for the installation of the exhibition, including their construction and installation of a great faux pylon. Many thanks go to the Registration, Education, Photography, and Secretarial Departments, whose members worked so diligently and enthusiastically right down to the finish line to make this exhibition happen on schedule.

Introduction

The period covered in the catalogue, from 1850 to 1930, considers the formative years in the development of photography and Egyptology. It was the time of great fascination with ancient Egypt and the sunrise for scholars and photographers of the Nile Valley. It was an exciting and dramatic stage in the emergence of an intense interest and study of Egypt and its treasures. Egypt experienced the development of museums that led to the emergence of the Egyptian Museum in Cairo. People were taken on a journey into that ancient world and experienced a sense of a truly remarkable culture.

This exhibition was sparked by a 1992 gift by Ms. Marcia S. Young to the Frank H. McClung Museum of a number of early albumen prints of the Nile Valley. These prints joined other similar photographs of Egypt in the Museum's photographic archives collection, given to the University of Tennessee in 1934 by Louis Bailey Audigier in memory of his wife, Eleanor Deane Audigier of Knoxville. The Audigiers bought the prints during a trip to the Nile Valley in 1913. I had become familiar with the prints and realized that with a few additions we had the makings of an exhibition. Fortunately, a number of prints for purchase came to my attention from John W. Pye of Brockton, Massachusetts. Using a modest fund set up a number of years ago by the Friends of Egyptology, a local group interested in ancient Egypt, I was able to acquire prints to fill in the gaps.

After recognizing that photography and Egyptology began to evolve around the same time, it seemed worthwhile to present a few of the first photographers who recorded the monuments of Egypt together with some of the first Egyptologists who documented ancient Egyptian culture. The importance of their respective contributions show that both promoted new knowledge of and interest in ancient Egypt. Both disciplines—photography and Egyptology—were emerging as exciting new tools of science and were, in their own way, describing the significance of ancient Egypt to the world. A bond developed between them. By 1869 the Egyptologists were progressing well with their excavations and extraordinary finds, and the photographers were busy capturing on film much that had long been hidden under Egyptian sands. As a result, a worldwide interest grew. Egypt realized the importance of its past, and a major museum eventually was established in Cairo by progressive thinkers who saw the need to preserve Egypt's heritage.

Some eighty original photographic images of both well-known and less-visited sites along the Nile were selected from the McClung Museum's collection of early prints, stereoviews, and postcards. The prints illustrate in great measure why people came to Egypt and what had seized their imagination. A number of special photographers produced remarkable images of the Nile Valley, and with this emerging technology they documented scenes of enduring value. They witnessed the state of monuments in the late Nineteenth and early Twentieth Centuries, and their photographs awakened a curiosity in people to learn more.

There are fifty-eight excavated objects in the exhibition, which mostly parallel the work of the commercial photographers. The objects were borrowed from several American museums to complement the prints and to illustrate the simultaneous development of both disciplines. The ancient pieces had been acquired as a share of their own museum's excavations, were gifts from Egyptological funding institutions as part of their archaeological work in Egypt, or were gifts to the museums from donors who had travelled in Egypt.

Also featured are selections from scholars active in Egypt between 1850 and 1930. The list is long of those who contributed in large and small ways toward the understanding of Egypt. A few of the important Egyptologists and archaeologists, photographers and studios, dealers and travellers, and pashas and khedives are highlighted. Among them were individuals who greatly distinguished themselves by creating countless photographic images, making important archaeological discoveries, producing eagerly awaited publications, or contributing in some other meaningful way. Mentioned are a few well-known Egyptologists active in Egypt between 1850 and 1930, such as Auguste Mariette, Gaston Maspero, George A. Reisner, James Henry Breasted, William Matthew Flinders Petrie, and Howard Carter. Among the many skilled commercial photographers who produced fine photographs of important monuments of Egypt are Félix Teynard, the Bonfils family, Antonio Beato, Francis Frith, J. Pascal Sébah, and Zangaki. A brief account is given of a few of the archaeological excavations going on during this eighty-year period, such as at Gizeh (the home of the Great Pyramid and eternal Sphinx); at the Apis bull cemetery of the Serapeum at Sakkara; at the temples at Abydos, Dendereh, Karnak, and Luxor; and at the royal tombs in the Valley of Kings at Thebes. Important work also was being done at Esneh, Edfu, Kom Ombo, and Philae; at such Nubian sites as the great mortuary temples of Rameses II and his wife, Nefretiri, at Abu Simbel; and in discoveries made further south at Kerma at the Third Cataract. The monuments at these and other sites became beehives of archaeological and photographic activity. Egyptian and foreign governmental officials, who also played a role in facilitating archaeological and photographic work, are touched upon. Other notables, and those not so notable, who had a connection to the sites and/or the objects in the exhibition were not forgotten.

In conclusion, the author apologizes and assumes responsibility for any important omissions or errors of judgment: the omissions are unintended, and the errors are strictly her own.

Elaine A. Evans

Elaine Altman Evans
Curator / Adjunct Assistant Professor
January, 2000

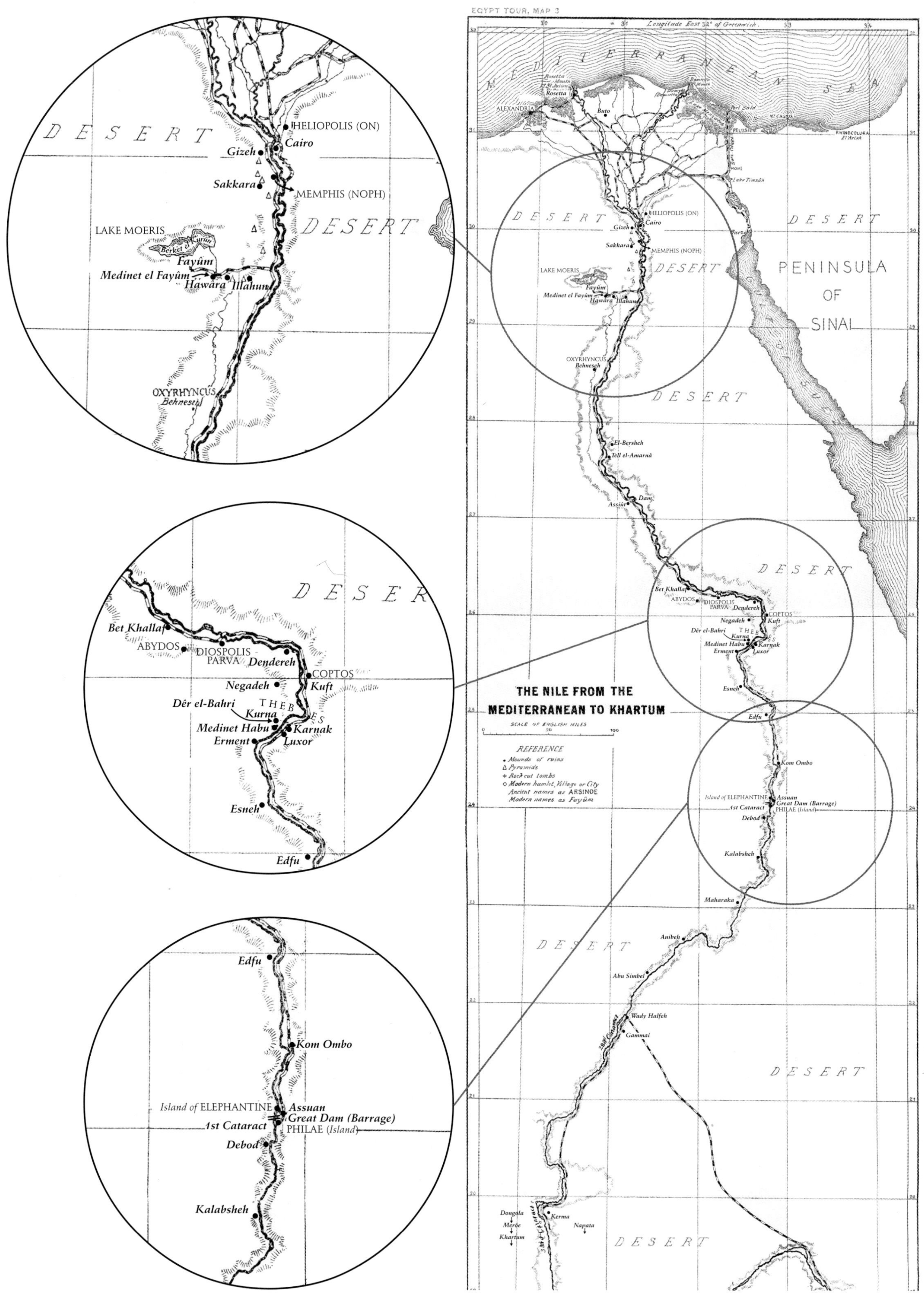
EGYPT TOUR, MAP 3
Longitude East 32° of Greenwich
MEDITERRANEAN SEA
Rosetta
ALEXANDRIA
Buto
Port Said
PELUSIUM
DESERT
PENINSULA OF SINAI
HELIOPOLIS (ON)
Cairo
Gizeh
Sakkara
MEMPHIS (NOPH)
LAKE MOERIS
Berket el Kurûn
Fayûm
Medinet el Fayûm
Hawâra
Illahun
OXYRHYNCUS
Behneseh
El-Bersheh
Tell el-Amarnâ
Assiût
Dam
Bet Khallaf
ABYDOS
DIOSPOLIS PARVA
Dendereh
COPTOS
Kuft
Negadeh
Dêr el-Bahri
THEBES
Kurna
Medinet Habu
Karnak
Erment
Luxor
Esneh
Edfu
Kom Ombo
Island of ELEPHANTINE
Assuan
Great Dam (Barrage)
1st Cataract
PHILAE (Island)
Debod
Kalabsheh
Maharaka
Anibeh
Abu Simbel
Wady Halfeh
Gammai
Dongola
Meroe
Khartum
Kerma
Napata
THE NILE FROM THE MEDITERRANEAN TO KHARTUM
SCALE OF ENGLISH MILES
0 50 100
REFERENCE
• Mounds of ruins
Δ Pyramids
+ Rock cut tombs
○ Modern hamlet, Village or City
Ancient names as ARSINOE
Modern names as Fayûm

Timeline

Egypt From the Predynastic Period to the Modern Era*

Predynastic Period	4000–circa 3200 B.C.	
Late Predynastic Period	3200–3000 B.C.	
Early Dynastic Period	3000–2700 B.C.	Dynasty I–II
Old Kingdom	2700–2230 B.C.	Dynasty III–VI
First Intermediate Period	2230–2050 B.C.	Dynasty VII–X
Middle Kingdom	2050–1750 B.C.	Dynasty XI–XII
Second Intermediate Period	1750–1552 B.C.	Dynasty XIII–XVII
New Kingdom	1552–1080 B.C.	Dynasty XVIII–XX
Third Intermediate Period	1080–525 B.C.	Dynasty XXI–XXV
Late Dynastic Period	525–332 B.C.	Dynasty XXVI–XXX
Ptolemaic Period	332–30 B.C.	Alexander the Great conquers Egypt and Ptolemaic royal house rules
Roman and Byzantine Periods	30 B.C.–circa A.D. 395	Egypt becomes a Roman province
Islamic Period	circa A.D. 639–1250	
Mameluke Period	A.D. 1250–1517	
First Ottoman Period	A.D. 1517–1798	
French Period	A.D. 1798–1805	
Second Ottoman Period	A.D. 1805–1952	
British Control	A.D. 1883–1936	

*Adapted from the chronologies in Michael A. Hoffman's *The First Egyptians*, Columbia, The McKissick Museum and the Earth Sciences and Resources Institute, the University of South Carolina, 1988, and from Joan W. King's *Historical Dictionary of Egypt*, African Historical Dictionaries, No. 36., New Jersey/London, Scarecrow Press, 1984.

NOTES

Spellings: Spellings of Egyptian place names and personal names used by scholars between 1850 and 1930 were not uniform and various Egyptologists continued to make changes. Therefore, in keeping with the period covered, the author has chosen, whenever possible, to use the orthography in James Henry Breasted's *A History of Egypt*, 1905, and in Gaston Maspero's *Egyptian Archaeology*, 1889.

Publications: The publications cited in text entries in the catalogue are selected research sources that were mostly published during 1850 through 1930. They are listed for those interested in further reading about the site or object being addressed.

Map: The map on the opposite page was adapted from James Henry Breasted's *Egypt Through the Stereoscope. A Journey Through the Land of the Pharaohs*, published by Underwood & Underwood, 1908.

Figure 3. Pot

Predynastic Period
Object: earthenware
21.8 high x 9.0 cm. diameter (8-5/8 x 3-1/2 inches)
Provenance: Diospolis Parva: HU H228
Excavated by Flinders Petrie, 1889–1890
Egypt Exploration Fund, 1900
The Carnegie Museum of Natural History, Pittsburgh: 11678-89

The long, rounded body of buff-orange, alluvial clay and red slip tapers to a pointed end. A ridge encircles a short, wide neck below a wide, convex, rolled rim. The jar is typical of a type which Petrie called "Rough-faced Pottery, Class R." They were found one to a grave and always at the end of the grave.

CHAPTER

The First Explorers of the Nile Valley

Exploration has been continuous and is as old as life itself. Every living creature in its own way possesses the need to search new terrain. People have naturally sought the excitement of exploring places where no one else has been.

This was no less true in the time of the early Egyptians. One of the earliest of human nomadic groups in the world was in the Nile Valley, where roving peoples looked to settle and took advantage of the great waterway as their source of survival. Exploration in Egypt was not confined to the Nineteenth century but began in the Paleolithic Period, 700,000 B.C., the time of the first appearance of humans in the Nile Valley. The earliest Egyptians themselves explored the land on either side of the Nile, the western shores of the Red Sea and down from Suez to what is now Eritrea and Somalia. But it was the Nile that was their focus in the search for likely places to settle. It was along those rich alluvial banks.

Later, as the population expanded and settlements were established, the people of Egypt developed into a complex society capable of building colossal monuments and deeply hidden tombs located on both sides of the Nile River, from Lower Nubia (Sudan) all the way to the Mediterranean Sea, a distance of some one thousand and seventy miles. These stone reminders preserve the history of a once-great civilization. The hieroglyphic inscriptions that decorate the columns, walls, pylons and the colorful tomb paintings and unique tomb and temple treasures all document important events, religious mysteries, and daily life of the ancient Egyptians. Tombs and temples also record some of the countless expeditions to and explorations of various foreign regions including Syria, Lebanon, southern Palestine, and Punt (probably Ethiopia).

One ancient Egyptian tomb that documents an important early explorer belongs to the nobleman Harkhuf, who was a governor of the South and wearer of the royal seal. His Old Kingdom rock tomb on the West Bank across from Assuan, discovered by the British excavator Francis W. Grenfell in 1885 and 1886, records four explorations to Nubia in the distant south. On his last significant expedition to Yam, a country possibly in the area of Dongola and Kerma, Harkhuf, accompanied by his army, returned with "all great and beautiful gifts" and including "a dancing dwarf...from the land of spirits...."[1] The dwarf was quite unique and so impressed the reigning pharaoh Pepi II that the king wrote the explorer Harkhuf a letter requesting him to

> *Come northward to the court immediately; ...thou shalt bring this dwarf with thee... for the dances of the god, to rejoice and [gladden] the heart of the king of Upper and Lower Egypt....*[2]

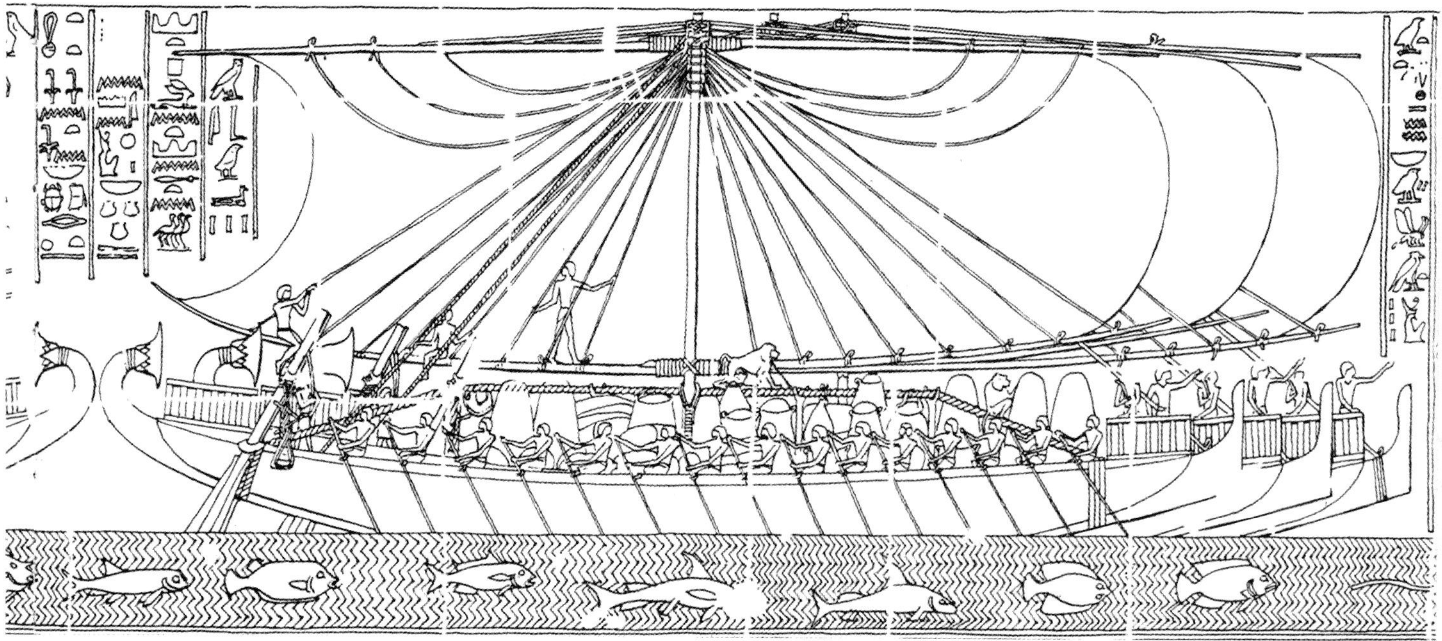

Figure 1–1. Queen Hatshepsut's fleet

The illustration is adapted from a relief in the mortuary temple of Queen Hatshepsut at Der el-Bahri of expeditionary ships sent in early Dynasty XVIII to the land of Punt for incense, myrrh, ivory, ebony and other valuables. Thebes, circa 1492 B.C.

Harkhuf had the esteemed letter inscribed on the facade of his tomb to record his historic and much appreciated discoveries in uncharted regions.

> *The majesty of Merinere…my lord, sent me, together with my father,…to Yam, in order to explore a road to this country. I did it in only seven months, and I brought all [kinds of] gifts from it….*[3]

Other explorers recorded their travels, such as the high-ranking nobleman and caravan leader named Pepi-nakht, whose titles included governor of foreign countries and ritual priest. His campaign-explorations in Nubia are found in seven columns on each side of the door of the facade of his Old Kingdom cliff-tomb near that of Harkhuf. The inscription tells of the commodities he brought back from his expeditions. However, an important assignment for him was the exploratory voyage he took along the coast of the Red Sea. There he was to recover the body of a certain slain captain of ships, royal companion and caravan leader. He had been killed while "…building a ship there for Punt, when the Asiatics…slew him…."[4]

An expedition carved in relief on the walls of the well-known mortuary temple of Queen Hatshepsut of the New Kingdom at Der el-Bahri, Thebes, shows an expedition to the land of Punt, circa 1492 B.C. Punt was a place no one really knew much about. Hatshepsut was able to boast of explorations to the mysterious land to collect valued ointments and gum of myrrh with which to please the god, Amen-Re, in offerings.

> *But I will cause thy army to tread them, I had led them on water and on land, to explore the waters of inaccessible channels, and I have reached the Myrrh-terraces [Punt].*[5]

This was no easy accomplishment. The expedition had to trek across a one hundred fifty-mile-wide Eastern Desert to the Red Sea and then navigate its waters some one thousand five hundred miles south for the return.

Many more in the ancient world were eager for knowledge of Egypt, having heard stories about this exotic land "where rain only seldom fell, and where the fields were fertilized by the annual inundation of a great river."[6] The early Greek travellers were amazed to find that a number of the gods worshipped there were their own but with different attributes or names. Ancient writers fanned the flame of interest in Egypt.

One such early scholar was Hecataeus of Miletus, an Ionian logographer, who was among the earliest Greeks to arrive in Egypt. His interest was in exploring the Nile River and its inundation, the Delta, and the animals of Egypt. He was less interested in the Egyptians themselves, or their history. However, a writer who was indeed curious about the Egyptians followed in his footsteps. He was the great Greek historian Herodotus of Halicarnassus, who wrote a valuable and extensive account of his expedition in Egypt, probably sometime after 449 B.C. He travelled to the First Cataract recording his thoughts as an explorer, observer, and listener to the stories related to him by the Egyptians he encountered along the way. Herodotus' visit included the Delta, Memphis, Thebes, and Elephantine. As a seeker of information with no knowledge of the Egyptian language, Herodotus does provide amazing details in much of his documentary about the wonders he found there and has added much, albeit not always accurately, to our understanding.

Another to be mentioned is Diodorus of Sicily, who was in Egypt in 59 B.C. for an unknown length of time. His famous "World History" written ca. 60-30 B.C., contains forty books.

Figure 1–2. Engraving of French soldiers at the Gizeh pyramids and the Great Sphinx

During his invasion of Egypt, Napoleon called his troops to the Battle of the Pyramids with the words: "Soldiers, forty centuries have their eyes on you." [7]

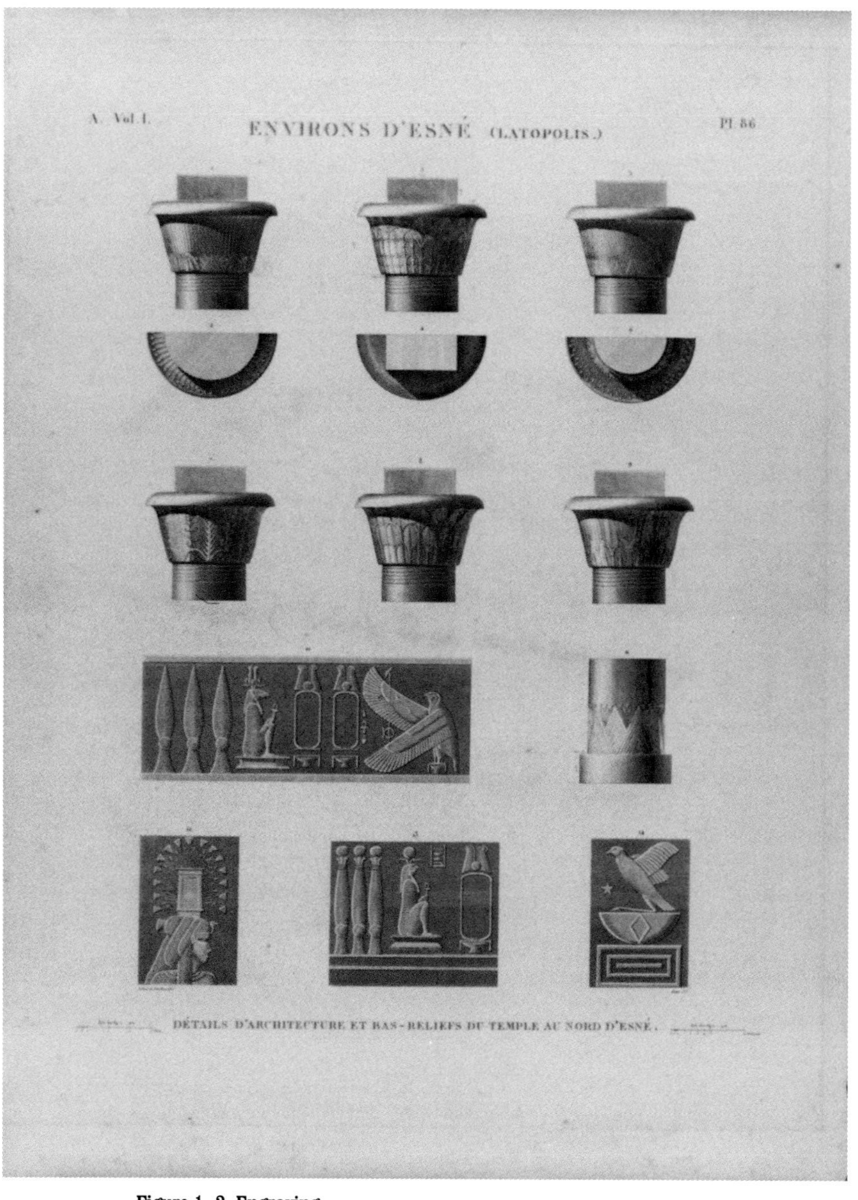

The first book is devoted to Egypt, its gods, ritual life of the kings, administration, justice and laws, and other customs.

The Greek historian and geographer Strabo (63 B.C.[?]-A.D. 21) went to Egypt to collect geographical information in 25-circa 19 B.C. Book Seventeen of his "Geography" includes Egypt, Ethiopia, and north Africa. Strabo remarks on some ninety-nine towns and settlements along the Nile to the border of Lower Nubia (Sudan).

Other ancients travelled to Egypt, such as the Romans who brought Egyptian obelisks back to Rome. But it was not until the Sixteenth and Seventeenth Centuries that various antiquarians explored Egypt to search for and study its ancient monuments and objects. In the Eighteenth Century fine books were published containing drawings, maps, and other more detailed illustrations, which proved to be invaluable documents that inspired a steady interest in Egypt. Hieroglyphic inscriptions were copied and studied. When the Rosetta Stone was discovered by a member of Napoleon Bonaparte's army in 1799, it caused another major flurry of scholarly excitement. The famous stone contained three inscribed registers written in demotic, in Greek, and in hieroglyphs. This important discovery led to the decipherment of Egyptian writing in 1822 to 1824 by the Frenchman Jean Françoise Champollion. By the Nineteenth Century not only were explorers attracted to Egypt, but ordinary travellers, who sought the delight of a fascinating and remote land. However, mostly only the wealthier could afford the trip. This created a certain status for those having made the journey.

Figure 1–3. Engraving

Object: Plate 86, A. Volume I: *La Description de l'Égypte.*
Paris: C.L.F. Panckoucke, 1821 [second edition]
51.8 wide x 71 cm. high (20-1/4 x 28 inches)
Frank H. McClung Museum: 1997.5.31
Gift of Friends of Egyptology, 1997

An original engraved plate illustrating architectural details and bas-reliefs from the Temple of Esneh. The plate is from the great publication produced after Napoleon Bonaparte's scientific commission went to Egypt in 1798. It comprises fourteen volumes of plates (eleven elephant size and three atlas size) and eleven letter press volumes.

Notes

1 *Records* I, p. 160.

2 ———, p. 161.

3 ———, p. 152-153.

4 ———, p. 163.

5 *Records* II, p. 117.

6 Gardiner, p. 1.

7 Clayton, *Rediscovery*, p. 15.

Credit

Figure 1–1 from *Ships of the Pharaohs* by Bjorn Landstrom, translated by Keith Bradfield, translation copyright © 1970 by International Book Production, Stockholm. Used by permission of Doubleday, a division of Random House, Inc.

Selected Bibliography:

Breasted, James Henry, *Ancient Records of Egypt*, Vols. I-V. New York: Russell & Russell, Inc., 1962.

Clayton, Peter, *The Rediscovery of Ancient Egypt*. London: Thames and Hudson, 1982.

Gardiner, Alan, *Egypt of the Pharaohs*. New York: Oxford University Press, 1966.

Godley, A. D., *Herodotus*, Book II. Cambridge: Harvard University Press; London: William Heinemann Ltd., 1936.

Jones, Horace Leonard, *The Geography of Strabo*, Vol. XVII. Cambridge: Harvard University Press, 1949.

Oldfather, C. H., *Diodorus of Sicily*, Book I. Cambridge: Harvard University Press; London: William Heinemann Ltd., 1936.

The long view of the Temple of Edfu, taken in 1850 by Félix Teynard, is the earliest represented in the exhibition. Teynard was one of the first commercial photographers to explore and record the Nile Valley. See Figure 3–55 on page 37.

Figure 2–1. Bonfils Photographic Expedition

Félix Bonfils, holding a parasol, is seated to the right of his son Adrien, while on a photographic expedition in Jordan in the 1880s. Their tent and attending butler are in the background.

Courtesy Archives of Historical Documentation (AHD). Fouad C. Debbas collection, Brighton, Massachusetts.

Commercial Photographers Set the Style

> *Were but the character of the pen for severe truthfulness as unimpeachable as that of the camera, what graphic pictures might they together paint!*[1]
>
> **—Francis Frith, 1860**

When one considers the type of temperament that was necessary for the taking of good photographs and making fine prints under often adverse conditions, one realizes the strength needed by these pioneers of photography in Egypt. They had to possess great perseverance under very difficult circumstances. There were many personal dangers, hardships, and perils, including the risk of exhaustion from the intense desert heat. They lugged cumbersome photographic equipment in rickety wagons from site to site across impossible roads and treacherous paths. Even when they used modest sailing vessels and were able to draw close to selected shores with all their photographic apparatus stored aboard, the site might be farther inland, and to reach it a laborious task. Much of the photographic process was done at the site.

Photographers came to the Middle East to establish themselves. Many had their own studios in the large cities, where they produced and sold their exotic products to the many travellers passing through Egypt. Not only were they taking commercial photographs of monuments for tourists, but a few, including Antonio Beato, were used by archaeologists and Egyptologists at their excavations as well. Photographers attracted the attention of such rulers as the Ottoman Sultan Abdül-Hamid II (1876–1909), a fervent photography buff. Photographers were encouraged in technical advances, and he patronized them and their studios. By his order, the empire was recorded in detail by photographers whom the Sultan commissioned. He collected photographs of the Middle East and compiled elaborate albums as well.

The world of Nineteenth Century photography in the Middle East was wide. Therefore, only those photographers whose work is in the exhibition will be mentioned below. It should be noted that these represent only a sampling of the hundred or more photographers that were active in the Middle East in the Nineteenth Century.

Figure 2–2. Francis Frith

The self-portrait shows Francis Frith dressed in an elaborate Turkish costume, 1856–1860.

The Photographers

Hippolyte Arnoux: In 1860 the French photographer established his studio in the environs of Port-Saïd where he often signed his photographs "Arnoux Photographie Port-Saïd." He photographed various stages during the building of the Suez Canal until its completion in 1869. A selection of albumen prints of the Suez Canal were brought together in *L'Album du Canal* in 1869. From 1869 his photographic work of genre scenes and studio-posed images was established. He was a partner to the ***C. & G. Zangaki Brothers.***

Antonio (Antoine) Beato (ca. 1825–ca. 1906): Possibly born on the Italian island of Venice, Antonio Beato and his younger brother Felice travelled to India in 1857, where they opened a studio in Calcutta. In 1862 Antonio Beato was making a living in Cairo and later in 1870 at Luxor, where he had also established a photographic studio near the Winter Palace Hotel. Antonio Beato is one of the first to photograph Egypt. His widespread coverage of Egypt was as monumental as the monuments he photographed. He may have been influenced in the 1850s by his brother-in-law, the photographer James Robertson. Robertson was working in Constantinople, the capital of the Ottoman empire, in 1852, probably with Felice Beato, who later went to China and then worked in Yokohama, Japan. "Robertson, Beato & Co." is on a number of circa 1857 photographs by Felice Beato.

The eminent Egyptologist Gaston Maspero engaged him as a photographer and also purchased his archives. A number of these are preserved today in Egypt. At his death in approximately 1906 in Luxor he had fifteen hundred negatives in his Luxor studio.

Henri Béchard: The dates of French photographer Henri Béchard, who appears to have arrived in Egypt before the opening of the Suez Canal in 1869, are unknown. He worked with Hippolyte Délié and ***Auguste Mariette.*** An association with ***J. Pascal Sébah*** developed, and they opened a second studio in the Garden of Ezbekiyah in Cairo. The Gold Medal at the International Exposition in Paris in 1878 was awarded him. His photographs were published in an album by his brother Émile and André Palmieri in 1887. However all his photographic production seems to have stopped around 1880.

The Bonfils Family: Originally from France, the Bonfils family opened their studio in Beirut, Lebanon, in 1867, then a country under Ottoman rule. The father, Félix Bonfils (1831–1885); the mother, Marie-Lydie Cabanis Bonfils (1837–1918); and later their son Adrien Bonfils (1861–1928) took numerous photographs of Egypt, in addition to other countries in the Middle East. Lydie Bonfils is credited with having taken many photographs of female subjects. Within four years the family business had a stock of fifteen thousand prints and nine thousand stereoviews taken from close to six hundred negatives of Egypt, the Middle East, and Greece. By 1888 they had a large stock totaling sixteen hundred eighty negatives. Lantern slides were also available. Félix Bonfils, his wife, and son continued to operate their studio in Beirut, with outlets in Cairo and Alexandria in Egypt, as well as a contact in New York.

The arrival of the Kodak box camera in 1888 which had so popularized photography spelled doom to the commercial studio photographer in the Middle East. It is difficult to precisely date the sale of "Maison Bonfils," as the plates were used after Lydie Bonfils died in 1918. The Bonfils were perhaps the most gifted and significant photographers of the Middle East. Their prints were excellently processed and encompassed a vast array of subjects with sensitivity. They were very popular and were produced in volume for rapid sale. It is often difficult to separate their individual work, but those photographs taken before 1878 are most certainly taken by Félix Bonfils. In 1871 he presented a paper in Paris before the Société française de photographie and was awarded a prestigious medal.

SUGGESTED READING: Félix Bonfils, *Souvenir d'Orient. Album pittoresque des sites, villes et ruines les plus remarquables.* Vols. 1–2: de l'Égypte de la Nubia. Alais: 1877.

Figure 2–3. Lehnert & Landrock advertisement

Advertisement for the art publishers, Lehnert & Landrock, Cairo, circa 1930. Many of the prints sold by them were of photographs taken by Rudolf Lehnert.

Émile Brugsch (1842–1930): The German Egyptologist went to Egypt in 1870 to assist his distinguished older brother Heinrich F. K. Brugsch. In 1871 he became a Conservator in the Egyptian museums in Cairo under ***Gaston Maspero*** and Keeper in 1883. He was a skilled lithographer and excellent photographer, who made numerous photographs of objects in the Egyptian Museum that appear in the *Catalogue Générale* of the Museum. The Khedive gave him the title *Bey* and later *Pasha*.

P. Dittrich: The German photographer came to Egypt and established a studio in Cairo in 1880. In 1885 he was associated with Heymann, Laroche and Company of Cairo, which also possessed a studio at Constantinople. This is the same ***Laroche*** that was a partner with ***J. Pascal Sébah*** at Constantinople at around the same time.

Francis Frith (1822–1918): The Englishman Francis Frith was the first photographer of note to use the wet-collodion process and was the most well-known of the more than one hundred photographers who worked in the Middle East during the Nineteenth Century.

Born in Chesterfield, England, of a Quaker family, he was at first a grocer, but in 1850 he opened a photography studio at Liverpool, England, and published his work in 1855. In 1856 he made his first trip to Egypt, where he produced numerous photographs on giant glass plates by the wet-collodion process. The prints immediately became a commercial success. From 1857 to 1859 they were distributed at the sites of the Grand Tour in Egypt, Palestine, and Syria.

In 1857 Frith published a hundred stereoviews through the house of Negretti & Zambra and a selection of large formatted prints for the house of Agnew. He was a skillful businessman, and on his return to England he opened an establishment selling multiple copies of prints from his negatives and stereoviews. He also published various albums and books containing his photographs.

The great difficulty in Photography is to get the Sitter to assume a Pleasing Expression of Countenance—Jones, however, thinks that, in this instance, he has been extremely successful.

Figure 2–4. Cartoon

A cartoon from an issue of *Punch* in 1862 shows Francis Frith (pseudonym "Jones") as he prepares a glass plate for a photograph of the Sphinx.

Lehnert & Landrock: The Austrian photographer Rudolf Lehnert (1878–1948) and German manager Ernst Landrock (1878–1966) opened their company in an old studio in Tunis, Morocco, in 1904. However, those who were unable to serve in the army were compelled to leave Tunis in 1914 for Switzerland or elsewhere. Their business confiscated, Lehnert and Landrock found themselves confined in Switzerland. In 1920, however, they started a new business, Oriental Art Publisher, in Leipzig. In 1923 Lehnert travelled the Middle East, taking photographs mainly in Egypt, Palestine, and Lebanon, and in 1924 a new business was opened in Cairo. The new enterprise seems to have satisfied Lehnert, but in 1930 he returned to Tunis where he opened his own photo studio producing mostly portraits.

G. Lékégian: A very prolific Armenian photographer who lived in Egypt, but whose dates are unknown. He was active in the Middle East between the 1860s to the 1890s. In 1887 he opened a studio in Cairo near the Shepheard's Hotel. Most of his work is signed "Photographie Artistique G. Lékégian & Co." As he focused on Egyptian everyday life, his photographs were often used as inspiration and documentation by Orientalist artists.

His photographs are carefully composed to create as natural an appearance as possible. Lékégian became the official photographer for the British occupation forces in Egypt.

Lichtenstern & Harari: Their dates are uncertain, but they were established in Cairo at the beginning of the Twentieth Century. In addition to photographs, vast quantities of postcards were produced and sold by them to eager tourists. They were the founders of the Cairo Post Card Trust.

Peridis: Active in the late 1870s, little is known about this Greek photographer. He was one of the many professional Greek photographers who came to Egypt when the Suez Canal was being built and then opened in 1869. It is known he was in partnership with a man named Georgiladakis. Albums of the late 1870s and 1880s contain their work, some have on them "Peridis & Co."

J. Pascal Sébah ([?]–1890): Possibly born in Turkey, Pascal Sébah had a large studio called *el Chark* (The Orient) in Constantinople and was among those photographers who had outlets in various cities with an associate, the Frenchman A. Laroche. His signature is nearly always on mixed albums from the 1870s to 1890. Among his numerous photographs of Egyptian landscapes, monuments and temples were fine images of Nubians and staged genre scenes. There are inconsistencies in his work suggesting borrowed negatives, including typographical differences in signature and titles on the photographs, which indicate he may have used local photographers. The numbers on his photographs run into the four hundreds. Nevertheless his work was much praised, and the Silver Medal was awarded him at the *Exposition universelle* of 1878 in Paris.

Félix Teynard (1817–1892): An engineer and French photographer, Félix Teynard was a student at Grenoble, France, of Jean Françoise Champollion, the decipherer of hieroglyphic writing. He travelled through Egypt photographing the monuments and sites between 1851 and 1852 and then again in 1859. Teynard brought back to France a collection of some one hundred sixty calotypes. Later he was again in Egypt for the opening of the Suez Canal in 1869.

C. & G. Zangaki Brothers: Active in Port-Saïd at the entrance to the Suez Canal from the 1870s, their exact Greek origins and birth dates are unknown. The brothers lived and travelled in Egypt and Palestine between 1870 and 1885. It is G. Zangaki who appears to be the camera man. At first the brothers were associated with the French photographer, ***Hippolyte Arnoux***, with whom they opened a first studio at Port-Saïd.

An 1870s photograph of the Sphinx reveals a photographer's cart with the Greek inscription *Adelphoi Zangaki* (Zangaki Brothers). There are other photographs which show a brother in a large-brimmed hat, a necessary aid for the relentless Egyptian sun. They produced numerous photographs of the Middle East and Egypt, mainly for the tourists and their travel albums; the artistic quality has been judged limited. No difference between the work of the two brothers can be detected. This suggests one was the photographer and one the technician. The Kodak box camera seems to have put the Zangaki brothers out of business.

Notes

1 Frith, "Egypt," p. 32.

Credit

Figure 2–2 from *Egypt and the Holy Land in Historic Photographs* by Julia Van Haaften and Jon Manchip White, 1980. Courtesy Dover Publications, Inc., Mineola, New York.

Selected Bibliography: Photographers

Bosticco, Sergio, *Photographers and Egypt in XIXth Century.* Firenze: Alinari, 1984.

Bull, Deborah and Donald Lorimer, *Up the Nile: A Photographic Excursion: Egypt 1839–1898.* New York: Clarkson N. Potter, Inc., 1979.

Chevedden, Paul E., *The Photographic Heritage of the Middle East.* Malibu: Undena Publications, 1981.

Fleig, Alain, *Reves de Papier. La photographie orientaliste 1860–1914.* Neuchatel: Ides & Calendes, 1997.

Frith, Francis, "Egypt and Palestine" in *The British Journal of Photography,* February 1, 1860.

Gavin, Carney E. S., *The Image of the East: Photographs by Bonfils.* Chicago: University of Chicago Press, 1982.

Howe, Kathleen Stewart, *Félix Teynard: Calotypes of Egypt. A catalogue raisonné.* New York: Hans P. Kraus; London: Robert Hershkowitz; Carmel: Weston Gallery, 1992.

Perez, Nissan N., *Focus East: Early Photography in the Near East (1839–1885).* New York: Harry N. Abrams; Jerusalem: The Domino Press and the Israel Museum, 1988.

Figure 3–1. Statue of Kemkare and Son

Old Kingdom, Dynasty IV–VI
Object: painted limestone
39.4 cm high (15-1/2 inches)
Provenance: Gizeh, Lower Egypt; Cemetery 1000, tomb 11
Excavated by George A. Reisner, 1903–1904
The Phoebe Hearst Museum of Anthropology, University of California at Berkeley: 6–19780

Before the right foot on the base of the once polychrome statue is the inscription: "the royal wig-maker *Kemkare*." The walking man wears a tight-fitting apron, pleated over on one side and secured by a knot through the slits of the apron band. His right hand holds a piece of folded cloth. His nude son stands at his left. The inscription on the base in front of the child's feet reads "His eldest son, *Ankhqakhes*."

The statue was found by the American Egyptologist George A. Reisner (1867–1942), Director of the tomb excavations at Gizeh, which were supported by the Hearst Egyptian Expedition of the University of California at Berkeley.

CHAPTER

The Age of Discovery in Egypt: *Birth of Egyptology and Photography*

In the early Nineteenth Century the camera was still imperfect, and color photography was a mere hope for the future. Therefore, engravings were the primary medium travellers and scholars relied upon to record their findings. But by the 1850s photography was in, and the rush to photograph Egypt was on.

Visitors to Egypt now had photographic souvenirs of the sites they visited to take home with them. No longer would there be total dependence on the romantic sketches, watercolors, and paintings made by professional and amateur artists to reveal Egypt.

Nor would there be the need to plan elaborate commissions such as the one Napoleon Bonaparte organized in 1798 when he sent some one hundred and sixty-seven scientists and technicians to explore and document Egypt. It had been the most important scientific expedition of the century, which resulted in the discovery of the Rosetta Stone and had a major impact on the awareness and study of ancient Egypt. As a result, Egyptologists and photographers were soon to shape new paths.

...he was observed climbing frantically to the top of the great pylon, camera-frame in hand, to "use up" the last streak of light.[1]

—Francis Frith, 1858

Photography Is In Vogue: 1850–1930

Although the ancient Egyptians did not have the camera, they clearly understood the idea of a lasting image and translated it into stone monuments and painted tomb walls for eternity. Trying to capture an image permanently is probably as old as human imagination.

Nineteenth Century photographers were to profit from this vision and more importantly to have a great impact on the emerging field of Egyptology. One person working alone could record monuments and copy countless hieroglyphic inscriptions with the greatest accuracy by using a camera. Photographs helped to document many Egyptian antiquities that were later removed from a site, that were subsequently plundered, that deteriorated through weathering, or that completely vanished due to environmental conditions. Through the work of early photographers, scholars can still study the printed images.

Beneath my eyes I had Giza, Abusir, Saqqara, Mitrahina. My lifelong dream took shape. There, almost within reach, was a world of tombs, stelae, inscriptions, statues.[2]

—Auguste Mariette, 1850

Archaeology Reaches New Heights: 1850–1930

During the 1800s, the fields of Egyptology and archaeology were continuing their development into academic disciplines with excavations and removal of ancient Egyptian treasures wildly thriving along the Nile. Some of the finds went to Egyptian and European museums while many objects went into private collections. Scholars were eager to interpret and document Egypt.

Many archaeologists working in Egypt became legendary. Only a few of the dominating figures can be touched upon in the exhibition, and their immense achievements and publications very briefly noted. The copious works of these pioneers are still consulted today.

Up the Nile: The Sites

Alexandria

...it is a subordinate monument that the accident of time has preserved: it is a part and a small one of the splendours of the Temple of Serapis.[3]

—E. M. Forster, 1922

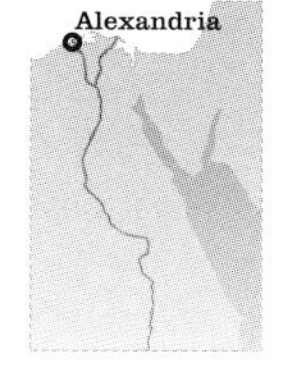

This majestic city founded by Alexander the Great in 332 B.C. is located in the northeast Nile Delta. The Hellenistic capital of Egypt was a major cultural center. Flowering under the Ptolemies, the Romans after 30 B.C., Alexandria later passed on to the Arabs in A.D. 642.

A red granite column approximately ninety feet high surmounted by a Corinthian capital marks the city, which had the most celebrated lighthouse, museum, and library in the ancient world. Early travellers marveled at the towering monument which reflected the once prosperous trade center and hub predominantly for Greek culture that was second only to the grandeur of Rome.

Figure 3–2. Pompey's Column

Roman Period
Albumen(?) print
Photograph: Edition Photoglob
McClung Museum: 1/655
Gift of Marcia S. Young, 1992

Mistakenly called "Pompey's Pillar" after the Roman general (106–48 B.C.), the column was probably raised to honor the emperor Diocletian (A.D. 245–313) as it once supported a now missing equestrian statue of him. It looms above the former citadel of Rhakotis, near the catacombs and Temple of Serapis.

Heliopolis

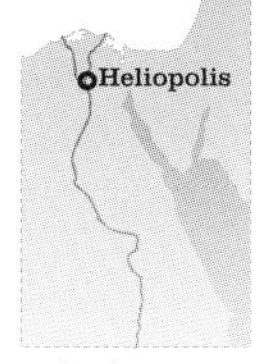

The city of Heliopolis, located around seven miles northeast of Cairo, was the oldest religious center in ancient Egypt and great seat of learning called On ("House of the Sun") in the *Bible*. The main cult center for the worship of the various forms of the great Egyptian sun god Re was at Heliopolis. There resided the most famous masters of all priestly knowledge in Egypt.

> *I then hired some land near the obelisk and cleared it...finding pieces of another obelisk....*[4]
>
> ***—Flinders Petrie, 1912***

In 1925 the area of Heliopolis was a modern city of some twenty thousand people. Travellers came by motorcar or railway, attracted to its Arabic style architecture, race course, and luxurious Palace Hotel, as well as to the famous obelisk.

In 1912 the British Egyptologist W. M. Flinders Petrie (1853–1942) discovered about two dozen obelisk fragments nearby, which he reassembled. As the restored obelisk was the same size, Petrie thought it might be the mate of the Sesostris I obelisk.

Additional Reading: W. M. Flinders Petrie and Ernest Mackay, *Heliopolis, Kafr Ammar and Shurafa*. London 1915.

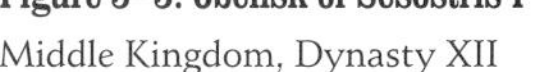

Figure 3–3. Obelisk of Sesostris I

Middle Kingdom, Dynasty XII
Albumen print
Photographer: J. Pascal Sébah
McClung Museum: 1996.10.1
Gift of Friends of Egyptology, 1996

This lone, red granite obelisk—sixty-seven feet high, and weighing one hundred and twenty-one tons—is the only one remaining from a city famed for them. It was one of a pair that once flanked the Temple of Amen built by Sesostris I. Hieroglyphic inscriptions on four sides record the titles and names of the pharaoh. The monument was probably raised to honor the celebration of his Jubilee, traditionally the thirtieth year of his reign. Part of the inscription reads: *...Son of Re "Sesostris," beloved of the Souls of Heliopolis, living forever, Horus of Gold....*[5]

Gizeh

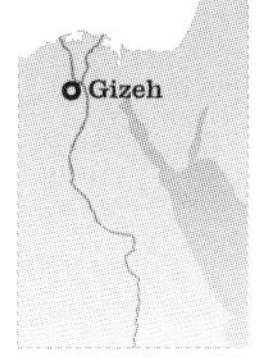

Gizeh is located on a long plateau on the western side of the Nile, about eleven miles south of Cairo. Travellers would enjoy the sights on the tramway for about one hour, or longer by horse cab to visit the most celebrated characteristic of Egypt. Here the three great pyramids of Khufu, Khafre, and Menkure dominated the sun-drenched, desert landscape. No less imposing was the Great Sphinx, a monument two hundred and forty feet long, rather weather beaten, punctured by treasure seekers and weapons, and hidden in part by the constancy of desert sands. Visitors were advised to select a non-windy day, as whirling sand is very irritating. Also "sun umbrellas" and "smoked spectacles" were the suggested protection against the bright sun.

> *The three largest pyramids, stand in line and visible for many miles up and down the Nile valley, had held the eyes of travelers ever since they were built....*[6]
>
> ***—George Reisner, 1930***

Beginning early in the Nineteenth Century a few dedicated excavators or researchers worked at Gizeh and published their important findings. By the mid-century more excavators and scholars from various countries worked at the Gizeh Complex, providing the world with their new findings. A few of the most prominent among them, beginning in 1850, was the French Egyptologist Auguste Mariette (1821–1881) followed by the German Egyptologist Ludwig Borchardt (1863–1938) and the eminent British Egyptologist Flinders Petrie (1853–1942) and later by the American Egyptologist George A. Reisner (1867–1942).

Additional Reading: Sir Flinders Petrie, *The Pyramids and Temples of Gizeh*. London 1883.

Figure 3–4. Trackway to the Great Pyramid of Khufu (Cheops)

Old Kingdom; Dynasty IV
Undetermined print
Photographer: unidentified
McClung Museum: A1: 161 C136 9P
Gift of Mr. and Mrs. Louis Bailey Audigier, 1934

In the foreground early travellers stroll along the old road that crosses the Gizeh plateau on the West Bank of the Nile River towards the Great Pyramid. At the upper left is the old Rest House. The entrance in the northern face is clearly visible in the core limestone blocks about fifty-five feet above the ground. After quite an energetic climb visitors entered into the Ascending Corridor and the Grand Gallery measuring one hundred and fifty-three feet long by twenty eight-feet high leading to the King's Chamber. Egyptian guides carried candles and torches to illuminate the long, dark way.

Gizeh

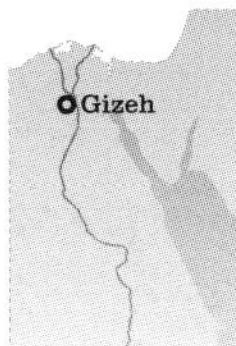

Figure 3–5. Khufu (Cheops) Pyramid

Old Kingdom, Dynasty IV
Silver print
Photographer: Zangaki
McClung Museum: A1: 121 C136 8P
Gift of Mr. and Mrs. Louis Bailey Audigier, 1934

Camels line up for the camera while their masters wait for riders. Tourists will pose on these camels for a traditional photograph with the pyramids and Great Sphinx.

Figure 3–6. Sphinx and Pyramid of Khafre

Old Kingdom; Dynasty IV
Silver print
Photographer: Zangaki
McClung Museum: A1: 121 C136 1P
Gift of Mr. and Mrs. Louis Bailey Audigier, 1934

Almost all of the original white Tura limestone casing is missing, but some upper courses remain intact. The wind-swept Sphinx has been freed of the continuous encroachment of sand numerous times since the days of Thutmose IV. Clearing was done again beginning as early as the Ptolemaic Period, and in Roman times.

At the beginning of the Nineteenth Century the sands of time buried the Sphinx up to the shoulders. It was cleared in 1818 by Giovanni Caviglia, an Italian explorer; in 1886 under the French Egyptologist Gaston Maspero (1846–1916); and again in 1925–1926 by Émile Baraize, a French archaeologist. This photograph was probably taken sometime before the clearance by Maspero.

I had the services of the greater part of our trained men, about one hundred in number, and purchased a light railway for use in the excavations.[7]
—George A. Reisner, 1903

Figure 3–7. Offering Basin

Object: limestone
36.5 high x 58 wide x 18 cm. deep (14-3/8 x 22-13/16 x 7-1/16 inches)
Provenance: Gizeh, Lower Egypt: Cemetery 1000, tomb 206;
Excavated by George A. Reisner, 1903–1904
The Phoebe Hearst Museum of Anthropology, University of California, Berkeley: 6–19752

The inscribed rectangular basin was made by *Akhethotep* for his father *Senenu* an "inspector of *Web*-priests." The cartouche on the rim bears the name of King Khufu (Cheops). Such basins were used by priests to pour liquid libations of thanks and present other offerings to the gods in the tombs and also temples. In the inscription is the wish for a western necropolis burial for *Senenu*.

Memphis

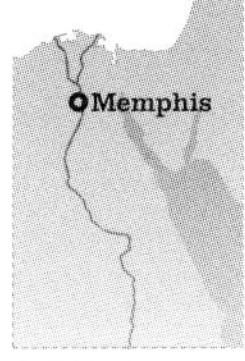

Memphis was the first capital of a united Egypt; in modern times the village was named Mit Rahina. Known as "The city of the White Wall," from the Egyptian *Aubu-Hat*, it was the great religious center located on the West Bank of the Nile just eight miles south of Gizeh and perhaps the greatest city in ancient Egypt. The first pharaoh and unifier of the two lands, the so-called King Menes, circa 3000 B.C., established his residence near there. Due to its strategic location he could control both Upper and Lower Egypt. The administrative capital was at its height during the Early Dynastic Period and Old Kingdom, mainly dynasties I through IV. Although Memphis as a capital was replaced by Thebes as the religious center and residence of kings, the city nevertheless continued to flourish into the Roman Period as a center for trade and international business.

> *Thus we worked out the western pylon of the great temple, finding many tablets engraved with ears, to entreat the hearing of the god.*[8]
> ***—Flinders Petrie, 1912***

From 1850–1854 the French Egyptologist Auguste Mariette excavated at Memphis. In 1851 he found there the Serapeum (named after the Greek god Serapis under King Ptolemy I), or underground Apis galleries, probably his greatest discovery. The subterranean tombs were carved in the rock in which the coffins containing embalmed sacred bulls of the god Ptah were interred after death. Nearby stood the house of Mariette.

ADDITIONAL READING: Auguste Mariette, *Le Sérapéum de Memphis*, folio. Paris 1857.

Figure 3–8. Statue of Rameses II

New Kingdom, Dynasty XIX
Albumen print
Photographer: Hippolyte Arnoux
McClung Museum: 1996.9.4
Gift of Friends of Egyptology, 1996

The colossus limestone statue lays face up in a palm-wood forest at the site of Memphis near Sakkara. The lone statue and a few ruins of the temples of Rameses II marked this historic place, once the site of a thriving city. The statue was later moved and stands outside the Cairo railroad station in Rameses Square.

Sakkara

A short two miles southwest of Memphis was the necropolis of Sakkara, the cemetery of the royal and non-royal. The first, great, free-standing, Old Kingdom monument is the royal pyramid tomb of Zoser. Built in Dynasty III it is the prototype for the Great Pyramid at Gizeh. The superstructure is built entirely of stone blocks, covering a substructure of a maze of passageways and rooms. The master architect of the pyramid complex was the highly esteemed Imhotep, a person of great religious wisdom, in architecture and medicine, who held the highest priestly titles during Zoser's reign.

> *Apis, the living image of Osiris revisiting the earth, was a bull, who, while he lived, had his temple at Memphis (Mitrahenny), and, when dead, had his tomb at Sakkárah.*[9]
> ***—Auguste Mariette, 1872***

ADDITIONAL READING: James E. Quibell, *Excavations at Saqqara*. Cairo 1907–1923.

Figure 3–9. The Step Pyramid

Old Kingdom, Dynasty III
Albumen print
Photographer: G. Lékégian & Co.
McClung Museum: 4/655
Gift of Marcia S. Young, 1992

Auguste Mariette excavated here in 1857. Later, early in the Twentieth Century the British Egyptologists James E. Quibell (1867–1935) and Cecil Firth (1878–1931) excavated several seasons at this important pyramid complex.

Sakkara

It remains the masterpiece of all Egyptian mastabas.[10]
—Georg Steindorff, 1913

Figure 3–10. Mastaba Tomb of Ti

Old Kingdom, Dynasty V
Albumen print
Photographer: Henri Béchard
McClung Museum: 1996.10.3
Gift of Friends of Egyptology, 1996

The sunken mastaba tomb, over a half mile from the Step Pyramid, belonged to a high court official and wealthy landowner named Ti. Facing the entrance to the colonnaded court on the central pillar just above the sand is a relief of Ti holding a staff. In the center a flight of stairs descends to the subterranean corridor leading to the tomb room. The tomb is important because of its finely executed, preserved reliefs, some still brightly painted, depicting daily life of the tomb owner.

Auguste Mariette discovered this principal tomb in 1860, bringing to light an early masterwork in the art of relief and inscription. The photograph was taken before excavators later cleared the tomb. In 1910 it was photographed in detail by Friedrich Koch of Berlin.

ADDITIONAL READING: Georg Steindoff, *Das Grab des Ti*, Vol. 2. Leipzig 1913.

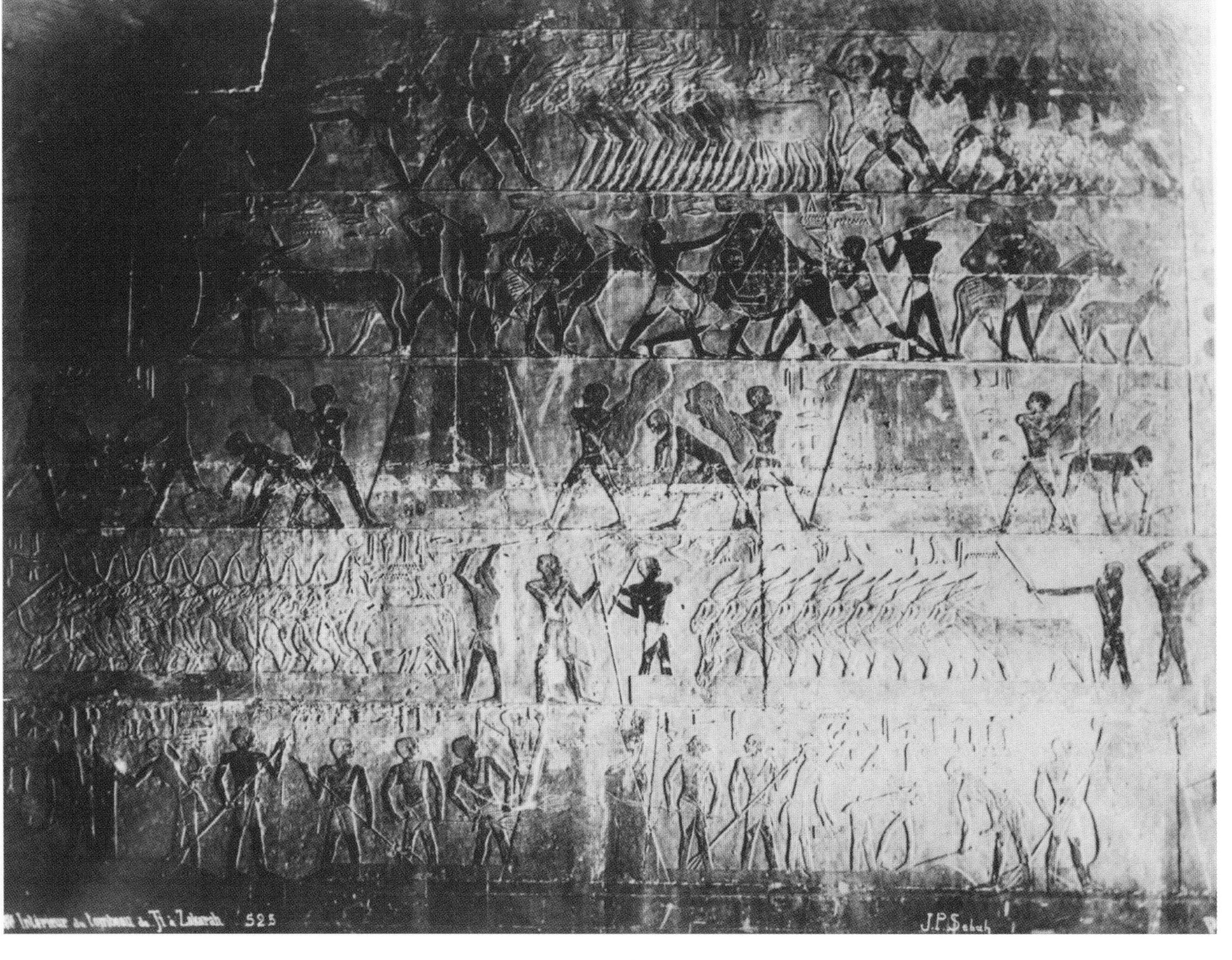

Figure 3–11. Relief from Tomb of Ti

Albumen print
Photographer: J. Pascal Sébah
McClung Museum: I/697
Gift of Friends of Egyptology, 1995

An interior view of the tomb chapel relief showing a harvest scene in five registers.

1. Herders drive asses.

2. Herders prepare a sack of corn for loading on asses that carry it to the threshing floor.

3. Ears of corn from sacks are piled up.

4. Asses thresh corn.

5. Threshed corn is piled up with long forks and put in a sack by a female worker.

Illahun

Located on the western side of the Nile southeast of the fertile Fayum on the edge of the Libyan Desert, the site is known for the Pyramid of Illahun. This was the burial place of the Dynasty XII pharaoh Sesostris II. All that remained was a mound of unburnt Nile bricks and low walls of huge limestone blocks. It was nearby, however, that Flinders Petrie excavated ruins of a town in 1889 founded by Sesostris I in Dynasty XII. Also found under Petrie's direction was the famous personal jewelry of Sit-Hathor-Yunet, daughter of Sesostris II, in her tomb at Illahun.

Some building also went on in this district under Khuenaten (Akhenaten).[11]

—Flinders Petrie, 1890

Figure 3–12. Building Block

New Kingdom, Dynasty XVIII
Object: limestone
23 high x 55 wide x 18 cm. deep (9-1/16 x 21-5/8 x 7-1/16 inches)
Provenance: Illahun
Excavated by W. M. Flinders Petrie, 1889–1890
The University of Pennsylvania Museum: E 325
(Neg. # S4-143034)

One arm of the unconventional, monotheist pharaoh Ikhnaton, which means "He who is useful to the sun disk," has tattooed cartouches of the creator god *Aton*, who was symbolized by the king as a sun disk with streaming rays. He holds one of his daughters, while another daughter raises her hands in adoration.

The block was uncovered in 1889 during explorations by Petrie at the towns of Illahun, Gurob, and Kahun. The fragment originally came from a building constructed by Ikhnaton, possibly from his city, Akhetaton at Tell el-Amarna, but it was found re-used in a unspecified tomb near the site of the pyramid of Sesostris II. The block was among some of the objects recovered and presented to various public collections such as at the University of Pennsylvania.

ADDITIONAL READING: W. M. F. Petrie, *Illahun, Kahun and Gurob, 1889–1890*. London 1891.

Fayum

The large fertile lowland area, bordered by Lake Moeris on its northern rim, is located on the western side of the Nile River southeast of Gizeh. Many fine fruits and other produce greatly prized by the Ptolemies and Romans were grown. For the modern visitors there were railways that radiated out from the main town, Medinet el-Fayum, to transport them to the nearby places of interest, including the pyramids of Hawara and Illahun.

ADDITIONAL READING: Bernard P. Grenfell, et al, *Fayum Towns and Their Papyri*. London 1900.

The first Greek papyrus which reached Europe from Egypt came from the Fayum.[12]

—Bernard Grenfell, 1900

Stylus (not illustrated)

Greco-Roman Period
Object: reed
9 long; 0.8 cm. diameter (3-1/2 x 3/8 inches)
Provenance: Fayum
Egypt Exploration Fund, 1901
The Carnegie Museum of Natural History: 1948–6

The medium brown, glossy, reed (*Phragmites aegyptiaca*) "pen" is cut on a slant and has a beveled, rounded end and tapered tip with a center slit. Such pointed implements were used in Egypt during Graeco-Roman times to incise characters on thin, wax-coated, wooden tablets, and other materials such as clay. Sizes vary as sometimes they were re-sharpened.

Hoop Earrings (not illustrated)

Roman Period (?)
Object: glass, gold (?), silver (?)
5.5 high x 3.2 wide x 0.5 cm. deep (2-3/16 x 1-1/4 x 3/16 inches)
Provenance: Fayum
Egypt Exploration Fund, 1901
The Carnegie Museum of Natural History: 2231–21

Dice (not illustrated)

Roman Period(?)
Material: ivory; pigment
0.9 long x 0.9 wide x 0.9 cm. square (3/8 inches)
Provenance: Behneseh
Egypt Exploration Fund, 1902–1903
The Carnegie Museum of Natural History: 2400–27

The six-sided cubes have incised concentric circles with a centered dot. The hand-carved gaming pieces were a popular form of entertainment for both Greeks and Romans, even for emperors. The dice were used alone or as part of board games. High stakes were often waged, and cheating with loaded dice was not unknown. During dynastic times the Egyptians tossed knucklebones for moves on board games, and, although not common, faience dice are known in the New Kingdom.

As usual, a large stone protected the doorway.... The chambers within were found to have been anciently plundered by a vertical hole sunk from above.[13]

—John Garstang, 1903

Bowl (not illustrated)

Old Kingdom, Dynasty III
Object: diorite (syenite)
11 high x 23.2 cm. diamenter (4-3/8 x 9-1/8 inches)
Provenance: Bet Khallaf, Tomb K 5
Collected by the Egyptian Research Account, 1901.
The University of Pennsylvania Museum: E 9788

The small, squat, double-handled bowl represents one of the known styles of stone vessels produced during the Old Kingdom. It has the weight and solid characteristics of the period.

Garstang, excavated for the Egypt Research Account during the 1900–1901 season at Bet Khallaf. He cleared three Old Kingdom, Dynasty III tombs near the tomb of King Neterkhet, of the same date. In the tombs he found various stone vessels and in K 5, the tomb of a prince, three diorite bowls.

The Temenos of Osiris I had wished to excavate since I first saw it in 1887. It was undoubtedly one of the oldest centres of worship.[14]

— Flinders Petrie 1902

Figure 3–13. Court and Entrance to Temple of Seti I

New Kingdom, Dynasty XIX
Albumen print
Photographer: Antonio Beato
McClung Museum: 1996.10.7
Gift of Friends of Egyptology, 1996

Two hopeful guides stand in front of the walled-up original temple entrance ways in the second court of the temple built by Seti I and completed by his son Rameses II, called the *Memnonium* by the Greek historian and geographer Strabo (64/63 B.C.–21 A.D.). The reliefs on the five pillars show Rameses II presenting offerings to various gods. The photograph was taken before the temple was fully excavated and cleared.

Behneseh

Behneseh (el-Bahnasa) is at the desert edge on the western side of the Nile over sixty miles south of the Fayum. It is the ancient site of Oxyrhynchus, once the capital of a nome. Later it was a small Roman district important for its corn crop. A fish by that name was highly esteemed by people there. The British papyrologists Bernard Grenfell (1869–1926) and Arthur Hunt (1871–1934) were the first to explore the extensive mounds at the site in 1897 and later made subsequent discoveries of valuable papyri of the Roman Period (written in Greek) for which the site is mainly known.

Bet Khallaf

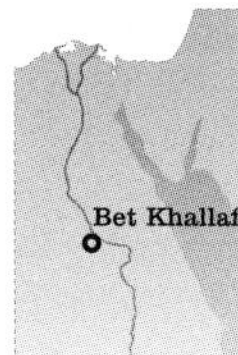

Bet Khallaf, a village some ten miles north of Abydos, is the site of a brick mastaba dating to Dynasty III and King Zoser. It was excavated by the British archeologist John Garstang (1876–1956).
ADDITIONAL READING: John Garstang, *Mahasna and Bet Khallaf*. London 1903.

Abydos

Abydos was one of the oldest and most important religious centers of worship in Upper Egypt. Osiris, the great God of the Dead, was worshipped there. It may have been his burial place and the birth place of King Menes, the pharaoh believed to have unified Egypt around 3000 B.C.

In 1859 Auguste Mariette vastly cleared the sand and almost fully excavated the temples of Seti I and his son Rameses II. The temple of Seti I had been covered with sand up to the roof with just the tops of the walls showing above the ground. Other Egyptologists ensued such as the Frenchman Émile Amélineau (1850–1915), who from 1894 to 1898 was the first person to clear early dynastic royal tombs at Abydos. Petrie also dug there from 1899 to 1903 and later. In 1903 British Egyptologist Margaret A. Murray (1863–1963) discovered the nearby cenotaph, or honorary tomb, of Seti I.
ADDITIONAL READING: W. M. Flinders Petrie, *Abydos.*, Part I; Part II. London 1902; 1903.

Figure 3–14. Relief from Temple of Seti I

New Kingdom, Dynasty XIX
Albumen print
Photographer: Zangaki
McClung Museum: 1996.10.5
Gift of Friends of Egyptology, 1996

The king stands before the enthroned goddess Isis in a detail from the doorway of the Sanctuary of Isis. Seti I wears the so-called Blue Crown and she the vulture headdress with a circlet of uraei surmounted by a horned sun disk. The goddess holds a "roqxute," an *ankh*-sign flanked by a *was*-scepter, symbols of life and stability, before the pharaoh's face.

Figure 3–15. Relief from Temple of Seti I

New Kingdom, Dynasty XIX
Albumen print
Photographer: Zangaki
McClung Museum: 1996.9.5
Gift of Friends of Egyptology, 1996

The deities Horus and Isis are at either end of the bier of Seti I who is represented in the form of the god Osiris. Isis as a falcon hovers over the mummy, while two other falcons spread their wings in protection at the head and foot ends. Beneath the bier are relief panels. At the left is the ibis-headed Thoth, god of divine intelligence; two royal cobras; and at the right is a standing baboon, also associated with Thoth. The relief is located in the South Wing in a small chapel.

Decorated Jar (not illustrated)

New Kingdom, Dynasty XVIII
Object: earthenware
109 cm. high (42-7/8" inches)
Provenance: Abydos, el-Arábah, Tomb E255
Gift of Egyptian Research Account, 1900
The University of Pennsylvania Museum: E 9180

El-Arábah is the modern town of the ancient Abydos, the site of a vast number of burials due to its extreme sacredness. John Garstang, who excavated at el-Arábah in 1900 found a scarab of Amenhotep II and a number of tools and vessels in Tomb E255. Among decorated jars, the one in this exhibit demonstrates the appearance of line decorations, color, and soft surface polish. Such changes in Egyptian pottery Garstang attributed to influences of "Mediterranean coasts and islands."

Model Bag (not illustrated)

New Kingdom, Dynasty XVIII
Object: bronze
7 high x 6.9 wide x 2 cm. deep
(2 x 2-7/16 x 13/16 inches)
Provenance: Abydos
Collected by the Egypt Exploration Fund, 1899–1900
The University of Pennsylvania Museum: E 9244

The tiny bag is inscribed with the name *Hekreshu*. Models were an important part of burial practices. They were scaled down versions of objects and activities in this life and therefore indispensable to serve the deceased in the afterworld as they had in the world of the living. There were a variety of models of butcher shops, bakeries, spinning workshops, granaries, various types of ships, rows of soldiers and types of implements and accessories made in painted wood and of metal.

Figure 3–16. Figurine of a Baboon

Dynasty I (Archaic)
Object: earthenware, faience glaze
109 cm. high (42-7/8 inches)
Provenance: Abydos, Tomb M69
Excavated by Flinders Petrie, 1902–1903
The Carnegie Museum of Natural History: 2400–7–B

The faint, green-blue glazed, squatting figure is supported by its extended forelimbs and projecting feet. The arms are not indicated. Except for the raised brow ridges, large frontal snout, and slightly open mouth, the face lacks detail. Animal worship was popular and lasted into the Roman Period. At least as early as Dynasty I, the baboon was one of the manifestations of the god Thoth, patron of the scribes. This was probably due to the baboon's intelligence and its ability to be easily taught.

Figure 3–17. Stela

Second Intermediate Period–
New Kingdom, Dynasties XIII–XVIII
Object: limestone
292 high x 25.5 wide x 6.9 cm. deep (11-13/16 x 10-1/16 x 2-3/4 inches)
Provenance: Abydos: Cemetery E78
Collected by the Egypt Exploration Fund, 1901
The University of Pennsylvania Museum: E 9952
(Neg. # S8-65465)

The stela has an unusual feature of a cutout *ankh*-sign (symbol of life) and is inscribed with the names of *Sebekhotep* and his wife *Neferuptah*. Some stelae were large and others were like small flat tombstones. Inscribed or decorated with reliefs, they were used as mortuary tablets placed in the tombs. Many list the names, prayers, and the good deeds of the deceased.

Hitherto it has been taken for granted that when no exact age could be stated...it must fall into a general limbo of "prehistoric times...." [15]

—Flinders Petrie, 1898–1899

Wavy Handled Jar (not illustrated)

Predynastic Period
Object: earthenware
27 high x 18 cm., diameter (10-5/8 x 7-1/16 inches)
Provenance: Diospolis Parva: HU U391
Excavated by Flinders Petrie, 1889–1890
Egypt Exploration Fund, 1900
The carnegie Museum of Natural History, Pittsburgh: 11678–71

The fine, buff, marl clay vessel tapers from its broad sloping shoulder to a flat bottom. Two applied, horizontal lugs of four wavy curves pinched by fingers decorate the jar at the upper sides. The jar represents the type of well-formed early stage of wavy handled types before the style "degraded" into a cylindrical shaped vessel. According to Petrie the jar was used to hold ointment, probably palm oil. When it changed to its final form, it held mud, but he offered no reason for such contents.

Diospolis Parva

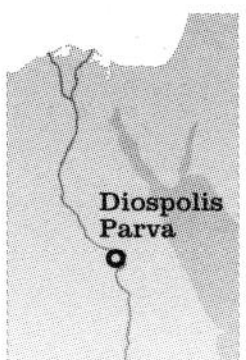

In 1898 and 1899 Flinders Petrie excavated the large predynastic burial site at ancient Diospolis Parva, located on the western side of the Nile, the area of the fellahin village of Hu mid-way between Abydos and Dendereh. Among the meager ruins, Petrie discovered evidence of predynastic settlements. The site was extremely important to Petrie. He was able to make additions to his classifications of predynastic graves and put in order the difficult subject of the earlier periods of Egypt. The result was his systematic method to "sequence date" predynastic periods. (Please see Figure 3 on page xii.)

ADDITIONAL READING: W.M. Flinders Petrie, *Diospolis Parva. The Cemeteries of Abadiyeh and Hu 1898-9*. London 1901.

We had therefore here a good opportunity of lighting one of the dark periods of Egyptian history.... [16]

—Flinders Petrie, 1898

Dendereh

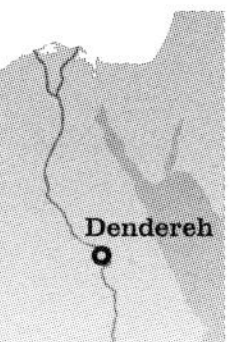

Dendereh is about four hundred and seventeen miles south of Cairo by river and some forty miles south of Diospolis Parva. It was the capital of the VIth nome (the Egyptian *Aati*) of Upper Egypt. This important site is among the best preserved although less characteristic of earlier architecture and decoration of the dynastic periods. The city is ancient in origin and was well-known in Egyptian legend as the place of one of the combats between the god Horus of Edfu and the evil god Seth.

It was not until Auguste Mariette worked for several seasons at Dendereh that much of the debris was cleared. Later, in 1897 and 1898, Flinders Petrie found nearby tombs of princes of the nome. These dated principally from the end of the Old Kingdom to the end of the Middle Kingdom, or dynasties VI–XII, which brought to light what Petrie called the "Dark Age," a time span about which little was known. Also uncovered were the later dated catacombs of sacred animals.

Dendereh was another important stopping place for most visitors. As was usual they were advised to hire donkeys at the train and tourist steamers for a ride of three quarters of an hour and have a supply of candles or an electric torch (flashlight). When they arrived at the site they saw mounds of sand and rubble that hid the lower part of the building.

ADDITIONAL READING: Auguste Mariette, *Denderah,* Vols. I–V. Paris 1870–1875; W. M. Flinders Petrie, *Dendereh 1898*. London 1900.

Figure 3–18. Temple of Hathor Facade

Ptolemaic-Roman Periods, circa 116 B.C.–A.D. 34
Albumen print
Photographer: Francis Frith
McClung Museum: 1997.5.6
Gift of Friends of Egyptology, 1997

The temple is dedicated to Hathor, goddess of love and joy, consort of Horus of Edfu and equated with the Greek goddess Aphrodite. Three Hathor-headed sistrum columns with screen walls between them are on either side of the entrance. Images of the goddess on the facade were defaced by Christian religious fanatics, and reliefs depicting the Roman emperor Tiberius (A.D. 14–37) were also badly damaged. Facade reliefs bear cartouches of the other Roman emperors—Caligula (A.D. 37–41) and Claudius (A.D. 41–54)—who worshiped Hathor.

Figure 3–19. Longview of Temple of Hathor

Ptolemaic-Roman Periods, circa 116 B.C.–A.D. 34
Albumen print
Photographer: J. Pascal Sébah
McClung Museum: 1996.10.8
Gift of Friends of Egyptology, 1996

A Greek inscription on a cornice dates the dedication of the temple to the reign of Tiberius Caesar (A.D. 14–37). The exterior rear wall has a centered image of Hathor in relief and Augustus offering an image of Maat, goddess of truth, and two mirrors to various deities. A large scene shows Caesarion (47–30 B.C.), presumed son of Cleopatra VII and Caesar, burning incense while Cleopatra holds a cult object behind him. The projecting lion's heads on the building sides are drains for rain water.

Village houses are built close to the temple walls submerged deep in sand. The remains of former local dwellings can be seen on the roof at the left. Villagers desired to live close to a sacred site.

Figure 3–20. Relief of Isis

Ptolemaic-Roman Periods, circa 116 B.C.–A.D. 34
Albumen print
Photographer: Zangaki
McClung Museum: 1996.10.9
Gift of Friends of Egyptology, 1996

The great mother goddess Isis (in Egyptian *Aset*) was worshipped throughout Egypt. Isis wears a long, plaited wig, the vulture headdress identifying her with the goddess Mut, a circlet of cobras, and a disk with horns associated with the cow-goddess Hathor. A broad collar decorates her pleated diaphanous dress. In her left hand is the papyrus scepter and in her right the *was*-scepter usually carried by goddesses. The relief, on an outside wall, shows how high the ground level was before being cleared during excavations.

Figure 3–21. Hypostyle Hall

Ptolemaic-Roman Periods, circa 116 B.C.–A.D. 34
Albumen print
Photographer: G. Lékégian & Co.
McClung Museum: 5/698
Gift of Friends of Egyptology, 1995

An interior view of the outer Roman Hypostyle Hall shows three of the meticulously carved columns surmounted by sistrum-capitals (barely visible in upper left corner). The sistrum was the favorite instrument of the cow-goddess Hathor. Egyptian guides stand on the base of a column testing its girth. Gouges of defacement are on the columns.

After the clearing of sand the columns and bases were revealed. The relief scenes are mostly of Emperor Nero, who seeks the waters of life from Horus and Thoth. Reliefs depict his being crowned by the cobra goddess, Buto (Lower Egypt), and vulture goddess, Nekhbet (Upper Egypt), and making offerings to various deities.

Temple Relief (not illustrated)

Middle Kingdom, Dynasty XII
Object: limestone
47.9 high x 40.3 wide x 13 cm. deep (18-7/8 x 15-7/8 x 5-1/8 inches)
Provenance: Coptos, Temple of Sesostris I
Excavated by W. M. Flinders Petrie, 1894
Gift of Mrs. Charles H. Cramp, 1894
The University of Pennsylvania Museum: E 943

The wall fragment is probably an image of the vulture goddess of Upper Egypt *Nekhebet*, who wears the vulture headdress with an uraeus over her forehead. Her usual White Crown of Lower Egypt is missing. *Nekhebet* was associated with the sun god *Re* and regarded as a mother goddess and the wife of the Nile God *Hapi*. She holds an unseen *ankh*-sign in one hand and a long-stemmed, lotus scepter in the other. According to Petrie the fragment of the goddess may date to the previous reign of Amenemhet I, father of Sesostris I.

Figure 3–22. Temple Relief

Second Intermediate Period, 1778–1567 B.C.
Object: limestone
55.5 high x 26.1 wide x 13.9 cm. deep (21-7/8 x 10-5/16 x 5-1/2 inches)
Provenance: Coptos: Temple of Nubkheperre-Antef
Excavated by W. M. Flinders Petrie, 1894
Gift of Mrs. Charles H. Cramp, 1894
The University of Pennsylvania Museum: E 941(Neg. # Roll.29:10)

Represented is the cosmic god *Montu* of Hermonthis, an important solar center and thought to be the Heliopolis ("City of the Sun"). The deity appears in the form of a falcon as *Re-Harakhte,* the great solar god "Horus of the Two Horizons," and wears the solar disk, uraeus, and double feather headdress.

So soon as we left, a native dealer ... went to work with a gang of men.... Whatever was left behind was absolutely lost to all record. [17]

—Flinders Petrie and J. E. Quibell, 1895

Figure 3–23. Jar

Predynastic Period
Object: earthenware
Provenance: Negadeh cemetery, Upper Egypt
10.8 high x 8 cm. diameter (4 x 3-1/8 inches)
Excavated by Flinders Petrie, 1895
The Peabody Museum of Archaeology and Ethnology: 07–40–50/72235

The handmade vessel, with a narrow, flat, painted rim, is a variation on typical types produced during the Gerzean Period, circa 3500/3400–3200 B.C. Decorating the ovoid pot are tapered bands enclosing nine rows of horizontal wavy lines painted in red on the lighter buff background. A small, string hole handle is on either side of the upper body. Pottery was generally for food, even in the tomb.

Coptos

Thirty miles north of Thebes is the site of the modern town Kuft, or the ancient Coptos, where the ruins of a once-great trading town are located. Caravans set out from Coptos to the Red Sea and the Sinai Peninsula and other exotic lands for precious goods. Mining expeditions went through the Wady Hammamat to quarries in the eastern desert. The protector of Coptos was the harvest-god, Min, who safeguarded travellers.

In 1893 and 1894 Flinders Petrie found at Coptos a large stone statue of Rameses II seated between Hathor and Isis, as well as numerous important relief fragments. Around 1909 the French Egyptologist Raymond C. Weill (1874–1950) excavated at Coptos with his associate A. Reinach. They discovered several Old Kingdom stelas containing royal decrees and the ruins of a temple dating to the Middle and New Kingdom periods.

Additional Reading: W. M. Flinders Petrie, *Koptos*. London 1896.

Negadeh

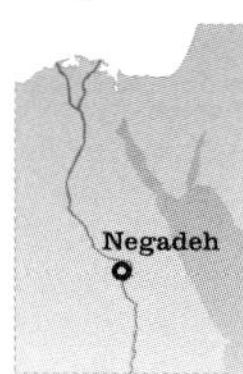

Negadeh (Naqada) was another important center in the predynastic and dynastic periods. It is located about twenty miles north of Thebes on the western side of the Nile. The origins of the Negadeh culture has been roughly dated from 5500 to 4000 B.C., in three phases down to 3100–3000 B.C. or about the beginning of the Early Dynastic Period.

It was along the edge of the desert, between Ballas and Negadeh, that Flinders Petrie and James Quibell discovered a large predynastic cemetery with more than three thousand tombs. The burials contained among other funerary items numerous decorated pottery jars buried with the deceased.

Additional Reading: W. M. F. Petrie & J. E. Quibell, *Naqada and Ballas, 1895*. London 1896.

Jar (not illustrated)

Predynastic Period
Object: earthenware
35.5 high x 15 cm. diameter at mouth (12 x 5-7/8 inches)
Provenance: Negadeh Cemetery A, Grave 1497
Excavated by W. M. Flinders Petrie, 1894–1895
Gift of the Egyptian Research Account, 1895
The University Museum, University of Pennsylvania: E 1492

Such black-topped jars were found in great quantity at Negadeh. The vessel has a flat base and high sides expanding to a wide mouth, one of the variations of this type. The red color of the body was produced by a hematite wash and the black by black peroxide of iron. By regulating the air in the kiln, the color contrast was created and the surface was burnished to give a lustrous sheen. On the upper body is an unidentified mark in the shape of a noose. The beautifully finished pot was made by hand and probably made specifically for burial with the deceased.

Thebes: West Bank
Valley of the Kings

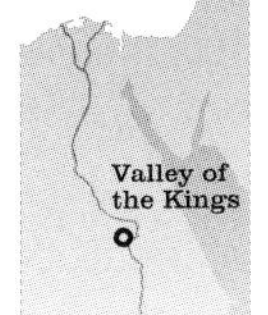

Thebes (Greek name) was no doubt the most important site in Egypt. The large, splendid and wealthy capital of the pharaohs was dedicated to its principal deity *Amen-Re* in imposing religious complexes on the East Bank. However, the royal tombs of the kings and queens, the ancient artisans' village of Der el-Medina, and mortuary temples located on the western side of the Nile River were also high points of interest. Visitors stayed in hotels on the eastern side of the Nile. A stop at Thebes was not advised between mid-April to mid-November as the weather was usually quite hot and the most fashionable Winter Palace Hotel was closed. For the more hearty and enthusiastic the equally attractive Hotel Luxor facing the Nile and its large garden were open all year. A launch took visitors across the Nile where donkeys and carriages waited to transport them to tombs and temples.

> *Amun-Re, Mut, and Khuns ..., were the Theban triad to whom the holy buildings of Thebes on the two banks of the Nile were dedicated....*[18]
>
> ***—R. Hitchens, 1910***

Probably the earliest scholar attracted to the West Bank was the French Jesuit Claude Sicard (1677–1726), who came to Egypt in 1712 and was the first to discover Thebes, where he effectively identified some monuments and tombs. James Bruce (1730–1794) was a British traveller who, around 1768, cleared the tomb of Rameses II, still called "Bruce's Tomb." The famous French expedition of scholars and scientists arrived in 1798, compiling much documentation. The great British Egyptologist John Gardner Wilkinson (1797–1875), well-known for his numerous books about Thebes, excavated there in 1824 and later. Jean François Champollion (1790–1832), the renowned translator of hieroglyphs, worked at Thebes in 1828–1829. Thebes soon became a beehive of archaeological activity where many others including Mariette, Maspero, Petrie, and Carter did extensive work.

Figure 3–24. Valley of the Kings

New Kingdom, Dynasties XVIII–XX
Albumen print
Photographer: unidentified
McClung Museum: 1997.5.11
Gift of Friends of Egyptology, 1997

One of the dusty roadways that leads into the necropolis of ancient Thebes, Valley of the Kings at Biban el-Muluk in the western mountains, where the pharaohs of Egypt were buried. The rocky peak of el-Qorn ("the Horn") rises in the background.

The British Egyptologist Arthur E. Weigall (1880–1934), as Inspector-General of Antiquities of Egypt from 1905 to 1914, worked closely with excavations of the Theban tombs. Wiegall initiated the numbering system for the tombs and helped to open and to conserve them.

Additional Reading: A. E. P.Weigall, *Guide to the Antiquities of Upper Egypt*. London 1910

> *I will state that we had definite hopes of finding the tomb of one particular king, and that king Tutankhamen.*[19]
>
> ***—Howard Carter, 1923***

Figure 3–25. Tomb of Tutankhamen

New Kingdom, Dynasty XVIII
Platinum(?) print
Photographer: Publisher's Photo Service Inc.
McClung Museum: 1996.10.12
Gift of Friends of Egyptology, 1996

The stone-walled tomb entrance at the left leads down to the unique burial place of Tutankhamen, discovered in 1922 by the British Egyptologist Howard Carter and his colleague and patron Lord Carnarvon. Clearing the tomb and transporting the artifacts to the Egyptian Museum in Cairo by Carter and his colleagues took ten years. At the right is the tomb of Rameses VI. Debris from constructing this later tomb had covered and hidden the entrance to Tutankhamen's burial place.

This disturbed but practically intact treasure-filled tomb became the most sensational archaeological find of all time. For Carter and Carnarvon it was a fulfillment of a long search that combined the skills of an archaeologist with a last minute stroke of luck. Discouraged at not finding the tomb, Carter was about to leave the Valley and dig elsewhere.

Figure 3–26. Colossi of Memnon

New Kingdom, Dynasty XVIII
Albumen print
Photographer: Edition Photoglob
McClung Museum: 10/655
Gift of Marcia S. Young, 1992

Two gigantic, weather beaten, sandstone colossi loom above the sands on the West Bank of the Nile at Thebes. They are statues of Amenhotep III—son of Thutmose IV and father of the monotheist pharaoh Amenhotep IV, called Ikhnaton. Next to the pharaoh's leg is the figure of his Great Royal Wife, Tiye. The colossi, which originally decorated the front of the pharaoh's mortuary temple, are all that remain.

Amenhotep III ruled over the most sumptuous court of the Mediterranean world. He had long and peaceful reign of thirty-eight years. The statues are mistakenly called the "Colossi of Memnon" after a mythical Ethiopian king who fought at Troy and was killed by Achilles.

Figure 3–27. Tomb of Seti I

New Kingdom, Dynasty XIX
Albumen print
Photographer: Zangaki
McClung Museum: 1996.10.11
Gift of Friends of Egyptology, 1995

The sun disk bears two important gods, Khepera and Khnum in the corridor to the burial chamber of Seti I, father of Rameses II. The gods precede the beginning of the Sun Litany, a hymn to the sun god which decorated most royal tombs. Khepera, the rising sun, or renewed life, is depicted as a large beetle. The ram-headed Khnum is the great creator of heaven, earth, and who with clay made the gods and humankind on his potter's wheel.

The tomb was one of six royal tombs in the Valley of the Kings, first discovered by the Italian excavator and explorer Giovanni Battista Belzoni (1778–1823) in 1817. Belzoni made wax impressions of the inscriptions and reliefs and indicated the colors at a time when the science of archaeology was in its infancy.

Thebes

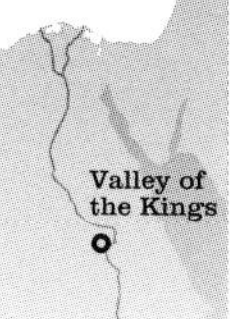

Figure 3–28. Tomb of Nakht

New Kingdom, Dynasty XVIII
Albumen print
Photographer: Antonio Beato
McClung Museum: 6/697
Gift of Friends of Egyptology, 1995

Scenes of daily life were painted in bright colors on the walls of the Theban tomb of Nakht, an official and priest of Amen-Re. An agricultural scene in the lower left register shows men hoeing, seeding, and driving cattle. In the upper register Nakht and his wife present a table of food and floral offerings to the god Amen.

The tomb was a photographic challenge as many tombs were blackened by fires built by Egyptians who lived in them. Candles and torches used with tin mirrors to reflect the sunlight into the tomb was the customary method of artificial illumination, but they blackened the paintings and sculptures. Beato probably used the new lamp invented around 1880 for burning magnesium.

Der el-Bahri

Der el-Bahri is the Arabic name meaning "Northern Monastery," suggested from a monastery formerly in the area. The bay of sandstone cliffs are in clear view from the opposite, eastern side of the river. The site is well-known for the stunning mortuary Temple of Queen Hatshepsut, built around 1500 B.C., the mid-point of her reign. Behind the cliffs are the royal tombs of the Valley of the Kings (in Arabic *Biban el Muluk*).

> *There can be little doubt as to the origin of this temple. Deir-el-Bahri was raised to the glory of queen Hatasu....*[20]
>
> ***—Auguste Mariette, 1880***

The Swiss Egyptologist Henri Edouard Naville (1844–1926) excavated at Der el-Bahri from 1893 to 1896 and later returned in 1903–1906, with the assistance of the British Egyptologist Henry R. Hall (1873–1930), to clear the temple of Mentuhotep. The American Egyptologist Herbert Winlock (1884–1950) continued Naville's work excavating the temples at Der el-Bahri for many years as Director of the Egyptian Expedition of the Metropolitan Museum of Art of New York.

Additional Reading: Edouard Naville, *The Temple of Deir el-Bahari*. Vols. I-VI. London 1895-1908; *The XIth Dynsty Temple at Deir el-Bahari*. Vols. I–III. London 1907–1913.

Figure 3–29. Shrine of Hathor

New Kingdom, Dynasty XVIII
Albumen print
Photographer: G. Lékégian & Co.
McClung Museum: 11/655
Gift of Marcia S. Young, 1992.

In the mortuary temple of Hatshepsut, above the doorway to the shrine of the goddess Hathor of the Theban necropolis, is the protective symbol of the Winged Disk. The solar deity spreads its wings over the rock hewn chambers of the holy dwelling. On either side of the doorway is the Horus name above the cartouches of Hatshepsut's half brother Thutmose II, who may have co-ruled with Hatshepsut. The shrine probably had a cow statue of Hathor in the inner chamber seen only by the queen and priests.

Figure 3–30. Temple of Hatshepsut

New Kingdom, Dynasty XVIII
Object: stereoview
Underwood & Underwood, Publishers, 1908
McClung Museum: 1998.10.4.70
Gift of Friends of Egyptology, 1998

Queen Hatshepsut dedicated her mortuary temple to Amen-Re, the patron god of Thebes and the kingdom, to support the belief in her divine birth as his daughter. It had sacred chapels devoted to Hathor and Anubis as well as chambers for other gods. The gleaming white limestone temple is finely defined against the cliffs of Der el-Bahri. The terraced structure is unique and unknown elsewhere in Egypt. However it endured much mutilation and erasure of her image by her successor and half brother, Thutmose III, the monotheistic religious zeal of Ikhnaton and later the early Christian fanatics.

Although Auguste Mariette excavated some areas of the temple it was Naville, who in 1893 began to excavate and further clear the temple, a work financed by the Egypt Exploration Fund. Naville's much important work had the assistance of the nineteen-year-old British Egyptologist Howard Carter (1874-1939) as draughtsman.

Der el-Bahri

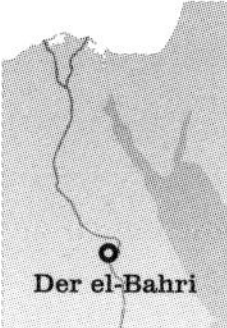

Figure 3–31. Hathor Chapel in Cairo Museum

New Kingdom, Dynasty XVIII
Sepia toned silver print
Photographer: Berthaud
McClung Museum: A1: 221 18th dyn. 9
Gift of Mr. and Mrs. Louis Bailey Audigier, 1934

The intact chapel, ten feet long and five feet wide, is brightly painted, with a vaulted roof of blue and yellow stars to create the illusion of heaven. The side walls show Thutmose III in adoration, presenting incense and water before Amen-Re and also before Hathor as a woman and in another scene in the form of a cow. Before the chapel stands a limestone statue of Hathor as a life-size cow. It is painted reddish-brown with black spots and indications of a gilded head, horns, and flanks. Papyrus stems and flowers hang from her neck and fall behind the standing King Thutmose III, who wears a kilt and the striped royal *nemes* headdress.

The Chapel of the Hathor Cow of Thutmose III was found in 1906 by Edouard Naville and British Egyptologist Henry R. Hall (1873–1930) during excavations at Der el-Bahri of the badly damaged Dynasty XI Temple of Mentuhotep II. The unique find was made possible by the Egypt Exploration Fund and was the first time that a statue of a goddess and her chapel were found intact.

Dra Abu 'n Neggeh

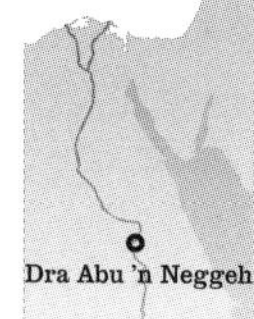

Located in the foothills of the Libyan desert north of Der el-Bahri, the village of Dra Abu 'n Neggeh (Dra Abu Naga) is one of the oldest burial places in Thebes, some graves dating to Dynasty XI. Rock tombs on the hills date to Dynasty XVIII–XIX and include the tomb of Neb-Amen, a king's doctor. Others were for a fan-bearer, steward to a queen, and a high-priest. The tomb of Roy, a Dynasty XVIII royal scribe of King Harmhab, was excavated by Howard Carter before his discovery of the tomb of Tutankhamen.

Funerary Cone (not illustrated)

New Kingdom, Dynasty XVIII
Object: earthenware
22.5 long x 9 cm. diameter (8-7/8 x 3-9/16 inches)
Provenance: Dra Abu 'n Neggeh: Surface debris: Tomb 162
Eckley B. Coxe, Jr., Expedition, 1922
The University of Pennsylvania Museum: 29–86–689

Two or more rows of red pottery cones decorated the top front of Theban tombs. They were approximately a foot long, set in point first with only the flat circular base visible, and looked like roof poles. The cones generally bear a stamped impression of the name and titles of the tomb owner as does the example in this exhibit. It is inscribed "*Qenamen,* the Mayor of Thebes and Overseer of the Double Granary of the god Amen-Re." Cones were made in great quantity and are valuable for names and titles of Theban officials and other notables that would otherwise remain unknown.

Figure 3–32. Model of the Hathor Cow

Early Twentieth Century
Object: painted plaster
28.5 high x 11 wide x 27 cm. long (11 x 4-3/8 x 10-5/8 inches)
Created by Henri Edouard Naville
The Peabody Museum of Archaeology and Ethnology: 09–20–50/74703

The three-dimensional model of the statue in the Hathor chapel was made for study purposes, but it may also have been in an exhibit by the Egypt Exploration Fund in London to publicize the successful 1903–1906 excavations at Der el-Bahri and the importance of the work. An article in *The Times,* February 24, 1906 stated "...we urgently solicit the support of all friends of antiquity, and especially of all who are interested in the land of the Pharaohs."

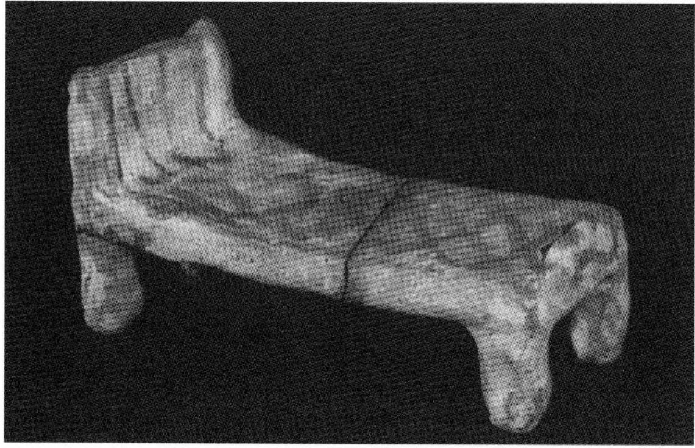

Figure 3–33. Model of a Bed

Middle Kingdom(?)
Object: earthenware; paint
9.5 high x 7.4 wide x 16.9 cm. long (3-3/4 x 2-15/16 x 6-11/16 inches)
Provenance: Dra Abu 'n Neggeh
Surface debris: Cemetery VI
Eckley B.Coxe, Jr., Expedition, 1922
The University of Pennsylvania Museum: 29–86–605
(Neg. # S4-143033)

Models played an important role in funeral practices. The red-ware bed was magically intended to serve the deceased as it had in life. A clay figure of a man or a woman made to scale may have originally been part of the model.

The site, located north of Der el-Bahri, was excavated by the American Egyptologist Clarence Fisher (1876–1941) during two seasons work from 1921 to 1923, with monies from the Eckley B. Coxe, Jr. Endowment of the University of Pennsylvania. The model bed was found during these excavations.

He smites millions, alone by himself; all lands are despised and contemptible before him.... Beautiful is the appearance of the king....[21]

—Pylon Inscription of Rameses III

Medinet Habu

The great complex of Medinet Habu had at its center the Great Temple of Amen with a royal palace and magazines surrounded by an inner and outer wall. There were dwellings for temple attendants, service and administration offices, a garden with a pool, and a smaller temple built in Dynasty XVIII. The fortress-like complex was protected by huge inner and outer walls.

Medinet Habu is three quarters of a mile from the Colossi of Memnon in western Thebes. Although an earlier, smaller, Lesser Temple exists at the site, the impressive, larger Great Temple was erected there by Rameses III of Dynasty XX on the same plan as the Ramesseum. Rameses III was the last of the great temple builders in the New Kingdom. Many reliefs in the great cult temple record his victories over his enemies, the so called Sea Peoples.

The principal excavator of Medinet Habu was the German archaeologist Uvo Hölscher (1878–1963). He worked at clearing, restoring, and recording the famous site for eleven years, setting new, high standards in field work. The result was a series of monumental publications.

ADDITIONAL READING: Uvo Hölscher, *The architectural survey of the great temple and palace of Medinet Habu*. Chicago 1929.

Figure 3–34. Great Temple of Amen at Medinet Habu

New Kingdom, Dynasty XX
Albumen print
Photographer: Antonio Beato
McClung Museum: 1997.5.7
Gift of Friends of Egyptology, 1997

On a doorway King Rameses III advertises his military prowess as he subdues his enemy. He grasps him by the topknot, holds a long, shafted spear posed to strike a blow, and tramples him with his foot. Cartouches with the pharaoh's prenomen (*Usermaatra-meryamen*) and nomen (*Rameses* III) are before his face.

Figure 3–35. Great Temple of Amen at Medinet Habu

New Kingdom, Dynasty XX
Albumen print
Photographer: Henri Béchard
McClung Museum: 1996.10.18
Gift of Friends of Egyptology, 1996

A partial view of the Hypostyle Hall of the Second Court terrace shows a row of round columns with calyx capitals and a row of square columns. On the far left column is a defaced image of the king with his hands in adoration wearing the White Crown of Upper Egypt. Stones and debris clutter the temple floor.

Medinet Habu

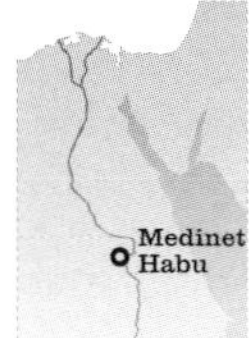

Figure 3–36. Rosette Tiles

New Kingdom, Dynasty XX(?)
Object: faience
3.2–5.5 cm. diameter (1-1/4 x 2-3/16 inches)
Provenance unknown
Old collection, 1890s
The Detroit Institute of Arts: 90.1S12821.2; 90. 1S12593.2–3

The round wall tiles have inlays of eight white petals joined at their narrow ends by a centered boss. No doubt they were inset decorations from a group that ornamented a palace wall. Similar inlays have been found at other sites, including the palace of Ikhnaton at Tell el-Amarna, of Rameses III at Tell el-Yehudiyeh and his palace at Medinet Habu. The rosette motif originated in Syria and appears in Egypt in the Old Kingdom on the headband worn by Princess Nofret in the Egyptian Museum.

Figure 3–37. Lesser Temple at Medinet Habu

New Kingdom, Dynasty XX
Albumen print
Photographer: Bonfils Family
McClung Museum: 1996.10.16
Gift of Friends of Egyptology, 1996

A longview of the smaller temple begun by Thutmose III and Queen Hatshepsut in Dynasty XVIII and later completed by Thutmose III after he became sole ruler. Alterations and additions were made by subsequent pharaohs particularly Rameses III. At the left are two central columns with elaborate floral capitals and high screens that are preserved from a colonnade that once faced the First Court. One of the gateways into the First Court bears an inscription with the name of Antoninus Pius, a Roman emperor in A.D. 138–161, attesting to additions in the Roman Period.

King of Kings am I, Osymandyas. If anyone would know how great I am and where I lie, let him surpass one of my works.[22]
—Diodorus of Sicily, circa 21 B.C.

Figure 3–38. The Ramesseum

New Kingdom, Dynasty XIX
Albumen print
Photographer: J. Pascal Sébah
McClung Museum: 1996.10.14
Gift of Friends of Egyptology, 1996

A long, side view of the ruins of the so-called Tomb of Osymandyas. The name was derived from the prenomen, *Usermare,* one of the names of Rameses II, by Diodorus Siculus ([?]–21 B.C.), a Sicilian historian. In the distance to the left is the Colossi of Memnon.

Ramesseum

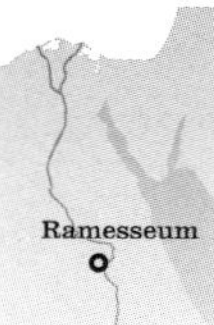

The mortuary temple of Rameses II to honor the god Amen-Re and to immortalize his own name is one of the most visited monuments in western Thebes. Unlike the more perfect Temple at Medinet Habu, the complex no longer had its it surrounding shell and side walls. Nevertheless, early visitors marveled at what remained of the monument although it appeared as a half-destroyed pile of blocks.

Visitors reached the temple by donkey from the West Bank landing in three quarters of an hour, but from the Colossi of Memnon or Der el-Bahri in fifteen to twenty minutes. Refreshments were available at the rest-house to special tourists and patrons of the Luxor and Winter Palace hotels.

The British Egyptologist James E. Quibell (1867–1935), who honed his archaeological skills under Flinders Petrie, was the discoverer of the famous Palette of King Narmer at Hieraconpolis. Quibell was the first to excavate at the Ramesseum, where he made important finds, including Middle Kingdom papyri, a library of the temple priests, and other inscribed items such as cartonnage fragments, painted inscriptions, stelae, brick stamps, and jar sealings.

ADDITIONAL READING: James E. Quibell, *The Ramesseum*. London 1898.

Ramesseum

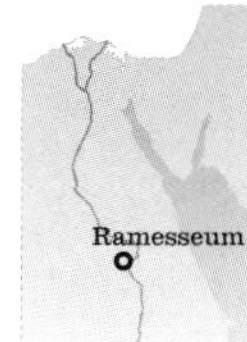

Figure 3–39. Colossus of Rameses II

New Kingdom, Dynasty XIX
Albumen print
Photographer: Peridis
McClung Museum: 3/697
Gift of Friends of Egyptology, 1995

A fragmented colossus of Rameses II, with the king's cartouche on its shoulder lays at the ruined First Court. Originally the polished, fifty-two-and-one-half feet high, seated statue was close in size to the largest known statues of him at Abu Simbel. At the left is one of the tall statues of Rameses II as Osiris. In the background is a section of the Great Pylon on the eastern wall of the Court.

Figure 3–40. The Great Hypostyle Hall

New Kingdom, Dynasty XIX
Albumen print
Photographer: Henri Béchard
McClung Museum: 1996.10.15
Gift of Friends of Egyptology, 1996

An interior view of the Great Hypostyle Hall with nine of its open papyrus capitals reminiscent of those in the great Temple of Amen-Re at Karnak in the foreground. A fallen, fragmented, colossal statue of the pharaoh is in the background.

Figure 3–41. Jar

Roman Period
Object: earthenware
22.2 high x 23.1 cm. diameter (8 -3/4 x 9-1/16 inches)
Provenance: The Ramesseum
Excavated by James E. Quibell, 1896
The Egyptian Research Account, 1896
The University of Pennsylvania Museum: E 1949
(Neg. # S35-143089:12)

The wide-mouthed, buff-ware jar is decorated with ridged bands around the upper half of a lobular shaped body, tapered to a pointed bottom. Two looped handles project just below the short neck. James Quibell found the jar in a long subterranean corridor of a disturbed Dynasty XII tomb at the Ramesseum, which had been entered at a later time.

In fact, the public buildings of Thebes, temples and palaces alike, must literally have blazed with color.[23]

—A. M. Blackman, 1923

Figure 3–42. Pillars of Thutmose III

New Kingdom, Dynasty XVIII
Albumen print
Photographer: G. Lékégian & Co.
McClung Museum: 16/655
Gift of Marcia S. Young, 1992

The broken archway in the background leads to the Hall of Records in which the Dynasty XVIII pharaoh Thutmose III erected two red granite pillars that once supported a roof. They are decorated with heraldic flowers representing the two parts of Egypt: at left are the papyrus blossoms of Lower Egypt for the Delta area, at the right the lotus flowers of Upper Egypt for the Nile Valley. The column drums remain from a colonnade of clustered papyrus-columns of sixteen shafts.

Thebes: East Bank

Karnak

Undoubtedly, Karnak is the home of the most impressive religious complex in all of Egypt, comprising some two hundred and fifty acres. The remains of the great temples of the sacred city of the god Amen-Re at Karnak and Luxor are on the East Bank. It is the home of the king of gods who lives there amid shrines, towering obelisks, a sacred lake, great gateways, avenues lined by recumbent sphinxes and rams, lesser temples, and the largest building ever erected in Egypt to honor him. The Great Temple of Amen was the location of the holy sanctuary for the bark and statue of Amen. Priests of the temple came daily to present food and beverage offerings. On feast days the sacred statue was carried around its holy precincts for everyone to gaze upon, and on great feast days it was transported by river to other temples while villagers lined the river banks in awe.

Few travellers to Egypt missed seeing this splendid complex of ruins. A bustle of guides, carriages, and donkeys waited outside the hotels and steamers along the river front to escort eager arrivals to the temples of the patron god of Thebes. In 1899 they would have seen eleven columns in the great Hypostyle Hall at Karnak that had collapsed. The calamity was due to the instability of the ground caused by changes in the levels of the Nile River and from the salts present in the heaped earth surrounding them.

The columns were subsequently re-erected by ramp and lever by the French Egyptologist Georges Legrain (1865–1917), who worked on a vast scale at the site from 1895 to 1917. He is remembered as the first Egyptologist to excavate and restore Karnak. Legrain cleared the Hypostyle Hall and the surrounding area and reassembled and rebuilt unsafe and toppled stones. In 1903 and 1905 he excavated a huge pit filled with mud and water to retrieve his famous hoard of objects, including some seventeen thousand bronzes and seven hundred and seventy-nine stone statues.

Additional Reading: Georges Legrain, edited by Jean Capart, *Le temples de Karnak*. Paris 1929.

Figure 3–43. Gateway of Ptolemy III

Ptolemaic Period, 332–30 B.C.
Albumen print
Photographer: Publisher's Photo Service, Inc.
McClung Museum: 1996.10.19
Gift of Friends of Egyptology, 1996

The sacred Karnak precinct was once enclosed by a thick mud brick wall. The entrance to the southwest entrance and the Temple of Khonsu, the Theban moon god, was built by Ptolemy III, also called Euergetes I. On its concave cornice is the Winged Disk with uraei. In relief on the front and inside jambs are scenes of the king presenting offerings to deities. A donkey boy poses at the front of the gateway. Evidence of restoration is seen at the bottoms of the jambs.

Figure 3–44. Gateway of King Hormheb

New Kingdom, Dynasty XVIII
Albumen print
Photographer: Edition Schroeder & Company, Zurich
McClung Museum: 19/655
Gift of Marcia S. Young, 1992

The ruinous Pylon X, the south entrance to the sacred precincts, was built by King Hormheb with stones taken from a temple of Ikhnaton (Amenhotep IV). Reliefs on the gateway jamb show Hormheb, the last pharaoh of Dynasty XVIII performing religious rites. Two headless limestone statues of Rameses II stand before the Pylon. Rounded Beduin tents are set up close before the holy gateway.

Figure 3–45. Bust of Sekhet

New Kingdom
Object: black basalt
75 cm. high (29-1/2 inches)
Provenance: Temple of Mut, Karnak
Gift of Mrs. Phoebe Hearst
Phoebe Hearst Museum of Anthropology, University of California at Berkeley: 5–365

The lion-headed bust of the goddess Sekhet, meaning "the powerful one," has the body of a woman broken away at the waist. Only half of her right arm and left shoulder are intact. The noble animal wears a lappet wig, detailed broad collar, and a close-fitting dress ornamented by a rosette on each breast. A large sun disk with uraeus that once surmounted her head symbolized the warlike quality of the fiery sun and its devastating strength that destroyed enemies of Egypt and Sekhet as the manifestation of the powerful fireball. Sekhet was also an aspect of the sometimes lion-headed goddess of Thebes, Mut, consort of Amen-Re, a mother deity and mother of their son the moon god, Khonsu. At one time seven hundred statues of Sekhet were at the Temple of Mut. The figure is one of numerous seated images of the goddess carved during the reign of Amenhotep III.

The British excavator Margaret Benson (1865–1916) excavated the Temple of Mut at Thebes in 1895–1897 in consultation with the British Egyptologist Percy E. Newberry (1868–1949). She was skilled, alert to construction details, and recorded her finds in the manner of the time. Her discoveries of several Sekhets among other important sculpture is discussed in her book *The Temple of Mut in Asher,* London, 1899.

Colossal are the statues of the king, solid, powerful, and tremendous, boldly facing the world with the calm of one who was thought,...to be not much less than a deity.[24]

—R. Hitchens, 1910

Figure 3–46. Colossus of Rameses II

New Kingdom; Dynasty XIX
Albumen print
Photographer: G. Lékégian & Co.
McClung Museum: 20/655
Gift of Marcia S. Young, 1992

One of several granite colossi of Rameses II that were placed between the columns in the Great Court of the Temple of Amen-Re. The striding pharaoh wears the striped *nemes* headdress, the royal beard and clutches a folded cloth in each hand as he looks to eternity. His kilt bears his cartouche.

Luxor

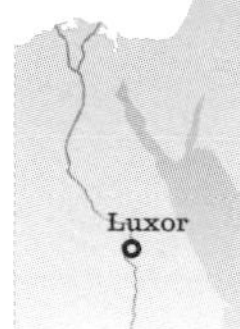

Located two miles south of Karnak, close to the river, is the site of the Temple of Luxor. Although less imposing and sprawled out than the Karnak complex, here elegant temples were built by Amenhotep III of Dynasty XVIII dedicated to the great Theban god Amen-Re, his wife Mut, and their son Khonsu. Subsequent pharaohs usurped the complex making changes and additions. However, Luxor still maintained its well-balanced architectural features originally established by Amenhotep III.

Luxor rose to importance in the Middle Kingdom and became the capital of the empire in the New Kingdom. The only change occurred during the brief reign of Ikhnaton, when the capital was at Tell el-Amarna. The New Kingdom was the period at Luxor for the local god Amen-Re to reach great heights. After Egypt had expelled the Hyksos invaders the New Kingdom period began and with it trade and the building of splendid temples to honor Amen-Re as the king of the gods.

Visitors stopping by steamer or crossing the Nile from the West Bank by ferry admired the impressive colonnades rising above the shimmering waters of the Nile.

ADDITIONAL READING: A. M. Blackman, *Luxor and Its Temples*. New York 1923.

Figure 3–47. Statue of Queen Nefretiri

New Kingdom, Dynasty XIX
Albumen print
Photographer: Zangaki
McClung Museum: 1997.5.14
Gift of Friends of Egyptology, 1997

The small statue of the Great Wife of Rameses II stands beside a colossal statue of her husband. The graceful figure is complemented by a long, elaborate wig, and her royal presence accented in the double cobra above her brow. Her headdress is surmounted by a sun disk and cow's horn, attributes that associate her with Hathor, goddess of love, joy, and beauty.

Figure 3–48. The Temple of Luxor

New Kingdom, Dynasty XVIII
Albumen print
Photographer: Francis Frith
McClung Museum: 1997.5.12
Gift of Friends of Egyptology, 1997

Two colossi of Rameses II buried in the sand, flank the pylon gateway. Reliefs on the pylon facade depict Rameses II during his famous Battle of Kadish in Syria, where in his fifth year of reign he is shown victorious over the Hittites.

In 1836 one of the two obelisks standing in front of the temple was re-erected in the Place de la Concorde in Paris. In the late Nineteenth Century the temple courts were cleared. The exterior areas with local village houses and pigeon coops were not removed until the 1940s.

Figure 3–49. Court of Amenhotep III

New Kingdom, Dynasty XVIII
Albumen print
Photographer: Zangaki
McClung Museum: 1997.5.13
Gift of Friends of Egyptology, 1997

The colonnades, a group of thirty-two clustered-papyrus columns with bud capitals, loom in the Second Court with their architraves, capitals, and shafts intact. Egyptian guides pose on a fallen block awaiting visitors to the site.

Figure 3–50. Temple of Erment

Ptolemaic Period, 332–30 B.C.
Albumen print
Photographer: Francis Frith
McClung Museum: 1997.5.15
Gift of Friends of Egyptology, 1997

Dedicated to the local war-god, the falcon-headed Montu and his consort Rat-tawy, the temple was erected by Cleopatra VII and Caesarion, her son by the Roman Emperor Julius Caesar. The columns bore images of Cleopatra and her son before local deities and other gods. The blocks in the right foreground are fallen columns and screen-walls. The center column bears a scene of Cleopatra holding a pair of sistra (a rattle-like instrument) followed by Caesarian in adoration before the god Ra-tawy.

...a temple neither ruined nor defaced, but buried to the chin in the accumulated rubbish of a score of centuries.[25]
—Amelia Edwards, 1872

Figure 3–51. Capitals of the Temple of Khnum

Ptolemaic-Roman Periods
Albumen print
Photographer: Zangaki
McClung Museum: 1999.2.2
Gift of Friends of Egyptology, 1999

Emerging from the sands are four of the twenty-four handsome floral capitals in the vestibule. They measure thirty-seven feet high and seventeen and three-quarters feet in circumference. A cartouche of the Emperor Trajan is on the abacus above the capital at left. The rails between the column shafts indicate the height of the sand before it was removed.

Erment

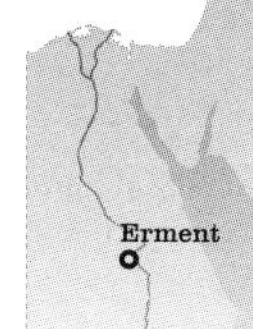

The site, named Hermonthis in antiquity, is nine miles south of Luxor on the western side of the Nile. The area was known for its temple built by Cleopatra VII to honor the goddess Isis. By 1929 the temple no longer stood, its stones having been used in building a sugar factory.

In 1927 the British excavator Robert Mond (1867–1938) and the American Egyptologist Walter B. Emery (1903–1971) excavated at Erment. There they discovered the graves of the Buchis bulls sacred to the god Montu.

Esneh

A charming site the Greeks called Latopolis is named for the fish *Lates niloticus*, or Nile perch.

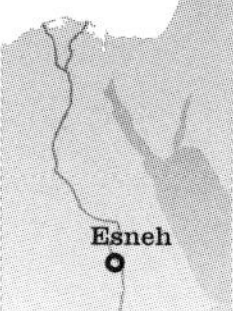

The fish was worshipped here as elsewhere in Egypt and reverently buried in extensive graves. The well-known Temple of Khnum was sacred to the local ram-headed god, the creator deity who fashioned humankind on his potter's wheel. Although the temple dates at least to Dynasty XVIII, the architecture is from the Ptolemaic Period, and most of the decorative elements are Roman. The temple probably was begun in 50 B.C. by the Roman Emperor Claudius and completed in A.D. 250 by Emperor Decius. Esneh is about four hundred eighty-five miles from Cairo.

Unfortunately the encroachment of the town almost obscured the temple. After a short walk from the moored steamers through the picturesque village, early visitors would see only part of the buried temple. They had to descend steps down many feet to reach the temple. In 1842 Mohammed Ali ordered the vestibule to be cleared, leaving the rest of the temple which was covered by village dwellings. This was done to safeguard a reserve of gunpowder!

Edfu

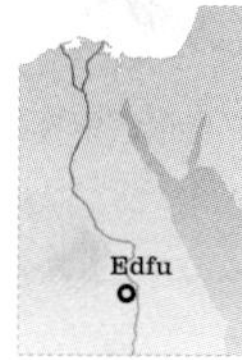

This remarkable site, which the Greeks called Apollonopolis Magna after the sun god Horus-Apollo, is located about sixty-five miles south of Luxor on the western side of the Nile. The almost perfectly preserved sandstone Temple of Edfu resembles that of Dendereh. The grand building was dedicated to the great solar deity Horus, his wife Hathor of Dendereh, and their son Harsomtus. Known at least from Dynasty XVIII, a new construction of a better temple was begun by Ptolemy III (Euergetes I) in 237 B.C. and finished in 57 B.C. during the reign of Ptolemy XII (Neos Dionysos).

> *...the huge building stands before us in the sunshine, erect and perfect. The effect at first sight is overwhelming.*[26]
> ***—Amelia Edwards, 1877***

In the early Nineteenth Century visitors were startled to see some sixty-four houses on the roof and the interior heaped with debris and dwellings. Before the front entrance, as in other temple sites, were more of the mud-brick huts and stables of villagers that almost reached to the top of the building. The traveller could also see various beautiful birds and waterfowl in a nearby marsh.

In 1860 Auguste Mariette discovered the site and began to clear the temple of all encroachments. As a result of his work countless inscriptions were for the first time fully seen.

Figure 3–52. Shrine in the Temple of Horus

Ptolemaic Period
Albumen print
Photographer: J. Pascal Sébah
McClung Museum: 1996.10.23
Gift of Friends of Egyptology, 1996

In the Sanctuary is the granite shrine from the earlier pre-Ptolemaic temple that was dedicated to Horus of Edfu by King Nectanebo II, Dynasty XXX. A winged solar disk, symbol of Horus of Edfu, protects the shrine, which at one time held behind its once bronze doors a statue of the sacred falcon. The wall reliefs bear witness to mutilation by Christian fervor.

Figure 3–53. Goddesses Crown King Nectanebo II

Late Dynastic Period, Dynasty XXX
Silver print
Photographer: Zangaki
McClung Museum: Al: 161 C136 2E
Gift of Mr. and Mrs. Louis Bailey Audigier, 1934.

Among the many rich reliefs decorating the temple is that of the vulture goddess Nekhbet and Buto the cobra goddess, representing Upper and Lower Egypt respectively, who endow the king with the Double Crown of Egypt. Each goddess wears her attribute. Such relief scenes were probably worked out from pattern books used by artisans.

Figure 3–54. Forecourt of the Temple of Edfu

Ptolemaic Period
Albumen print
Photographer: Antonio Beato
McClung Museum: 1996.10.22
Gift of Friends of Egyptology, 1996

In the spacious court a colossal statue of the god Horus stands at the proper right of the entrance of the Vestibule, or *pronaos*. A cavetto cornice decorates the roof and below are six, low, stone screens decorated with ceremonial reliefs between six columns surmounted by plant and palm leaf capitals.

Figure 3–55. Longview of the Temple of Edfu

Ptolemaic Period
Salt print
Photographer: Félix Teynard
McClung Museum: 1997.5.16
Gift of Friends of Egyptology, 1997

Exterior of the southwest great pylon entrance of the temple when in the 1850s it was much obscured by sand. On the left side of the pylon King Ptolemy XII smites his enemies, while Horus of Edfu and his wife Hathor of Dendereh look on. In the two rows above, the king makes offerings before Horus and Hathor and other deities of Edfu. Two recesses flank the gateway that held large flagstaffs clamped to the masonry. Small square openings allowed air and light to the stairways inside the pylon.

Now there remain only a few giant columns buried to within eight or ten feet of their gorgeous capitals....[27]

—Amelia Edwards, 1872

Figure 3–56. Longview of the Temple of Kom Ombo

Ptolemaic Period
Albumen print
Photographer: Francis Frith
McClung Museum: 1997.5.19
Gift of Friends of Egyptology, 1997

A gateway was found at the temple dedicated by Thutmose III, Dynasty XVIII, to the crocodile god Sobk. However, most of the reliefs that decorate the walls were made by several Ptolemaic kings. Later, Roman emperors added additional reliefs. Emperor Tiberius Caesar decorated the Court columns and outer walls, which bear depictions of him performing religious ceremonies.

Kom Ombo

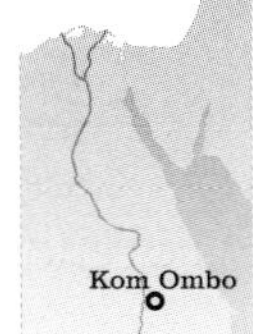

The ancient town of Ombos, located twenty-five miles from Assuan, was in modern times named Kom Ombo, or "Hill of Ombos." It was long buried beneath the desert sands. Only the ruined great temple survived, unique with its two sanctuaries in the one building each dedicated to an important god: Sobk, the crocodile god, and Haroeris, an early form of the falcon god Horus, patron of the blind. The building is uniformly divided into two halves along its longitudinal axis, each having its own gateway and chapel.

Visitors arriving by steamer had not far to walk to study the striking building standing deep in sand overlooking the Nile. Also, travellers took a half-hour ride from the railway station by a trolley-line leading to the temple. At the temple were mummiform crocodiles from the nearby crocodile necropolis to amaze them.

The French Egyptologist Gaston Maspero discovered evidence in 1882 that the earlier pharaohs Amenhotep I and Thutmose III had been associated with the temple. With the approval of Maspero, Director of the Antiquities Service, the French archaeologist Jacques de Morgan (1854–1900) began in 1893 to clear the mostly Ptolemaic Period temple.

ADDITIONAL READING: Jacques J. M. de Morgan, *Catalogue des monuments et inscriptions de l'Égypte antique*, Nos. 2–3: *Description du Temple d'Ombos*. Vienna 1895–1909.

Figure 3–57. Wall Relief

Ptolemaic Period
Albumen print
Photographer: unidentified
McClung Museum: 1996.9.8
Gift of Friends of Egyptology, 1996

Ptolemy XII wears the *hemhem*-crown and is blessed and given long life by the lion-headed goddess Sekhet(?). Behind her is the falcon-headed patron of the blind Haroeris, who wears the Double Crown and Harsiesis the son of Isis, who wears the White Crown and holds a *was*-scepter, symbol of stability. At left the great mother goddess Isis, and the ibis-headed god of learning Thoth, bless the king.

Assuan

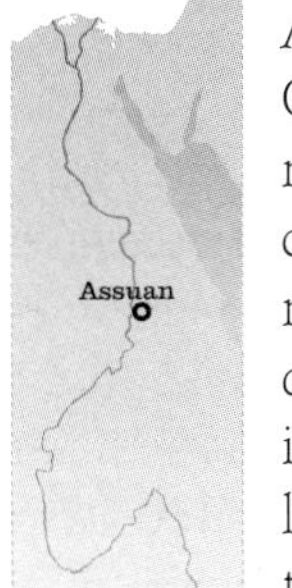

Assuan is five hundred and ninety miles south of Cairo. The Egyptian name for Assuan was *Swenet*, meaning making business or trade. The Greeks called it Syene in the Ptolemaic Period. Perhaps the most compelling attraction of all were the granite quarries south of the city and the famed Unfinished Obelisk that lay there. It was abandoned due to a flaw in the reddish granite of a single piece one hundred and thirty-seven feet long. It has been estimated to weigh one thousand and sixty-eight tons. Visitors would also cross to lush Elephantine Island to visit the treasures in the Assuan Museum, such as the mummy and gilded coffin of a ram, sacred to the god Khnum of Elephantine, found in the nearby ram necropolis. The Nilometer restored in 1870 under the rule of Khedive Ismail was another attraction.

> *Beggars—oh, well, they are everywhere in Egypt, again, like the flies; but they do bite so hard at Assouan as elsewhere.*[28]
>
> ***—John C. Van Dyke, 1930***

Beyond was the West Bank of the Nile, where important rock tombs of the nobles—dated to the Old Kingdom, Middle Kingdom, and later—were cut into the rock face. These belonged to powerful noblemen, the "Keepers of the Southern Gate," the starting point for important caravan routes. In 1885 and 1886 the tombs were opened by the British excavator Francis W. Grenfell (1841–1925) who was Commander-in-Chief of the Egyptian Army and who also collected antiquities.

Figure 3–58. Assuan

Silver print
Photographer: Peridis
McClung Museum: A1: 161 A849 1A
Gift of Mr. and Mrs. Louis Bailey Audigier, 1934

Ideally located on the East Bank below the First Cataract, its mosques, churches, markets, and fashionable hotels that seem to float in sunlight near the river's edge. *Felukas* (boats) with their sails furled are moored at the right.

Old Assuan Dam: Lower Nubia

Since the days of the rule of Mohammed Ali the irrigation of Egypt had been modernized by several, costly water-controlling barrages, or dams, that spanned the Nile River. One of the most important was the larger old Assuan Dam, called the Barrage, located just north of Philae at the First Cataract. It was constructed between 1898 and 1903, and later expanded.

After a short excursion from Assuan visitors sat in cars on rails and were pushed by Egyptian boys across the Barrage to the western side. There they could also enjoy pleasurable picnics in nearby gardens, tea in the open air, or a sail on the smooth waters of the lake at sunset.

Figure 3–59. Assuan Barrage

Platinum(?) print
Photographer: A. Marouez
McClung Museum: A1: 161 A849 1A
Gift of Mr. and Mrs. Louis Bailey Audigier, 1934

Built with granite from the nearby Assuan quarries, the Barrage had one hundred and eighty sluice gates to regulate the water. These were opened in July when the Nile began to rise. When the river subsided in December they were gradually closed. In 1929 the storage lake above the dam held a capacity of almost six hundred trillion gallons. The reservoir supplied necessary water for irrigation during months when the gates were closed.

Assuan Dam

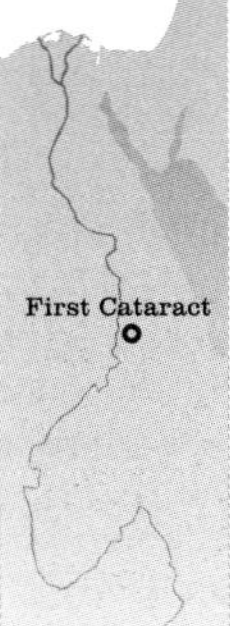

Figure 3–60. First Cataract

Color tinted silver print
Photographer: Lichtenstern and Harari, Cairo
McClung Museum: A1: 161 A849 1A
Gift of Mr. and Mrs. Louis B. Audigier, 1934

The foaming rapids of the Cataract swirl around a few fearless youngsters. From the Cataract Hotel in Assuan travellers could take a riverside route by boat, or make their way by rail to see the churning waters tumbling over shimmering, dark granite rocks, one of the natural wonders of the Nile.

Philae

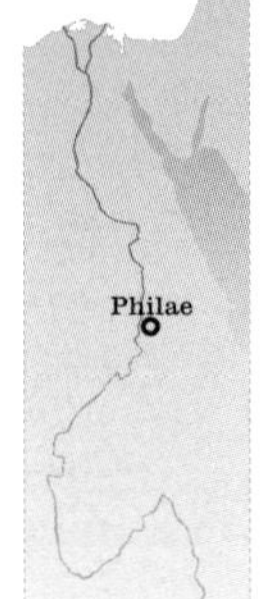

The dam at Assuan has raised the current over its foundations and the waves now swirl into the sanctuaries where processions of priests once walked.[29]
—Archie Bell, circa 1915

Touched by palm trees and called the "Pearl of Egypt," Philae was a most remarkable complex situated on the picturesque island of Philae. But after 1898 the site was to feel the impact of progress from the waters of the gigantic old Aswan Dam, although the stabilization of the buildings had been assured. The temples were only partially submerged in flood waters, but algae was soon found discoloring the stone and the reliefs were slowly eroding away.

At the time, the dam proved far more necessary to the people of Egypt than possible damage to a few antiquities. However, most of Philae was later saved and re-assembled stone by stone on nearby Agilkia Island, or New Philae, after the new Aswan High Dam was begun in 1960.

Figure 3–61. General View of the Temple of Isis

Ptolemaic-Roman Period
Albumen print
Photographer: J. Pascal Sébah
McClung Museum: 2/698
Gift of Friends of Egyptology, 1995

The temple of Isis at left and the Kiosk of Trajan at right is seen before the site was cleared. Nectanebo I in Dynasty XXX built the entrance between the sixty-foot-high pylon. Most of the temple is Ptolemaic, begun by Ptolemy II (308–246 B.C.), who also built the famous Pharos, or lighthouse, the museum, and the library at Alexandria. Reliefs on the towers depict Ptolemy XI (99–80 B.C.) in battle and making offerings to various deities. Other decorations were made by Roman emperors such as Tiberius Caesar (A.D. 14–37). On the island at the right and in the foreground are the mud brick remains of a destroyed Coptic village.

Figure 3–62. Second Pylon of the Temple of Isis

Ptolemaic-Roman Period
Albumen print
Photographer: Zangaki
McClung Museum: 25/655
Gift of Marcia S. Young, 1992

Scenes from the Forecourt on the forty-foot-high pylon face shows Isis and Horus being offered sacrificial meat by Ptolemy XII in his outstretched hand. In the relief above he presents a wreath at the right and at the left offers incense and pours liquid on an offering table. The stone at the base of the pylon was carved into a stela inscribed with a text concerning a land grant to the Temple of Isis in 157 B.C. The entrance between the pylons, decorated by Ptolemy VIII, was defaced as found in numerous other temples. A ruined Roman chapel is in the foreground.

Figure 3–63. Colonnade of the Birth House

Ptolemaic-Roman Period
Albumen print
Photographer: J. Pascal Sébah
McClung Museum: 3/698
Gift of Friends of Egyptology, 1995

Egyptian guides rest in the Forecourt of the Temple of Isis next to the Birth House, dedicated to the goddess Hathor-Isis. It contains scenes of the birth and early life of her son the god Horus. Its columns have floral capitals surmounted by sistrum-capitals, several of which were defaced. Cartouches and the *heb*-sign decorate the far right column. The next column has the *kheper-sign, Isis*-knot and *ankh*-sign encircling its shaft. The screens between the columns bear reliefs depicting several pharaohs attended by gods.

Figure 3–64. The Kiosk of Trajan

Ptolemaic-Roman Period
Color tinted silver print
Photographer: Lichtenstern & Harari, Cairo
McClung Museum: A1: 161 P578 1P
Gift of Mr. and Mrs. Louis Bailey Audigier, 1934

The unfinished Kiosk of Trajan is probably the best-remembered and charming building at Philae. One screen-wall has carved reliefs of Osiris, great Judge of the Dead, with the goddess Isis, receiving incense from the Roman Emperor Trajan (A.D. 98–117). Between August and December it was free from the elevation of the Nile waters after the completion of the old Aswan Dam.

Philae

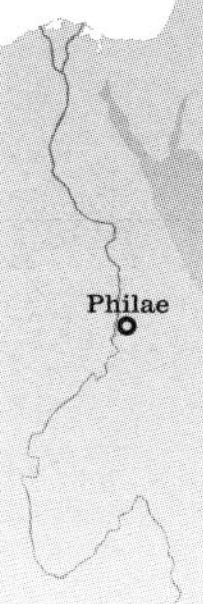

Figure 3–65. Wall Relief

Ptolemaic Period
Albumen print
Photographer: unidentified
McClung Museum: 1997.5.21
Gift of Friends of Egyptology, 1997

The two registers show Ptolemy VIII, son of Ptolemy V and Cleopatra I of the famed Rosetta Stone, presenting offerings. Above him are cartouches that bear his name. Unfortunately, the reliefs are greatly flattened, parts are illegible, and many areas are damaged.

Figure 3–67. Head of a God

Roman Period
Object: molded terra cotta
10.8 high x 10.2 cm. wide (4-1/4 x 4 inches)
Provenance: Alexandria(?), Egypt
Old Collection of 1890s
The Detroit Institute of Arts: 90.1S12162

Represented is a combined form of two deities: the god Horus, with the characteristic Double Crown of Egypt centered in the rays of the important Roman deity Helios, the Sun god. In the ancient world when Christianity was established, the production of terra cotta figurines declined. By the late Nineteenth Century, Greek and Roman figurines were a popular collector's item.

Figure 3–66. Head of a God

Roman Period
Object: molded terra cotta
8.6 high x 8.3 cm. wide (3-3/8 x 3-1/4 inches)
Provenance: Alexandria(?), Egypt
Old Collection of 1890s
The Detroit Institute of Arts: X 1989.195

The fragment represents the Egyptian god Horus, called Harpocrates, usually with a finger to his chin. Centered on his head is a Double Crown, a combined form of the White Crown of Upper Egypt and the Red Crown of Lower Egypt. Early artisans modelled by hand figurines of deities, but after the Sixth Century B.C. they were produced by molds. Small statuettes of sacred figures were among those made as votives for sanctuaries, tombs, and house shrines.

Debod

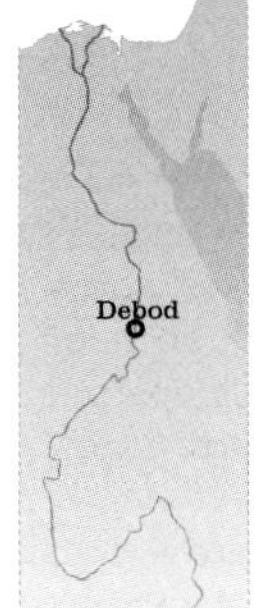

The village of Debod, or Dabud, was situated south of Philae on both banks of the Nile. A temple to honor its principal deity, Isis, along with Osiris and their child Horus, originally stood a short distance in on the West Bank. It was built by a king of Ethiopia, Ezekher-Amen. As with other structures around the same date additions were made by several Ptolemies and Roman emperors.

After walking along a quay and paved causeway visitors gazed at the first pylon. Here they looked up at the usual protective winged sun disk flanked by a cobra over the gateway. On the second pylon was an inscription by Ptolemy VI and his wife Cleopatra II dedicating the temple to Isis. The ruined condition was due to weakening by the flooding from the old Assuan Dam and theft of stone blocks by villagers. In 1963 the temple was transferred to the Parque de la Montaña in Madrid, Spain.

Additional Reading: Gunter Roeder, *Debod bis Bab Kalabsche.* Cairo 1911–1912.

Figure 3–68. Temple of Debod

Ptolemaic-Roman Period, IInd Century B.C.
Albumen print
Photographer: J. Pascal Sébah
McClung Museum: 1996.10.28
Gift of Friends of Egyptology, 1996

The standing first and second pylon entrances were built close to one another. The third pylon tumbled into a pile of shattered blocks. In the background are the ruined temple proper and the entrance to the Vestibule.

Kalabsheh

At the site of the ancient town of Talmis, about twenty-three miles south of Debod, stood the Temple of Mandulis, or Kalabsheh. Reliefs suggest the temple existed in the New Kingdom during the reign of King Amenhotep II of Dynasty XVIII. However, the temple dates mostly to the reign of the first Roman Emperor Augustus (27 B.C.–A.D. 14), grandnephew of Julius Caesar, who had it restored. Additions were made later by the despotic Emperor Caligula (A.D. 37–41) and the popular Trajan (A.D. 97–117), who made its final enlargement.

Visitors arriving by boat alighted on to the quay, walked along a causeway one hundred feet long and up some steps to pause before the pylon gateway. One had to step carefully to avoid toppled pillars, broken blocks, and other architectural parts to get a sense of the temple plan. After the completion of the old Assuan Dam, the site was submerged during the winter season. In planning for the new Assuan High Dam the structure was dismantled in 1962 and reassembled some thirty-one miles north on a hill overlooking Lake Nasser near the new Assuan High Dam.

From the river, it looks like a huge fortress; but seen from the threshold of the main gateway, it is a wilderness of ruin.[30]
—Amelia Edwards, 1877

As he had done at other sites, including Edfu, Kom Ombo, and Abu Simbel, the Italian conservator and excavator Alexandre Barsanti (1858–1917) began work to strengthen and restore the temple in 1895 and 1896, a necessary measure due to the building of the old Assuan Dam. The French Egyptologist Henri L. Gauthier (1877–1950) copied its important inscriptions, as did the German Egyptologist Gunther Roeder (1881–1966).

Additional Reading: Henri L. Gauthier, *Le Temple de Kalabchah.* Cairo 1911, 1914, 1927.

Figure 3–69. Temple of Mandulis

Roman Period
Albumen print
Photographer: J. Pascal Sébah
McClung Museum: 1996.10.29
Gift of Friends of Egyptology, 1996

Mandulis is the Greek name for a Nubian solar god associated with the temple. Facing the Forecourt is the entrance to the Hypostyle Hall, decorated by four columns with elaborate floral capitals and alternating screens. The short walls bear a ritual scene of Augustus with the Egyptian gods, Horus, Thoth, and Harsiesis, and contain Greek inscriptions.

Kalabsheh

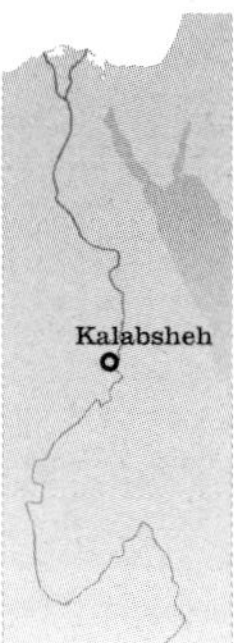

Figure 3–70. Longview of the Temple of Mandulis

Roman Period
Albumen print
Photographer: Francis Frith
McClung Museum: 1997.5.22
Gift of Friends of Egyptology, 1997

Although the temple was dedicated to the local Nubian god Mandulis, the Egyptian deities Isis, Osiris, Horus, and others were also worshipped there. On the exterior of the temple at the rear are large waterspouts. Surrounding the temple are the ruins of mud-brick dwellings.

Figure 3–71. Temple of Maharaka

Ptolemaic-Roman Periods
Albumen print
Photographer: Francis Frith
McClung Museum: 1997.5.25
Gift of Friends of Egyptology, 1997

The shrine has a small, rectangular court, and on either side are six columns and an intact entablature. A unique architectural feature that intrigued visitors was the spiral stairway leading to the roof that provided a far-reaching view. The damaged blocks that tumbled from the temple and were buried by invading sands posed a challenge to the most sure-footed traveller.

Maharaka

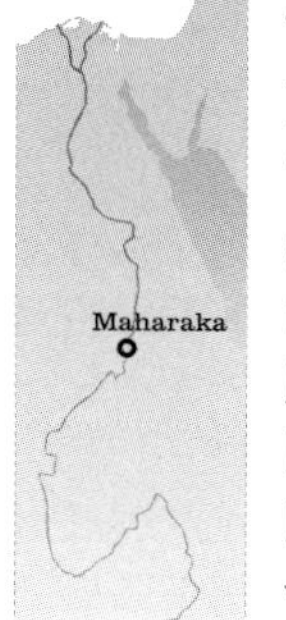

The town was called Hierasykaminos, or the "sacred sycamore," in antiquity and marked the southern boundary line of Egypt during the Ptolemaic and Roman Periods. Later the border was moved further south. The small temple at the site was dedicated to Serapis. At the time of the construction of the new Assuan High Dam in 1960 the small temple was moved twenty miles south of its original location to avoid the floods.

The cult of the god Serapis developed in Memphis in the temple located above the underground burial galleries of embalmed Apis bulls. Serapis was a combination of powerful Hellenic gods with the Egyptian god Osiris, particularly in his character as God of the Dead.

Anibeh

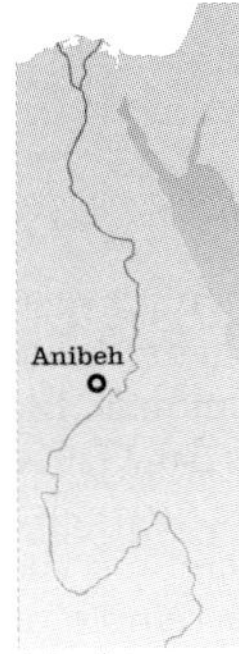

About two hundred and thirty kilometers south of Assuan is the palm-shaded modern village of Anibeh, possibly a center ruled by a chieftain subordinate to the capital of Nubia, Meroë, located between the Fifth and Sixth Cataracts. The ancient people of Anibeh were a pastoral and hunter culture, who constructed their dwellings and great buildings in brick. New Kingdom brick pyramids and tombs are nearby and an earlier Nubian necropolis of the Middle Kingdom and later.

In 1907–1908 the British archaeologists C. Leonard Woolley (1880–1960) and D. Randall-MacIver (1873–1945), began excavations at the Roman-Nubian necropolis on the West Bank at Karanòg three miles north of Anibeh, funded by the Eckley B. Coxe, Jr. Expedition to Nubia. Excavations at the pharaonic city and nearby cemeteries were also made from 1912 to 1914 and later by the German Egyptologist Georg Steindorff (1861–1951) and others.

...the forms of Egyptian worship had imposed themselves fairly effectually upon the beliefs of the non-Egyptian peoples of the South.[31]
—C. Leonard Woolley and D. Randall-MacIver, 1908

ADDITIONAL READING: D. Randall-MacIver and C. Leonard Woolley, *Karanòg: The Romano-Nubian Cemetery. University of Pennsylvania Museum, E. B. Coxe Jun. Expedition to Nubia, Vols. 3–4.* Philadelphia 1910.

Figure 3–72. Head from a *Ba* Statue

100 B.C.–A.D. 300
Object: sandstone
18 high x 15 cm. wide (7-1/8 x 5-7/8 inches)
Provenance: Anibeh, Upper Nubia
Eckley B. Coxe, Jr., Expedition, 1908
The University of Pennsylvania Museum: E 7036 (Neg. # S4-141631)

The head was among fragments of *Ba* statues found scattered around the Anibeh necropolis. It appears religious beliefs of the culture group were a blend of Egyptian, Greek, and local cults. The idea of the "soul," or *Ba*, in other areas developed differently than in Egypt, although related in concept. A sun disk missing from the top of the head associated the *Ba* with the Egyptian sun god Re.

Standing Lamp (not illustrated)

A.D. 275 –325
Object: bronze
34 cm. high (13-3/4 inches)
Provenance: Anibeh: Grave 187
Eckley B. Coxe, Jr., Expedition, 1908
The University of Pennsylvania Museum: E 7147

The thin shaft on the round foot supports a shaped cup that once probably contained olive oil and a wick. When the wick was lighted the flame brightened interiors. Such lamps were also used as votive offerings to deities and were part of tomb furnishings as well.

The vessels are without exception of a foreign type...that prevailed uniformly throughout the Roman Empire.[32]
—C. Leonard Woolley and D. Randall-MacIver, 1908

Figure 3–73. Flask

Ist Century A.D.
Object: blown glass
10 high x 7.9 cm. diameter (4 x 3-1/8 inches)
Provenance: Anibeh, Lower Nubia
Grave 384
Eckley B. Coxe, Jr., Expedition, 1908
The University of Pennsylvania Museum: E 7340 (Neg. # S4-143054)

The thin-walled, transparent, greenish-brown vessel has a pear-shaped body and splayed bell mouth and is decorated by a spiraled thread of white opaque glass around the body. The flask clearly exhibits the conventional characteristics of similar vessels of Roman manufacture used to hold oils and unguents. Such flasks were not made in Nubia as they show no regional or individual Nubian features.

Figure 3–74. Mortuary Temple of Rameses II

New Kingdom, Dynasty XIX
Albumen print
Photographer: J. Pascal Sébah
McClung Museum: 1996.10.27
Gift of Friends of Egyptology, 1996

The Great Temple, dedicated to the sun gods Amen-Re of Thebes and falcon-headed Re-Harakhte of Heliopolis, was created to celebrate the thirtieth year of the pharaoh's reign. Rameses reigned for thirty-six more years, from 1304–1237 B.C., enabling him to erect numerous monuments and usurp many others. The great pharaoh sits for eternity before his temple. In the distance is a *feluka*, a typical sailboat which has mostly remained unchanged since pharaonic times.

Old Rameses II did not intend that his praises should go unsung even in Nubia, nor that any of his brilliant deeds should go unrecorded.[33]

—Archie Bell, 1916

Abu Simbel

The famed temples of Rameses II were created on the shores of the Nile River, one hundred and seventy miles south of Assuan and twenty-five miles north of the border between Egypt and the Sudan. At one time an ancient town thrived near the site. The two temples carved out of the living sandstone rock face are unusual being so far south of Cairo and from ancient religious centers. No doubt they were intended to impress the Nubians with the greatness and power of the Egyptian monarch. When the new Assuan High Dam was begun in 1960 the temples were moved to higher ground at the same site, beginning in 1964.

As early as 1813 the temples were investigated by the Swiss traveller John Burckhardt, and in 1817 the Italian explorer Giovanni Battista Belzoni began excavations there. In less than a week he removed twenty feet of sand. The huge figure of Re-Harakhte in its niche above the entrance, the name of the owner of the temple, and a colossal head of Rameses II were exposed. Later excavations by the German Egyptologist Karl Lepsius (1810–1884), Auguste Mariette, and Alexandre Barsanti, made further headway in clearing sand and rubbish. The excavations uncovered previously unknown chapels, statuary, and stelae.

Figure 3–75. Mortuary Temple of Rameses II

New Kingdom, Dynasty XIX
Albumen print
Photographer: Antonio Beato
McClung Museum: 1997.5.24
Gift of Friends of Egyptology, 1997

Four seated figures of the pharaoh, sixty-five feet high and wearing the Double Crown of Upper and Lower Egypt, command attention on the facade. In the foreground is the colossal head from a seated statue above felled by an earthquake. Sand obscures the lower part of the colossi. The smaller figures standing next to the pharaoh's enormous legs are from the left his Great Wife, Nefretiri, a daughter, the Queen-Mother, and a son. On either side of Re-Harakhte are inscriptions and figures of the king honoring the god.

Figure 3–76. Temple of Hathor

New Kingdom, Dynasty XIX
Albumen print
Photographer: Antonio Beato
McClung Museum: 1997.5.23
Gift of Friends of Egyptology, 1997

The smaller temple adjacent to the larger monument honors the goddess Hathor and was created by Rameses II for Nefretiri his Great Wife. The facade, ninety-two feet long, is adorned by six monumental standing figures; two of his wife alternate with four of the king. Their children stand close to their legs.

Gammai

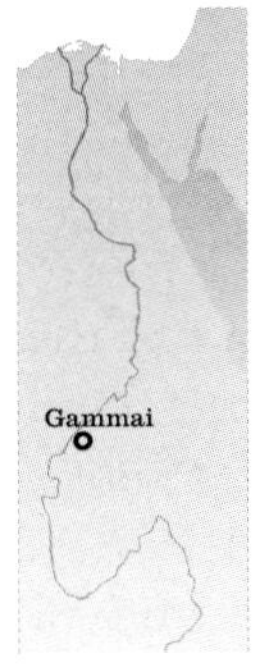

Gammai, located fifteen miles south of Wady Halfeh below the Second Cataract on the east side of the Nile, was of modest political or economic significance. Nevertheless the site did offer scholars comparisons with finds from other more important neighboring Nubian cemeteries.

The excavations at Gammai in 1915 by the American Egyptologists Oric Bates and Dows Dunham brought to light numerous predynastic and early dynastic grave sites, but the burials were badly damaged. Tomb robbers had tunneled into the cemeteries and burial mounds. Among the objects they uncovered were a series of thirty-four polished, black ware vessels in the typical southern style similar to those found from Kerma down to Meroë. Also, they made an unexpected discovery of a feather cap and cloak that had never been recorded before.

> *Gammai is at best a poor place, a backwater of civilization, and it will hardly have been more than that in ancient times.*[34]
>
> ***—Oric Bates and Dows Dunham, 1927***

Figure 3–77. Beaker

Nubian Middle Kingdom(?)
Object: black ware
15.5 high x 10.8 cm. diameter (6-1/8 x 4-1/4 inches)
Provenance: Gammai: Cemetery 100, Mound U33
Excavated by Oric Bates and Dows Dunham, 1915
The Peabody Museum of Archaeology and Ethnology: B4117

The slightly tapered, straight-sided, black, polished ware vessel is decorated with white-filled, incised triangles and geometric decoration encircling its body. The beaker resembles pottery forms found at other Nubian sites such as those at Kerma.

Kerma

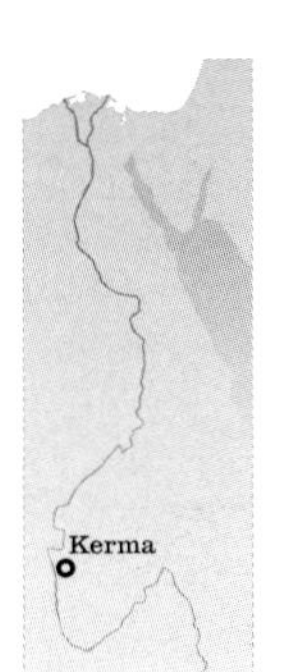

The Egyptian colony of Kerma was located two hundred and forty-six miles south of Wady Halfeh on the East Bank of the Nile. Its main importance was as guardian of the southern roads and protector of southern goods on route to Egypt.

> *The bed-burial, in this period so rare in Egypt, was the usual type of burial at Kerma.*[35]
>
> ***—George Reisner, 1923***

George Reisner made extensive excavations at the Kerma site from 1913 to 1916. It was important to excavate there as the area was to be flooded by irrigation and agricultural schemes of the government. His work on several mud funerary mounds and several hundred Nubian graves turned up numerous examples of a distinctive, fine black-topped, red-polished ware. This pottery and other arts and crafts found at Kerma greatly advanced knowledge of Egyptian influences in Nubia.

Additional Reading: George A. Resiner, *Excavations at Kerma*. Cambridge, Massachusetts 1923.

Figure 3–78. Bed Leg

Classic Kerma Period:
Second Intermediate Period
Object: wood
41.8 high x 16.6 wide x 5 cm. deep (16-7/16 x 6-1/2 x 2 inches)
Provenance: Kerma: Grave: K1085
Excavated by George A. Reisner, 1915
The Peabody Museum of Archaeology and Ethnology: 15-12-50

The wooden leg, shaped like an ox leg, had been part of the common type of bed (*angareeb*) upon which the deceased was placed. These beds had four legs supporting a rectangular frame, and a foot board, sometimes decorated with inlaid ivory geometric forms, and later replaced with animal inlays. It was probably webbed with rawhide straps or cord to support the body.

Hardwoods seem to have been in plentiful supply as ample acacias (*acacia nilotica*) grew nearby and African blackwood was easily imported from the southern Sudan. The carpentry of the furniture material found at the site reflects the typical work of Egyptian artisans working in an Egyptian colony located in Nubia.

Notes:

[1] Frith, *Francis Frith's Travels*, p. 14.

[2] Greener, *The Discovery*, p. 178.

[3] Forster, *Alexandria*, p. 160.

[4] Petrie, *Seventy Years*, p. 224.

[5] Habachi, *The Obelisks*, p. 49.

[6] Reisner, *Mycerinus*, p. 3.

[7] Reisner, *A History*, p. 23.

[8] Petrie, *Seventy Years*, p. 210.

[9] Mariette, *Monuments*, p. 116.

[10] Steindorf, *Das Grab des Ti*, p. 1.

[11] Petrie, *Illahun*, p. 20.

[12] Grenfell, *Fayum Towns*, p. 17.

[13] Garstang, *Mahasna*, p. 15.

[14] Petrie, *Abydos, 1902*, p. 1.

[15] Petrie, *Diospolis Parva*, p. 4.

[16] Petrie, *Dendereh*, p. 2.

[17] Petrie & Quibell, *Naqada*, p. vii.

[18] Hitchens, *Egypt*, p. 96.

[19] Carter, *Tutankhamen*, p. 76.

[20] Mariette, *The Monuments*, p. 256.

[21] Breasted, *Records*, p. 36.

[22] Oldfather, *Diodorus*, p. 169.

[23] Blackman, *Luxor*, p. 62.

[24] Hitchens, *Egypt*, p. 99.

[25] Edwards, *A Thousand Miles*, p. 159.

[26] Edwards, *A Thousand Miles*, p. 401.

[27] Edwards, *A Thousand Miles*, p. 393.

[28] Van Dyke, *In Egypt*, p. 138.

[29] Bell, *Spell*, p. 241.

[30] Edwards, *A Thousand Miles*, p. 376.

[31] Woolley and Randall-MacIver, *Karanòg*, Vol. III, p. 4.

[32] Woolley and Randall-MacIver, *Karanòg*, Vol. IV, p. 74.

[33] Bell, *Spell*, p. 249.

[34] Bates and Dunham, "Excavations at Gammai," p. 115.

[35] Reisner, "Excavations at Kerma", p. 17.

Selected Bibliography

Bates, Oric and Dows Dunham, "Excavations at Gammai" in *Harvard African Studies*, Vol. VIII. Cambridge, Massachusetts: Peabody Museum of Harvard University, 1927.

Bell, Archie, *The Spell of Egypt*. Boston: The Page Company Publishers, 1916.

Blackman, A.M., *Luxor and Its Temples*. New York: The MacMillan Company, 1923.

Breasted, James Henry, *Ancient Records of Egypt*, Vol IV. New York: Russell & Russell, Inc., 1962.

Carter, Howard, *The Tomb of Tutankhamen*. Vol. I. New York: Cooper Square Publishers, Inc. 1963.

Edwards, Amelia B., *A Thousand Miles Up the Nile*. Second Edition. Glasgow/ Manchester/New York: George Rutledge and Sons, Ltd., 1891.

Forster, E.M., *Alexandria: A history and a Guide*. Garden City, New York: Anchor Books, Doubleday & Co., Inc.1961 [repro of first edition, 1922].

Garstang, John, *Mahasna and Bet Khallaf*. London: Bernard Quaritch, 1903.

Greener, Leslie, *The Discovery of Egypt*. New York: The Viking Press, 1966.

Grenfell, B.P., et al, *Fayum Towns and Their Papryri*. London: Egypt Exploration Fund, 1900.

Habachi, Labib, *The Obelisks of Egypt*. New York: Charles Scribner's Sons, 1977.

Hitchens, Robert S., *Egypt and Its Monuments*. New York: Century Co., 1912.

Mariette, Alphonse, *The Monuments of Upper Egypt*. Translated from Auguste Mariette-Bey, "Itinéraire de la Haut Égypte." Boston: J. H. Mansfield & J. W. Dearborn, 1890.

Oldfather, C. H., *Diodorus of Sicily*. Book I. Cambridge, Massachusetts: Harvard University Press, 1946.

Petrie, W. M. Flinders, *Abydos. Part I, 1902*. London: Egypt Exploration Fund, 1902.

———, *Dendereh 1898*. London: The Egypt Exploration Fund, 1900.

———, *Diospolis Parva. The Cemeteries of Abadiyeh and Hu*,1898-9. London: Egypt Exploration Fund, 1901.

———, *Illahun, Kahun and Gurob 1889-1890*. London: David Nutt, 1891.

———, *Seventy Years in Archaeology*. London: Sampson Low, Marston & Co., Ltd., n.d.

Petrie, W.M. Flinders, & James Quibell, *Naqada and Ballas. 1895*. London: Bernard Quaritch, 1896.

Reisner, George A., *A History of the Giza Necropolis*, Vol. I. Cambridge, Massachusetts: Harvard University Press, 1942.

———, "Excavations at Kerma, Parts IV-V" in *Harvard African Studies*, Vol. VI. Cambridge, Massachusetts: Peabody Museum of Harvard University, 1923.

———, *Mycerinus*. Cambridge, Massachusetts: Harvard University Press, 1931.

Steindorf, Georg, *Das Grab des Ti*. Leipzig: J. C. Hinrichs, 1913.

Van Dyke, John C., *In Egypt. Studies and Sketches Along the Nile*. New York: Charles Scribner's Sons, 1931.

Woolley, C. Leonard and D. Randall-MacIver, *Karanòg. The Romano-Nubian Cemetery*, Vol. III. Philadelphia: The University Museum, 1910.

———, *Karanòg. The Romano-Nubian Cemetery*, Vol. IV. Philadelphia: The University Museum, 1910.

Funds Are Established

Figure 4–1. Seal of the Egypt Exploration Fund

A most important and enduring organization to further the study of ancient Egypt was the **Egypt Exploration Fund** (EEF). This society was founded in Great Britain in 1883 by the inspired zeal of the British Egyptologist Amelia B. Edwards, supported by the Orientalist R. Stuart Poole as honorary secretary, and benefactor Sir Erasmus Wilson as treasurer. In 1883–1894, a branch of the Fund opened in Boston, Massachusetts, under the leadership of the Reverend William C. Winslow. These dedicated individuals and influential backers were to greatly influence the course of Egyptology. Their principal objective:

> *To obtain and disseminate information respecting ancient and modern Egypt, and all or any of the countries adjacent, or being near thereto, and the ancient and modern inhabitants thereof, respectively, and respecting the history, religion, arts, literature, ethnology, archaeology, mineralogy, numismatics, topography, geography (physical and political), geology, zoology, botany, meteorology, and natural history and the manners and customs of the same countries respectively.*[1]
>
> **—The Egypt Exploration Fund, 1888**

The first excavations were in the Delta in Lower Egypt. In the 1880s archaeological excavations were still highly unscientific, a form of licensed—or unlicensed—destruction that mostly concentrated on large and impressive finds rather than the careful examination of a site and its contents. The objective was to find as much as possible in as short a time as practicable. However, change was on the way. The Swiss Egyptologist Henri Édouard Naville (1844–1926) was the first excavator to work for the EEF in British Egypt. His first excavations were in 1883 at Tell el-Maskhuta in the Delta, which resulted in a report that set the format and standards for future publications.

Edwards and Poole were gravely overworked. Between them, they had the whole responsibility for the day-to-day running of the Fund: collecting subscriptions, recruiting new members, corresponding with the press, lecturing to the public, and dealing with inquiries and complaints—all before the era of telephones and typewriters. They had to write everything by hand themselves as there was no money for a secretary.

Figure 4–2. Amelia Blandford Edwards

Amelia Blandford Edwards, founder of the Egypt Exploration Fund and the Department of Egyptology at University College, London.

Pen (not illustrated)

Roman Period
Object: reed
14.6 cm. long (5-3/4 inches)
Provenance: Oxyrhynchus
Gift of the Egypt Exploration Fund, 1904
The University of Pennsylvania Museum: E 11722

Pens like this were used to inscribe the many thousands of Roman papyri written in Greek found at Behneseh, called Oxyrhynchus by the Greeks, in Upper Egypt. The British papyrologists Bernard Grenfell (1869–1926) and Arthur Hunt (1871–1934) began exploration of the site in 1897 for the EEF and found there the richest source of papyri known.

String of Beads and Amulets (not illustrated)

New Kingdom
Object: faience, jasper, carnelian, glass
60 cm. (23-5/8 inches)
Provenance: Dendereh
Rosher Excavation, 1898
Sponsored by the American Exploration Society, 1898
The University of Pennsylvania Museum: E 3757

The reconstructed strand is composed of disc, barrel, ridged and ribbed-shaped faience, spheroid red jasper, barrel-formed glass and carnelian, and ridged carnelian. The necklace represents a type within the combinations of components found in less opulent Egyptian jewelry.

Necklace (not illustrated)

New Kingdom, Dynasty XVIII
Object: faience, carnelian
30 cm. (11-13/16 inches)
Provenance: Abydos: Tomb E255
Purchased from Egyptian Research Account, 1900
The University of Pennsylvania Museum: E 6732

Egyptian faience came in several variants. Generally the ware for jewelry was made of powdered quartz paste, shaped by pottery molds and decorated with a colored glaze. Carnelian is a semiprecious stone which was abundant as pebbles in the Eastern Desert of Nubia. It was prized for its rich red to red-brown color for beads and amulets and was a talisman to transfer potential harm. The necklace was probably among the finds made by the British Egyptologist Flinders Petrie during his excavations at Abydos from 1899–1904.

In Egypt, an important component was the Egyptian Antiquities Service, a branch of the government. It had been founded in the 1850s after Khedive Said (1854–1863) recognized the importance of taking steps to protect his country's heritage. It was the first time sites and monuments in Egypt were officially protected. The organization made certain sites accessible to excavators, maintained them, helped to safeguard sites from pillagers, and presided over the division of discovered antiquities. In the Nineteenth and early Twentieth Centuries distinguished European Egyptologists held the post of Director-General of the Service. But it was not until the 1920s that the training of Egyptian Egyptologists began.

Through the years the Fund, which was to change its name in 1919 to the Egypt Exploration Society, worked with the Egyptian Antiquities Service. The Fund was able to sponsor numerous archaeological excavations in Egypt followed by the rapid publication of the results. There were three administrative units: a department to support general work of exploration and discovery; an "Archaeological Survey" section to record ancient texts and scenes before they were destroyed; and a "Graeco-Roman Branch," a unit that furthered discovery and translations of classical, religious, or secular papyri. In 1897 a new department was established for the discovery and publication of excavated finds.

Activities abounded. Grants were pursued to aid in financing surveys, explorations, and excavations. New information was distributed, and antiquities were publicly exhibited in educational institutions, libraries, or similar institutions. Throughout the years some remarkable discoveries were made regarding the religious practices, laws, artistic developments, sciences, and the social and political climate of ancient Egypt. Each season the subsidized work effected positive results. By 1900 the notable officers in charge of explorations were the Swiss Egyptologist Henri Édouard Naville and British Egyptologists W. M. Flinders Petrie, Bernard P. Grenfell, and Norman de Garis Davies.

Another important operation was the distribution of antiquities and papyri to museums and universities including those in the United States. Such "gifts" were made proportionate to the incoming subscriptions, which the EEF depended upon for finances to continue its work. American subscriptions, which came from Boston and chapters in other cities, attracted antiquities to a number of American museums. In turn, excavations were supported each season. In this way, American institutions not only supported Egyptological research, but also obtained authentic objects of known origin that were historically important. Some of the objects recovered were received by such institutions as the University Museum at the University of Pennsylvania and the Carnegie Museum, Pittsburgh, as evidenced by the examples in this exhibition. The organization's publications continue to be a valued and useful research resource.

The EEF Meets the Egypt Research Account

In 1905, unable to accept the EEF Committee's intrigues and resistance to his terms regarding his work, Flinders Petrie left the Egypt Exploration Fund and established the British School of Archaeology in Egypt at the University College in London. However, the financing of such an operation became dependent on the already existing "Egyptian Research Account" (ERA), a small student fund founded by him in 1894, which raised money for archaeologists and excavations. Petrie had wanted the ERA broadened so students could go with him to Egypt, have their travel and living expenses covered, and work in Egypt for a season. He personally worked hard to increase subscribers and thereby expand his ambitions for the study of Egypt. An annual excavation report was published for subscribers, and excavated objects were placed in pubic museums.

Figure 4–3. Myrtle Broome and Amie Calverley

Flowers bloom in the desert for British excavation artists, Myrtle Broome (1888–1978) and Amie Calverley (1896–1959) at the Egypt Exploration Society House. Abydos, circa 1930. Photograph by Lindsley Hall.

Courtesy Lindsley Foote Hall Photograph Collection, Division of Special Collections & University Archives, University of Oregon library system.

British Excavations in Egypt

The excavations sponsored by the EEF allowed discoveries of numerous important city sites, including Biblical sites such as Pithom-Succoth, the city of Goshen, and the Greek Naukratis, where antiquities in papyrus, metals, ceramics, and glass were found. Ruins were surveyed and studied. Most impressive was the work in Upper Egypt at the Mortuary Temple of Queen Hatshepsut at Der el-Bahri, Thebes, followed by the discoveries at Deshasheh, Behneseh, tombs of Beni Hasan and el-Bersheh, and numerous other sites.

Excavations by eminent archaeologists were supported through publications—particularly those of the British Egyptologist Flinders Petrie (1853–1942) and his work at Negadeh, Dendereh, Coptos, and Thebes, to name just a sampling of his extraordinary range of excavations. Some of the material Petrie recovered was received by institutions in a variety of countries, including the United States, that contributed to the Fund and in turn were given antiquities. This was also the case with the ERA. Such arrangements supported Petrie's excavations, where he scientifically directed and compiled information in order to provide documented and provenanced objects.

Figure 4–4. Fragment of a Cartouche

New Kingdom
Object: red quartzite
20 cm. long x 9 wide x 3.7 deep (7-7/8 x 22-7/8 x 1-7/16 inches)
Provenance: Tell el-Amarna
Egypt Exploration Fund, circa 1900
The Carnegie Museum of Natural History: 7043–2

The carved relief fragment bears the name of Ikhnaton, or "Pious one of the Aton," a name change he made from his birth name, Amenhotep IV. The so-called heretic pharaoh established a religious cult in his new city called Akhetaton ("Horizon of the Aton") at Tell el-Amarna, where he decreed only one god was to be worshipped, the physical sun disk, Aton.

In 1912 the German Egyptologist Ludwig Borchardt (1863–1938), while excavating for the German Oriental Society, found the famous bust of Queen Nefertiti, wife of Ikhnaton, in a sculptor's studio at the site. It has been said he cleverly negotiated the bust out of Egypt avoiding possible sanctions related to the distribution of finds. Earlier, in 1887, a peasant woman found over three hundred official letters written in cuneiform on clay tablets in building ruins at Tell el- Amarna that documented correspondence between Ikhnaton and his father with foreign rulers.

Figure 4–5. Double Kohl Jar

New Kingdom (?)
Object: wood
6 cm. high x 2.9 wide x 2.1 cm. deep (2-3/8 x 1-3/16 x 7/8 inches)
Provenance: Abydos: D111
Egypt Exploration Fund, 1917.
The Carnegie Museum of Natural History: 1917 284

The small tubular container was designed to hold finely ground malachite, a basic green carbonate of copper, made into a powder to use as eye-paint. Also galena, a sulphide of lead, was made into a mixture and applied to the eyes as was oxide of manganese. The two holes in the lid supported kohl sticks, applicators used to apply the cosmetic. Such jars were created in other materials including faience and alabaster.

Figure 4–6. Six Shawabtis of Peduasar

Late Dynastic Period, 380–343 B.C.
Object: faience
9.8 cm. high (3-7/8 inches)
Provenance: Abydos: Cemetery G, Tomb 50
Egypt Exploration Fund, 1900–1902
The Detroit Institute of Arts: 90.310–314; 334

The nicely modeled figurines, glazed in bright light-blue, with the arms crossed over the chest hold a pick in the left hand and a *mr*-hoe in the right hand, along with a rope extending to a basket on the left back shoulder. A pillar at the rear extends from the bottom of the lappet wig to the small rectangular base the figure stands on. The uninscribed shawabtis of Dynasty XXX belonged to the prophet Peduasar, a priest of Hathor, to serve him as laborers in the fields of the Afterworld. Three hundred and eighty-five shawabtis of Peduasar were found buried in the sands of the tomb by Flinders Petrie.

American Excavations in Egypt

One development that greatly influenced the future direction of American Egyptology was the founding of the EEF in England. Money for the fund's projects was raised by subscription from museums, universities, and individuals. When excavations were concluded at a Fund site, the Egyptian Antiquities Service and the Fund made an initial division of the recovered material. The Fund then distributed its share among its subscribers.

American museums initially depended on donations from private collectors, but by the end of the Nineteenth Century many institutions were making financial contributions to excavations carried out by two British organizations, the EEF and Flinders Petrie's British School of Archaeology and Egyptian Research Account. In return they received a share of each season's finds. For fledgling American museum collections the advantages of acquiring antiquities in this manner were obvious. These institutions were not only supporting scholarly research, they were also receiving objects of a known provenance and well-documented archaeological data. However, American individuals and institutions eventually started to conduct their own major excavations in Egypt.

Shortly after the advent of American participation in EEF and the ERA, a significant number of museums and universities began to undertake their own systematic archaeological and epigraphic research in the Nile Valley. Among the pioneers was Phoebe Apperson Hearst (1842–1919), who in 1899 began financing the University of California at Berkeley's expeditions to Egypt. Another pioneer was Sara Yorke Stevenson (1847–1922), curator in the University of Pennsylvania's museum and the founder and driving force for the American Exploration Society. The Rhode Island businessman Theodore Munroe Davis (1837–1915), between 1903 and 1912, sponsored a series of highly successful excavations in the Valley of the Kings for the Metropolitan Museum of Art.

This tradition continues today. An institution that subscribed to the EEF, and later the EES, experienced the benefits of objects from the finds. This in turn inspired the start of American excavations in Egypt. Throughout this exhibition are examples of this exchange.

Private Gifts Enrich American Museums

For archaeological excavations to have taken place ample funding was crucial. The governmental funding agencies or private support in Britain, Germany, Austria, Italy, France, the United States, and other countries were depended on to finance excavations in Egypt. Museums and universities were able to sponsor their own excavations only with substantial financial backing. In the late Nineteenth Century, American collections of Egyptian antiquities kept pace with the growth of American industrial wealth; therefore, one source of revenue came from the enthusiastic private patronage of affluent donors.

Represented in the exhibition are some of the ways ancient Egyptian antiquities became a part of American collections. Certain contributions were big and others small. Each in its own way reflects a particular type of support that museums have long been accustomed to receiving to sustain their purpose. Generosity comes in many sizes and is a museum collection's lifeline.

The American benefactor **Eckley Brinton Coxe, Jr.** (1872–1916), who was born in Philadelphia, became an avid supporter of excavations in Egypt and Egyptian research for the University of Pennsylvania. After Coxe had graduated from the University in 1893, he began his many journeys to Egypt, including travels through the Sudan and to Khartum. During this time he developed his knowledge of Egypt's monuments and temples. An enduring bond began when, in 1907, the Eckley B. Coxe, Junior, Expedition to Nubia, under the direction of the British Egyptologist David Randall-MacIver brought back to the United States the first objects and knowledge from that culture. Other museums followed by example and acquired similar collections. Coxe's interest in Egypt was intense and is reflected in the endowment he established for excavations in Egypt. Every detail of the operation was closely followed by him. In 1903 he had been made a member of the Board of Managers of the University Museum and in 1910 its president, a post he held until his death in 1916. Due to his leadership the University Museum enjoyed its greatest period of growth and its creation of Egyptological research with excavations in Nubia, 1907–1910; Gizeh, 1914–1915; Dendereh, 1915–1918; Memphis, 1915–1923; Thebes, 1921–1924;

Figure 4–7. Eckley Brinton Coxe, Jr.

Eckley Brinton Coxe, Jr., benefactor of the University Museum and the Egyptian Section, has before him a Middle Kingdom, steatite statuette of the priest, Merer, discovered in Nubia. From a painting by Adolphe Borie, 1910.

Courtesy The University of Pennsylvania Museum, (Neg. #S8-137270)

Figure 4–8. Phoebe Hearst and Party at the Sphinx

Phoebe Apperson Hearst, back row, third from right, and the American Egyptologist George A. Reisner, at the far left on a donkey, pose with a group of friends. The pyramid of King Khufu (Cheops) looms in the background. Mrs. Hearst was the major patron of Reisner's excavations at Gizeh. Due to her efforts a museum was established at the University of California, Berkeley in 1901.

Courtesy of the University of California at Berkeley.

Figure 4–9. Double Pot

Predynastic Period
Object: painted earthenware
Provenance: unknown
8.5 high x 12.5 cm. wide (3-3/8 x 4-15/16 inches)
From the Louis Palma di Cesnola Collection, 1865–1870.
Gift of Albert Gallatin, 1934
Peabody Museum of Archaeology and Ethnology: 34-30-50/ 248

The two small, ovoid binocular pots are joined at one side of the upper bodies and have everted rims. Two string hole handles project at the upper unconnected sides. Decorated in red-brown paint, one jar has a shield shaped standard on a pole which is found on boats. It may represent a sacred emblem and symbol of a clan or nome. The other jar has nine, long, thick, horizontal lines with a center wave in each, above a row of long legged and long necked birds (ostriches or flamingos) that stand in water indicated by several rows of horizontal lines. The pot was produced during the Gerzean Period, circa 3500/3400–3200 B.C.

Figure 4–10. Head from a Coffin.

Late Dynastic Period
Object: painted wood
34.3 cm. high x 16.5 wide (13-1/2 x 6-1/2 inches)
Provenance: unknown
Gift of Frederick K. Stearns, 1901
The Detroit Institute of Arts: 69.4

The features of the wood face once covered in gesso show large eyes outlined in black, extended eyebrows, an aquiline nose, a light smile on thin lips above a small chin. Such details suggest the painted head is of a young man and was once part of the lid of his coffin. Various grades of coffins were produced, the more elaborately decorated being the more costly.

Figure 4–11. Cosmetic Dish

New Kingdom
Object: stone
8.6 cm. long x 6.4 wide (3-3/8 x 2-1/2 inches)
Provenance: unknown
Gift of Frederick K. Stearns, 1901
Detroit Institute of Arts: 90.1S14131

The dish is fashioned in the form of the sacred lotus flower and once had a sliding cover. In the creation myths the deity Nefer-Tum came forth from a lotus blossom floating on the sacred primordial waters of Nun in his role in making all things. Nefer-Tum, whose name means lotus, was the god of the lotus and the source of precious unguents.

and Medum, 1929–1932. The goal was to develop an Egyptian Section of the University Museum's collections and to establish a permanent gallery of Egyptian art. Provisions in Coxe's will of 1916 made it clear that "continuous and unremitting field work" was expected. His generous bequest enabled the University Museum to permanently continue its excavations and research.

Another benefactor to archaeology and anthropology in Egypt was the American heiress **Phoebe Apperson Hearst** (1842–1919) who supported systematic excavations and the efforts of ethnologists associated with the University of California. Hearst, a prominent member of the American Exploration Society, wanted the first anthropology department and first museum west of the Mississippi to be a center for the study of anthropology. Through its major patron, the University of California was provided with material for a museum to supplement the anthropology department. In 1901 the museum was established, and with Hearst's efforts the museum's core grew from some two hundred thirty thousand objects into the millions. Extensive and important finds were made under the auspices of the Hearst Egyptian Expeditions, including important excavations of the royal monuments at Napata and the pyramid tombs of Kabushiya in Upper Nubia. Beginning in 1903, the American archaeologist George Andrew Reisner undertook his life's work of excavating numerous mastabas in the vicinity of the Great Pyramid, and later the Valley Temple of Menkure and other pyramids and cemeteries at Gizeh. These endeavors were supported by the Hearst Expedition until 1905.

A slightly different type of support came from **Louis Palma di Cesnola** (1832–1904), who became the first director of the Metropolitan Museum of Art in 1878. Cesnola had amassed an enormous collection of material from his countless archaeological explorations and offered this prize to the museum for purchase in 1872. After a distinguished military career the controversial Cesnola was appointed United States consul at Cyprus, 1865–1877, where he unearthed and procured statues, inscriptions,

Figure 4–12. Alabastron

New Kingdom (?)
Object: alabaster
8.8 cm. high x 3.2 diameter
(3-1/2 x 1-1/4 inches)
Provenance: unknown
Gift of Frederick K. Stearns, 1901
The Detroit Institute of Arts: 90.1S11820

The vessel, decorated by natural striations in the stone, was used for perfumes, oils or ointments.

coffins, bronzes, and other ancient treasures. These and the Egyptian antiquities he acquired from Gaston Maspero and Émile Brugsch of the Egyptian Antiquities Service became the central feature in the museum's first building in New York.

Although not an actual benefactor, the excavator **Charles H. Rosher** might be mentioned here. Flinders Petrie recommended him in 1897 as a capable engineer to Sara Yorke Stevenson, curator of the Egyptian and Mediterranean section of the museum at the University of Pennsylvania. Rosher briefly joined Petrie at Dendereh to learn some basic excavation skills, as he was not a trained archaeologist. Later Rosher went on to excavate at Dendereh, under the sponsorship of the American Exploration Society in Philadelphia of which Sara Stevenson was an influential member. He drew plans of some tombs at the site. A large number of artifacts from Dendereh went into the museum's Egyptian collection.

In the category of private donors was **Mrs. Charles Cramp** of Philadelphia. In 1894 the University Museum of the University of Pennsylvania acquired some excellent examples of ancient Egyptian art from her. Little is known as well about another private donor, **Mrs. Dillwyn Parrish**. In 1914 Mrs. Parrish gave some significant ancient Egyptian objects to the University Museum. One donor to the Detroit Museum of Art, as it was once called, was **Frederick Stearns** (1831–1907). In his youth he had been an apprentice to a druggist, and in 1855 he moved to Detroit where he soon prospered as the owner of a successful drug manufacturing company. After retiring he traveled to many parts of the world including Egypt. In 1890 the Detroit Museum received a large number of the objects Stearns had amassed during his excursions.

Figure 4–13. Jar with Lid

New Kingdom
Object: faience
7.2 cm. high x 3.9 diameter, with lid (2-7/8 x 1-1/2 inches)
Provenance: unknown
Gift of Frederick K. Stearns, 1901
The Detroit Institute of Arts: X1989.143

The small, bright blue covered jar was made to hold ointments.

Figure 4–14. Broad Collar

Middle and New Kingdom Style
Object: faience
25.4 cm. high x 30.5 wide (10 x 12 inches)
Provenance: unknown
Gift of the Egypt Exploration Fund, Frederick Stearns and Dr. Henry Gillman, circa 1900
The Detroit Institute of Arts: F1989.51

The beaded *wesekh*-collar was reconstructed from jewelry elements similar to those found belonging to the Middle and New kingdoms. Characteristically the necklace is almost circular. Eight rows of slender, tubular, front beads are longer on the bottom row, decreasing to the top row and graduating in length to the ends. Decorating the outer row are drop-shaped pendants. A pair of half-circle shoulder plates have cords for tying. A nearly identical collar belonged to the Estate Manager Wah, found on his mummy by the 1919–1920 expedition of the Metropolitan Museum of Art at Der el-Bahri at Thebes.

Figure 4–15. Mr. and Mrs. Louis Bailey Audigier at Gizeh

Sepia toned silver print
Photographer: unknown
McClung Museum: A1: 161 C136 1P
Gift of Mr. and Mrs. Louis Bailey Audigier, 1934

The Audigiers and a friend pose before the Great Sphinx in 1913. Mr. Audigier, a photographer for *The New York Times,* holds his twin-lens reflex camera.

Model Situla (not illustrated)

New Kingdom
Object: bronze
11 cm. high x 2.8 wide (4-3/8 x 1-1/8 inches)
Provenance: unknown
Gift of Mrs. Dillwyn Parrish, 1914
The University Museum, University of Pennsylvania: E 12578

The squat, drop-shaped vessel, decorated by a band of engraved figures, has a short neck, a wide mouth, and is fitted with two rings for its handle. The model represents in miniature the type of metal container that functioned as a drinking cup.

Necklace with Shawabti (not illustrated)

Late Dynastic Period (?)
Object: faience
23 cm. long (9-1/16 inches)
Provenance: unknown
Gift of Mrs. Dillwyn Parrish, 1914
The University Museum, University of Pennsylvania: E 12657

The long string of thin, tubular blue faience beads supports a faience shawabti. The beads and shawabti formerly had been associated with a mummy.

On a Local Note...

In 1934 there was the generous donation of art given by **Louis Bailey Audigier** in memory of his wife, Eleanor Deane Audigier (1864–1931) of Knoxville, to the University of Tennessee. Part of the gift included a sizable photographic print and postcard collection which he and his wife had acquired during an extended residence abroad. These are now housed in the McClung Museum's Photographic Archives, and selections were made from them to enhance this exhibition.

More recently, in 1992, **Marcia S. Young** donated a small group of albumen prints to the McClung Museum. The prints, several of which were chosen for the exhibition, had belonged to her grandmother, who collected them. The photographs are now part of the McClung Museum's Photographic Archives.

The Friends of Egyptology was established following the opening of a small exhibit in 1984 at the McClung Museum entitled *Burial Practices in Ancient Egypt*. When James E. Harris, well known for his work with the royal mummies at the Egyptian Museum in Cairo, came to the McClung Museum as a guest lecturer, he suggested an interest group be started. As a result, two local people who are committed to ancient Egypt—Egyptologist Louise Bradbury and author Thelma Present—were instrumental in organizing film and event programs, such as McClung Museum sponsored tours to exhibitions about ancient Egypt. These programs were designed to encourage activities and flame and extend interest in ancient Egypt. Funds were raised which allowed the McClung Museum to purchase objects for its ancient Egyptian collection, including photographs, some of which are in this exhibition.

Notes

[1] *Memorandum*, p. 1.

Selected Bibliography

Drower, Margaret S., *Flinders Petrie, a Life in Archaeology*. London: Victor Gollancz Ltd., 1985.

"Eckley Brinton Coxe, Junior" in *The Museum Journal*, Vol. VII, No. 3. Philadelphia, September 1916.

Expedition. The University Museum Magazine of Archaeology/Anthropology University of Pennsylvania. Vol. 21, No. 2. Winter 1979.

Howe, Winifred E., *A History of the Metropolitan Museum of Art*. New York: The Metropolitan Museum of Art, 1913.

James, T.G.H. (ed.), *Excavating in Egypt: The Egypt Exploration Society, 1882–1992*. Chicago: University of Chicago Press, 1982.

Memorandum and Articles of Association of the Egypt Exploration Society. London: Perowne & Co., 1920.

CHAPTER 5

Egyptologists Make Important Discoveries

Gizeh, Early Nineteenth Century

The prospect of excavating in Egypt is a most fascinating one to me, and I hope the results may justify my undertaking such a work.[1]
—Flinders Petrie, 1883

A list of deserving names would be much longer than can be included here, unfortunately. Therefore, only some of the foremost Egyptologists who were associated with the material in the exhibition shall be touched upon and a few of their achievements noted. The catalogue and exhibition highlight the period from 1850 to 1930, although much had been done before 1850. Significant inroads were made by a few pioneer excavators from various countries in the very early Nineteenth Century. Their work stimulated interest in excavating and influenced later archaeologists. Only one location with explorations prior to 1850 has been chosen to spotlight, as it was pivotal.

Just eleven miles southwest of Cairo is the famous site of Gizeh, one of the oldest in the world. The attractions there were so well preserved that it was a natural place for early explorers and excavators to focus their attention, paving the way for succeeding Egyptologists. The Italian excavator Giovanni Battista Caviglia (1770–1845) brought information about the interior of the Great Pyramid to light, completely excavated the Sphinx, and uncovered steps up to that monument. The Italian explorer Giovanni Battista Belzoni (1778–1823) opened the second, Khafre's Pyramid. The British army officer and excavator R.W. Howard Vyse (1784–1853), assisted by a British civil engineer John S. Perring (1813–1869), published an important three-volume account of his pyramid operations, which included a survey by Perring. Karl Richard Lepsius (1810–1884), the German Egyptologist and one of Egyptology's most renowned scholars, excavated at Gizeh, made plans of chapels and almost a hundred tombs there, and mapped the whole Gizeh necropolis.

Early on, scholars copied the reliefs and inscriptions found in the Gizeh mastaba tombs. Among them was the French decipherer of hieroglyphs Jean-François Champollion (1790–1832), the Italian Egyptologist Ippolito Rosellini (1800–1843), British Egyptologist John Gardner Wilkinson (1797–1875), British traveler and collector Robert Hay (1799–1863), British Egyptologist James Burton (1788–1862), French archaeologist Nestor L'Hote (1804–1842), and the French Egyptologists and linguists Emmanuel (1811–1872) and Jacques (1842–1928) de Rouge. These trail blazers also worked at and studied sites other than Gizeh, providing abundant material towards the strengthening of Egyptian scholarship.

Figure 5–1. Auguste Mariette at Sakkara

Mariette supervises the removal of objects from an Old Kingdom mastaba tomb. A mummy and two large coffins of later date were removed near the edge of a deep square hole leading to the tomb chamber, where vases and canopic jars were also found, 1850–1854.

1850–1930
Auguste Mariette (1821–1881)

By the mid-Nineteenth Century the most outstanding Egyptologist in Egypt was Auguste Mariette. Born in Boulogne-sur-Mer, France, to a town hall official, Mariette studied at the College de Boulogne and traveled to London, England, where he taught French and worked as a designer. Later, in 1843, after he returned home he was appointed a professor of French at Boulogne.

No doubt, his reading the papers of the French Egyptologist, Nestor L'Hote, a family relative, had propelled Mariette towards learning and deciphering hieroglyphs. He was also fascinated by the extensive Egyptian collection of Baron Dominique Denon in the Boulogne Museum. Denon had been a diplomat, a playwright among other things, an artist, and a collector of antiquities for the Scientific Commission sent to Egypt by Napoleon in 1798 to 1801. In 1847 Mariette published his first article; it was about the objects on view in the Egyptian gallery of the museum. After assuming a small post in 1849 at the Louvre Museum in Paris, Mariette transcribed all the inscriptions in the Museum's collection. In 1850 he was sent to Egypt and began excavating at Sakkara. Here he soon made his greatest discovery, the Serapeum and its subterranean galleries with embalmed sacred bulls. This find secured his fame. In 1853 he was at Gizeh excavating areas near the Sphinx when he discovered the Valley Temple of King Khafre, the entrance to the walkway leading up to the mortuary temple, and the great pyramid of that pharaoh. Another challenge was met in 1859 when he almost completely excavated the Temple of Seti I at Abydos, financed by Khedive Saïd.

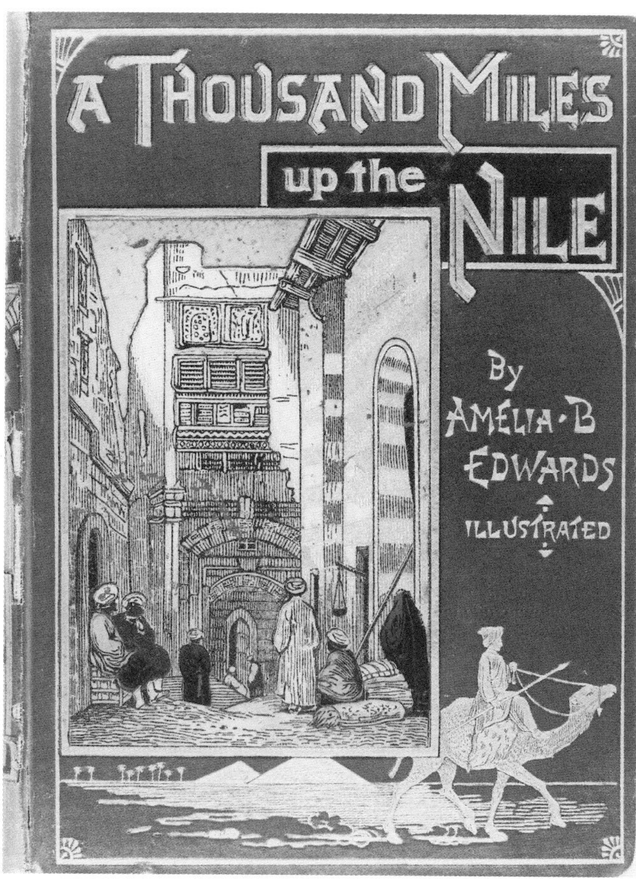

Figure 5–2. Cover of Amelia Edwards' book, *A Thousand Miles Up the Nile.*

The first publication in 1877 of *A Thousand Miles Up the Nile* by Amelia B. Edwards inspired the excavations of many Egyptologists. The book traces a delightful winter she spent in 1873-74 in a dahabiyeh gliding along the Nile and contains many engravings based on her expert drawings of the sites. This illustration of the cover is from the 1891 second revised edition.

Mariette's archaeological excavations were astonishing in number as were his unpublished writings and notes, which are now housed at the Louvre Museum in Paris, France and Griffith Institute, Oxford, England. Although his excavation techniques were criticized by later archaeologists such as Flinders Petrie, who complained about the condition of his predynastic site "after it had been ransacked by Mariette," [2] Mariette's work can be judged superior to others of his time.

An enormous debt of gratitude has been granted this giant figure active in the youthful stages of Egyptology. Mariette received many honors from several different countries including the distinguished Commander of the Legion of Honor in 1877 from his own country. Perhaps his greatest achievements were as founder of the Egyptian National Antiquities Service, creator of the Egyptian Museum in Cairo (the first National Museum in the Near East), the first to promote a sensitivity on a worldwide scale to the importance of preventing the destruction and removal of antiquities, and the preservation and conservation of monuments.

Amelia Blandford Edwards (1831–1892)

The childhood years of the British Egyptologist Amelia Edwards were filled with an ardent interest in ancient Egypt and a fascination influenced by the books of the eminent British Egyptologist Sir John Gardner Wilkinson (1797–1875). Although she had no formal academic training, she later became an Egyptologist and founder of both the Egypt Exploration Fund and the Department of Egyptology at University College, London. As a graceful writer and a keen observer of detail she authored eight novels, wrote numerous articles, and edited popular books on history and art. After her visit to Egypt in 1873 she was inspired to study hieroglyphics and Egyptology. From then on her devotion was intense.

One purpose directed Edward's life. She worked tirelessly as a strong advocate of accurate and scientific records being kept about monuments she observed were being destroyed and mutilated. To this end she founded the Egypt Exploration Fund in 1882 to save the monuments under siege along the Nile and to publicize their deteriorated condition. She wrote a number of popular articles and reports about excavations in Egypt. The Cypriote, Phoenician, and other writings on shards uncovered in the Fayum by Flinders Petrie, a close friend and colleague, were first identified by her. Edwards was a glowing light in the Nineteenth Century field of Egyptology.

The contributions of this extraordinary woman of the Victorian Age were remarkable. Edwards was not only well respected abroad but also in the United States, where her work did not go unnoticed. She received an LL.D. at Columbia University in New York in 1887, an L.H.D. from Smith College and a Ph.D. from the College of the Sisters of Bethany in Topeka. A lecture tour of the United States in 1889 and 1890 flamed interest in the Egypt Exploration Fund (EEF) and secured for her an American recognition. In October of 1891 while attending the dispatch of antiquities from an EEF excavation she became ill with influenza and later developed a lung condition from which she was unable to recover. In April 1892 she died at Westbury-on-Trym, England. On her grave lies a large stone *ankh*-sign, the hieroglyphic emblem of life. The enduring vision of this Victorian woman was tireless as was her devotion to Egyptologists and their work.

Henri Édouard Naville (1844–1926)

Édouard Naville was a Swiss Egyptologist and Biblical scholar who was born in Geneva, Switzerland, educated at the University of Geneva, and at King's College in London, and studied under the great German Egyptologist Karl Lepsius (1810–1884). Naville created a new format for publishing reports, formulated fundamental theories about the Egyptian language, and dispelled the ideas of others regarding the Exodus. Most of his published works contained the drawings made by his wife Marguerte de Pourtales, the talented daughter of a French Count. Unlike Flinders Petrie, Naville was interested in excavating and researching the grand temples and monuments.

Naville went to Egypt in 1868 for the first time and copied the Horus inscriptions at the Temple of Edfu. After having acquired standing as an Egyptologist, he was the first excavator to be sponsored in 1882 by the recently established Egypt Exploration Fund. He dug at many sites, beginning in 1883 at Tell el-Maskhuta and followed by a succession of others in Upper and Lower Egypt. In 1893 to 1896 he cleared the Temple of Hatshepsut at Der el-Bahri, with three British excavators: David G. Hogarth (1862–1927), Somers Clarke (1841–1926), and Howard Carter, who produced splendid drawings of sculptures for the fine, six-volume work of the site published in 1895–1908. After a period of absence he returned in 1903 to clear the Temple of Mentuhotep II at the same site with the British Egyptologist Henry R. Hall (1873–1930).

The British Museum has the colossal head of Amenemhet III of the Middle Kingdom which was found during Naville's excavations at Bubastis in 1886 to 1889. Many other important objects went to the Egyptian Museum in Cairo, the Museum of Fine Arts in Boston, and other museums. Various honors were bestowed upon Naville, and an extensive number of publications were produced during his distinguished career. Although he was really more a scholar than an archaeologist, according to a colleague Naville could not think of anything more rewarding for an Egyptologist to do than to excavate.

Gaston Maspero (1846–1916)

Another eminent figure and associate of Mariette was the incomparable French Egyptologist Gaston Maspero, who rose to prominence during the days of Egypt's greatest Egyptological development. His name is synonymous with Egyptological events in Egypt between the 1880s and 1914 in terms of archaeology and scholarship. He was Director of the Egyptian Antiquities Service and Head of the Egyptian Museum. Maspero was matchless in his contributions and number one in his field.

Although Italian by birth, the son of an Italian political refugee, Maspero as a child became a naturalized citizen of France. At age fourteen he was studying hieroglyphics while pursuing his formative education in Paris at the Lycée Louis-le-Grand, the École des Hautes Études. In 1873 he was awarded Docteur des Lettres. The following year he was appointed Professor of Egyptian Philology and Archaeology at the College de France. At age twenty-one he had met the celebrated Auguste Mariette, who showed him a couple of newly discovered texts which he quickly translated and published, an achievement that created a lasting bond between them. Also, he was immensely grateful to the French Egyptologist Emmanuel de Rouge from whom he learned much about the Egyptian language.

Figure 5–3. Gaston Maspero

Maspero at his desk later in his career.

In 1880 Maspero went to Egypt for the first time to become the first director of a new organization, the Institut français d'archéologie orientale in Cairo, and began to record important tomb reliefs and inscriptions. It was the same year Flinders Petrie arrived. Sadly, a year later Auguste Mariette died. Maspero took over as the Director of the Boulaq Museum and continued Mariette's unfinished archaeological work, giving particular regard to his wishes for opening several smaller pyramids at Sakkara. Within a short time Maspero found inside the pyramid of King Unis, last pharaoh of dynasty V, the king's untouched stone sarcophagus in the tomb chamber. More importantly, the central chamber and tomb chamber had pointed roofs and walls covered with the oldest known Egyptian inscriptions, the so-called "Pyramid Texts." These religious texts about the afterlife were cut into the walls and filled with blue pigment, a celestial color. As a result of this discovery he copied and translated some four thousand lines of inscription, which he published for the first time.

That same year of 1881 his career took another extraordinary turn. A cache of royal mummies hidden in the cliffs of Der el-Bahri came to Maspero's attention. Within two weeks Maspero had the tomb emptied and its contents on their way by steamer to the Boulaq Museum. Among the thirty-two intact royal remains found in the cache was the intact mummy of Seti I and his son, Rameses II.

As the Director of the Cairo Museum Maspero contributed much to its *Catalogue Général,* editing the contributions of other scholars. He had previously prepared comprehensive guide books to the Boulaq, Gizeh, and Egyptian Museums. As the chief regulator of archaeology in Egypt, he also was

Figure 5–4. Petrie at Abydos

Flinders Petrie and Amy Urlin, his sister-in-law, spend a moment in conversation during excavations at Abydos, 1899–1903.

Courtesy Egypt Exploration Society, London

helpful and supportive of the excavations by various visiting Egyptologists, including Flinders Petrie, John Garstang, George Reisner, Howard Carter, and Édouard Naville. As its Director, Maspero's improvements and development of the Egyptian Antiquities Service, his systematic clearing and preservation of the Karnak and Luxor sites, and his long list of scholarly publications are his golden legacies.

William Matthew Flinders Petrie (1853–1942)

William Matthew Flinders Petrie, called the "Father of Archaeology," is undoubtedly the world's best-known and most prolific excavator. When he was thirteen, books about the Great Pyramid by Charles Piazzi Smyth captivated him, inciting his interest in Egypt. Although he lacked a formal education, he nevertheless trained himself with intensity and developed a disregard for the archaeological methods and theories of others, deciding about procedures himself. In 1896 he married an Egyptologist, Hilda Urlin, his true and devoted helpmate.

Petrie was born in Charlton, England, to a civil engineer and surveyor and the daughter of an explorer of Australia. In his teens he worked with his father. Together they surveyed Stonehenge, an experience that shaped his interest in weights and measures. Petrie surveyed and drew plans of numerous archaeological sites in southern England, building a basis for new methods that were to become legendary. In 1880 Petrie went to Egypt for the first time to inspect and survey the Gizeh pyramids. Through his energy and enthusiasm a loan exhibition of ancient Egyptian art was held at the Burlington Fine Arts Club in London in 1894. In 1887, after a falling out with the Egypt Exploration Fund, his desire for independence from controlling forces was recognized and he excavated on a regular basis, with the aid of private support.

In his lifetime Petrie made more important discoveries than any other Egyptologist. He introduced new and improved archaeological field methods and classifications. He invented sequence dating, established relationships between Egyptian and Greek pottery, and emphasized the importance of examining everything, even the smallest and of seemingly little significance. The number of sites Petrie excavated from 1884 to the 1930s in Upper and Lower Egypt, Palestine, and Israel was staggering. One of his many great contributions was the discovery at Negadeh in Upper Egypt of early dynastic and predynastic sites, thereby bringing to light for the first time important data about the very first cultural remains in Egypt. Petrie held the first chair in Egyptology at the University College, London, created the journal *Ancient Egypt* and was its editor for twenty years. Petrie received numerous honorary degrees, and in 1923 he was knighted. The publications of his books, articles, and reviews number some one thousand!

Alexandre Barsanti (1858–1917)

Alexandre Barsanti is important to Egyptology especially because of the extraordinary skills he had as an artist, restorer, and technician. The Italian excavator was born in Alexandria, Egypt, and was educated at the Institute of Fine Arts in Florence, Italy. Barsanti became a most valuable engineer and official under Maspero in the Egyptian Antiquities Service and contributed articles for its *Annales*.

Barsanti was appointed by Maspero as the Conservator-Restorer of the Egyptian Museum in 1891. There he mended, restored, and mounted broken objects and united and strengthened numerous monuments. In 1892 he went to Upper Egypt with the French archaeologist Jacques de Morgan (1854–1909). In 1894 and 1895 he assisted the French Egyptologist Georges Daressy (1864–1938) to clear and restore the Temple of Medinet Habu. The following year he set off for Nubia, where he directed the consolidation and restoration of the temples and monuments affected by the Assuan Barrage. At Sakkara in 1899 to 1904 he restored and repaired numerous mastabas and tombs of later date at the site. While at Sakkara he also excavated areas of the pyramid of Unis and the remains of the funerary temple as well as other pyramids and sites. During excavations at Tell el-Amarna he discovered several fragments of delicately painted pavements which are in the Cairo Museum. While at Abu Simbel in 1909 he discovered a small court, cleared debris from one of the colossi of Rameses II, and built walls on the plateau to keep sand from the temple.

Victor Loret (1859–1946)

Born in Paris, the French Egyptologist Victor Loret was the son of an organist and a musician himself as well. As a child he saw a few pages from Jean-François Champollion's "Egyptian Grammar," which sparked his life-long fascination with Egypt. Later he studied under Gaston Maspero at the École des Hautes Études and the College de France, a vital beginning in his training.

In 1881 Loret went to Egypt as a member of the newly organized French Institute of Archaeology and shortly set out to work with the French Egyptologist Eugène Léfebure (1838–1908), copying inscriptions in numerous tombs in the Valley of the Kings. In 1886 he became Director of the Institute and that same year he assumed the post of Reader in Egyptology at the University of Lyons, where he taught until 1929.

Although Loret was Director-General of the Antiquities Service only from 1897 to 1899, he nevertheless completed much important work in the Valley of the Kings. He also cleared the tombs of Thutmose III and Amenhotep II, the latter with its ten royal mummies hidden by high priests from tomb robbers, including that of Dynasty XVIII King Thutmose IV and Dynasty XIX King Seti II.

Loret, who founded a school of Egyptology at Lyon, was a popular and successful professor of Egyptian studies. In honor of his contributions to Egyptology he was awarded the Grand prix Maspero of the Academy des Inscriptions and a Chevalier of the Légion d'Honneur. One of his most important works was his grand "Dictionary of Hieroglyphics."

Georges Legrain (1865–1917)

Georges Legrain, born in Paris, France, studied art and architecture, Egyptian archaeology, and languages under well-known French architects and Egyptologists.

In 1892 Legrain began his work for the Institut français d'archéologie orientale in Cairo, working at copying graffiti at Assuan and recording important tomb scenes from there to Kom Ombo, where he completely copied the temple. In 1893 and 1894 he worked at Tell el-Amarna making watercolor paintings. He also worked at other sites, including Dashur, where he produced lovely paintings of the famous Treasure of Dashur, consisting of elaborate gold necklaces, bracelets, pendants, and mirrors found in 1894–1895 in subterranean tombs by the French archaeologist and Director-General of the Egyptian Antiquities Service Jacques de Morgan (1857–1924). The precious jewelry belonged to several Dynasty XII princesses and is housed in the Cairo Museum. But his principal focus was at Karnak at Thebes. In 1895 Legrain was chosen to work there by de Morgan, an assignment that lasted until 1917, and where in 1903 he found an extraordinary cache of seventeen thousand statues and figures. In 1894 he had been appointed Inspecteur-Dessinateur and before World War I Chief Inspector of Luxor, where he worked during World War I.

Legrain was a careful and exacting excavator and record keeper. Not only did he clear the Great Hypostyle Hall at Karnak and surrounding areas, but he restored and rebuilt the unstable blocks and columns that had fallen. The enormous scale of this work was a first, and his techniques continued to be used to great advantage by those that followed.

Figure 5–5. James Henry Breasted

James Henry Breasted does what he did so well. He carefully copies a temple wall of hieroglyphic inscriptions, while assisted by a helper at Wady Halfeh, 1906.

Courtesy Museum Archives, Oriental Institute Museum, University of Chicago

James Henry Breasted (1865–1935)

James Henry Breasted was one of the most distinguished American Egyptologists of his time and true founder of Egyptology in the United States. During his long and distinguished career Breasted made many important milestones in increasing knowledge of ancient Egypt. He had, according to the British Egyptologist Sir Alan Gardiner (1879–1963), "an unbounded enthusiasm," which "gave a singular attraction to his conversation...."[3]

Breasted's birthplace was Rockford, Illinois. As a young man he worked locally for a time as a drugstore clerk and in 1886 graduated from Chicago College of Pharmacy, afterward working as a pharmacist. In 1892 he was granted a Master of Arts degree from Yale University, New Haven, Connecticut, and then went to study under the innovative, German Egyptologist Adolf Erman (1854–1937) at the University of Berlin, receiving a doctorate in 1894. The same year, at age twenty-nine, he published his mentor's "Egyptian Grammar" in English. Breasted took his bride, Francis Hart, to Egypt in 1894 for a honeymoon and returned to work in the Haskell Oriental Museum at the University of Chicago as an assistant in Egyptology and assistant director. In 1905 he reached the rank of Professor of Egyptology and Oriental History and received the first chair in Egyptology in the United States. The copying of important hieroglyphic inscriptions for German scholarly institutions and European museums inspired his great corpus in English. He copied, collated, and reconstructed countless texts in Egypt, which resulted in some ten thousand pages of text for his *Ancient Records of Egypt,* a five-volume work.

From 1905 to 1907 Breasted was the Director of the Chicago Egyptian Expedition and traveled to Egypt, where he made copies of hieroglyphic inscriptions from sites at Assuan to Meroë. In 1919 he founded the Oriental Institute at the University of Chicago, which became a leading Egyptological research institution up to this day. That same year the Oriental Institute Museum was established with a core collection acquired by Breasted beginning in 1894 in Egypt. In 1920 he was translating the "Edwin Smith Papyrus," a medical treatise purchased at Luxor by Smith in 1862, which had him tapping into his pharmacy skills. Through his efforts the Epigraphic Survey of Egypt was organized in 1924, which published books on Medinet Habu, the temples at Karnak and Luxor, and other sites. Breasted's *A History of Egypt* is considered by some a masterpiece.

George E. S. M. Herbert, Fifth Earl of Carnarvon (1866–1923)

The Earl of Carnarvon was a modest scholar, who refrained from boasting about his contributions to Egyptology, and a dedicated excavator with a strong sense of purpose. These were the qualities that rewarded him in the end with the discovery of the greatest tomb find in the history of Egypt. On November 26, 1922, Carnarvon and Howard Carter gained a glimpse into the Tomb of Tutankhamen, a burial place that had remained hidden under a pile of rubble since the late XIXth Dynasty. It was an incredible moment and a stunning realization that all his efforts had been realized.

George E. S. M. Herbert, Fifth Earl of Carnarvon, was born in Highclere Castle, Hants, England. After an education at Eton and Trinity College, Cambridge, he spent several winters in Egypt to regain his health after a nasty motor accident. These visits whetted his intense interest in Egypt.

In 1906 Carnarvon began to excavate at Thebes and with the assistance of Howard Carter made several important finds, which he published in *Five Years' Explorations at Thebes* in 1912. The year after the incredible discovery of the Tutankhamen tomb he died in Cairo at age fifty-seven. At the time, his death was attributed by many to the curse of Tutankhamen, but in fact it was an infection from a mosquito bite, occurring at the site, which caused blood poisoning and finally pneumonia. Carnarvon accumulated a highly prized collection of Egyptian antiquities, which was later bought by the Metropolitan Museum of Art in New York. It was said he was "a true friend of Egyptology, an excavator of endless patience and perseverance..." [4]

Figure 5–6. George A. Reisner

Reisner smiles for the camera between puffs on his favorite pipe.

Courtesy The University of Pennsylvania Museum (Neg. #S8-65488)

James Edward Quibell (1867–1935)

James Quibell had the good fortune to be trained under Flinders Petrie. This experience equipped him extremely well for the archaeological tasks ahead. He also had the devoted assistance throughout his life of his wife, Annie A. Quibell (1862–1927), a gifted artist who made drawings for his publications.

Quibell was born in Newport (Shropshire), England. He was a graduate of Christ Church, Oxford, and in 1893 went to Egypt to work under Petrie. That same year he dug at Coptos, an important site that dated back to Dynasty I. In 1894 he was with Petrie at Negadeh and Ballas and uncovered important material of the Predynastic Period. At the predynastic site at Hieraconpolis he and his colleagues, Frederick Green (1869–1949) and Somers Clarke (1841–1926), made the major discovery of the famous Narmer Palette. During his clearing of the Ramesseum at Thebes he found papyri dating to the Middle Kingdom and inscribed jar sealings. From 1899 to 1904 he served as Inspector-in-Chief of Antiquities in the Delta and Middle Egypt and in 1904–1905 of Luxor. Quibell published a catalogue of objects from the tomb of Yuia and Tuiu, parents-in-law of Amenhotep III, for the Cairo Museum in 1908, and excavated the important mastaba tomb of Hesire at Sakkara. In 1914 he was appointed Director of the Egyptian Museum, making many improvements and in 1923 was made the Secretary-General of the Antiquities Department. Following his retirement in 1925, he continued to excavate. In 1931 he became director of the Step Pyramid site at Sakkara, finding and restoring a large number of objects.

George Andrew Reisner (1867–1942)

The American Egyptologist George Andrew Reisner was born in Indianapolis, the son of a shoe store administrator of German birth. After receiving a Ph.D. from Harvard University he went to Berlin, Germany, to study Semitics and Assyrian and Babylonian texts. However, he found Egyptology more appealing and studied under the renown German Egyptologist Kurt Sethe (1869–1934). Following a year as an assistant in the Berlin Museum he returned home and became a member of the faculty at Harvard University, Cambridge, Massachusetts, and accepted the post of Curator in the Egyptian Department at the Museum of Fine Arts in Boston, posts he held the rest of his life. At this time both institutions funded his excavations at Gizeh, where he worked for four decades until his death in 1942.

Reisner's long excavating career was launched in 1899 as Director of the Harvard-Boston Egyptian Expedition, which was sponsored by Phoebe Hearst, a newspaper heiress and avid devotee of anthropology and Egyptology. The Hearst sponsorship started him on a long series of excavations in Egypt and in Lower Nubia. At Gizeh he was appointed the Director of the German, Italian, and American mission. Colleagues Ludwig Borchardt (1863–1938), Director of the German Institute of Archaeology, was assigned to excavate the Khafre Pyramid, Ernesto Schiaparelli (1856–1928), representing the Egyptian Museum in Turin, Italy, excavated the Khufu Pyramid, and Reisner was assigned the Menkure Pyramid. Three years later the Italians gave their concession to Reisner, including all of its Eastern Cemetery. In 1907 he opened up the valley temple of King Menkure and numerous tombs at the site. The dynasty IV–VI mastaba cemeteries there belonged to royal relatives and important officials of the government. It was in these tombs he discovered some outstanding treasures of the Old Kingdom as well as the names of their owners, titles, and family relationships. But perhaps his most important find was in 1925 of the intact tomb of Queen Hetep-heres, mother of King Khufu, located near her son's Great Pyramid. He also dug at a number of cemeteries and settlements in Nubia, where he found the pyramids of sixty-eight Ethiopian Kings and five other kings and revealed important information about the material culture of a little studied region.

Reisner was the first person to develop more systematic excavation methods and brought the technique of recorded digging much further than either Petrie's efforts or the work of other earlier archaeologists. He devised a system for numbering each mastaba and organized the information in a format Egyptologists still use. His attention to record keeping, with such scrupulous care, meant that his reports were much more complete than those of his colleagues, but also required much more time to prepare. Reisner was such a detailist and exacting archaeologist it took him much time writing up his findings for publication. Therefore, much of his work remained unfinished and unpublished before his death, but was later compiled by others from field notes.

Howard Carter (1873–1939)

The name Howard Carter remains bonded to the Pharaoh Tutankhamen and the discovery in 1922 of the famous tomb of treasures in the Valley of the Kings. The British Egyptologist spent his childhood in Swaffham (Norfolk), England, the son of an artist specializing in animals, a skill his father taught him that Carter was to use during his archaeological career.

Although Carter's career seemed at first a bit bumpy he eventually proved himself. Flinders Petrie said he had his reservations when the young Carter arrived in 1891 at Tell el-Amarna in Upper Egypt to work under his supervision, and with a view of collecting for his sponsor, William Amhurst Tyssen-Amherst (1835–1909), a British collector. At that time Carter was solely interested in painting and natural history. Petrie had strong doubts he would have what it would take to become an excavator. While keeping a close watch on his work, separate from his own, Petrie left him to clean out the temple site. There Carter found broken statues of the queen, some torsos, and a large number of stone chips.

After his debut at Amarna, Carter was employed as a draughtsman for the Egypt Exploration Society. He spent several seasons as an artist and photographer at the Temple of Hatshepsut at Der el-Bahri at Thebes, producing extremely skillful epigraphic records. His signature or initials are on numerous, beautifully executed plates for Édouard Naville's six-volume publication on the Temple of Der el-Bahri, work that involved copying scenes and inscriptions on the temple. At the end of this endeavor in 1899 he was made Chief Inspector of Antiquities in Upper Egypt in the Egyptian government's Antiquities Service, supervising excavations under Gaston Maspero. Under the direction of Maspero, Carter spent the first

Figure 5–7. Howard Carter

The photograph by Harry Burton shows Howard Carter using a soft brush to dust the remains of a shroud once covering the magnificent middle coffin of King Tutankhamen, depicted as a human form of Osiris, God of the Dead. The extraordinary gold and colored glass decorated coffin was inside a gilt coffin. Inside the middle coffin was the solid gold coffin containing the mummy of the king. The three coffins were enclosed by an outermost sarcophagus of quartzite and granite.

Courtesy The Metropolitan Museum of Art

years of this century as an energetic and active inspector of all the monuments of Upper Egypt. He was working in direct contact with the great archaeological sites of Egypt and gathering excellent experience of the vast terrain. In 1905, suddenly after a dispute with Egyptian officials, he left his post and had to support himself for a time as an artist and guide. Bolstered by his patron, the Earl of Carnarvon, he returned to the Valley of the Kings. But it was not until 1916–1917 that he was able to search the Valley again, when he found a tomb of Queen Hatshepsut. In 1922 the find of all finds was his as he descended the sixteen steps to the entrance of the Tomb of Tutankhamen and made the greatest discovery in Egyptian history. It took Carter and his associates ten years to finish the work. During his career the British archaeologist also discovered the royal tombs of King Mentuhotep II of Dynasty XI, of Dynasty XVIII King Amenhotep III, and of Queen Hatshepsut as well as her later tomb and that of King Thutmose IV.

It was said by the French Egyptologist Jean Capart (1877–1947) that "the public is often ill informed and regards Carter a poor Egyptologist. It is a way to diminish the value of an archaeologist, who by his marvelous knowledge of the land, was able to enrich our science with exceptional documentation." [5]

David Randall-MacIver (1873–1945)

David Randall-MacIver was a British Egyptologist educated at The Queen's College at Oxford. He worked with Flinders Petrie at Dendereh and Abydos from 1898 to 1901. From 1906 to 1911 he was Curator of the Egyptian section at the University Museum of the University of Pennsylvania. He went to Egypt and the Sudan as the Director of the Eckley B. Coxe, Jr., Expedition, sponsor of excavations in Egypt for the University of Pennsylvania. In Nubia he excavated the site at Karanòg with Charles Leonard Woolley from 1907 to 1910.

Arthur C. Mace (1874–1928)

Arthur C. Mace, the British Egyptologist, was educated at Keble College at Oxford. He joined Flinders Petrie at Dendereh in 1897–98 and at Abydos in 1899 to 1901 joining David Randall-MacIver who also worked under Petrie at these sites. Then in 1901 he went to Gizeh and Naga ed-Der, where he worked with George Reisner for five years. From 1906 to 1922 he was on the curatorial staff at the Metropolitan Museum of Art in New York, taking a leave in 1922 to assist Howard Carter in the immense work of clearing the tomb of King Tutankhamen. Mace was a co-author with Howard Carter on the first volume of the publication *The Tomb of Tut-ankh-amen.*

John Garstang (1876–1956)

The British archaeologist John Garstang, born in Blackburn (Lancaster), England, completed his education at Jesus College, Oxford. He was a faculty member for four years as a Mathematical Scholar. Later he went on to receive several advanced and honorary degrees and distinguished himself in Egyptian and Near Eastern studies. He became an Honorary Reader in Egyptian Archaeology at the University of Liverpool in 1902, and in 1907 he assumed the position of Professor of Methods and Practice of Archaeology until his retirement in 1941.

Early in his career Garstag directed excavations of Roman sites in Britain, and while he was teaching he worked in Egypt. In 1900 he was excavating at Bet Khallaf for the Egypt Research Account, and between 1900 and 1914 he dug at a number of sites including at Negadeh, Edfu, Nubia, Esneh, Abydos, and Meroë in the Sudan. A prominent scholarly figure, Garstang was awarded honorary medals, including the King's Silver Jubilee Medal in 1935, for his achievements and publications.

Henri Gauthier (1877–1950)

Henri Gauthier was a French Egyptologist of distinction. Born in Lyons, France, he was educated at the Faculté des Lettres at Lyons, where from 1897 to 1900 he studied under Victor Loret and later under Adolf Erman at Berlin.

In 1903 Gauthier joined the French Institute of Archaeology in Cairo and from 1913 to 1918 served as its secretary and librarian. From 1907 to 1910 he prepared data for the *Catalogue Général* of the Cairo Museum. At the request of Maspero he copied the inscriptions of three Nubian temples including the Temple of Kalabsheh. Following excavations in 1906 at Dra Abu 'n Neggeh on the West Bank of Thebes and at el-Qatta, he began his masterpiece *Le Livre des rois d'Égypte*, a five volume work published in 1907–1917. He served as Secretary-General of the Egyptian Antiquities Service from 1927 to 1937.

Figure 5–8. David Randall-MacIver and Charles Leonard Woolley

Randall-MacIver, second from right, and Woolley, at far right, enjoy refreshments during a pause in their excavations funded by the Eckley B. Coxe, Jr. Expedition, the University of Pennsylvania. Anibeh, Nubia, 1908.

Courtesy The University of Pennsylvania Museum, (Neg. #S4-1140721)

Uvo Hölscher (1878–1963)

The German archaeologist and architect Uvo Hölscher suitably combined both these subjects to serve him in his work in Egypt. He became a Lecturer at the Technical High School in Hanover, Germany, in 1921 an Assistant Professor, and in 1937 Professor. The Oriental Institute of Chicago awarded Hölscher an Honorary Chair and for eleven years he directed their excavations at the Temple of Medinet Habu.

In 1906 Hölscher was working with his countryman, the esteemed Egyptologist and architect Ludwig Borchardt (1863–1938), at the pyramids of Abusir. Later, in 1912, he dug the causeway area of the pyramid of King Khafre at Gizeh, producing a standard publication on the architecture of the complex.

Hölscher established, by far, the most intensive and complete recording of temple complexes than had been done before, particularly at Medinet Habu, and on the palace structure of Rameses III. He set new standards and published many important architectural volumes of his work at temple sites.

Charles Leonard Woolley (1880–1960)

One of the more industrious and dynamic personalities excavating in Egypt was the British Archaeologist Charles Leonard Woolley. He received a degree in Theology at New College at Oxford, and an M.A. at Oxon. During his career he was awarded a number of honorary degrees and received the Order of the British Empire. His knowledge of ancient cultures was wide and included the major discovery in 1934 of the royal tombs at Ur in Mesopotamia. Prior to this find, Woolley had been an Assistant Curator in the Ashmolean Museum at Oxford from 1905 to 1907 working under Arthur Evans (1851–1941), the great discoverer and excavator of The Palace of Minos in Crete.

In Egypt, Woolley excavated from 1907 to 1911 at Karanòg in Nubia for the Eckley B. Coxe, Jr., Expedition of the University of Pennsylvania. In 1912 he dug for the Oxford University Expedition to Nubia, and in 1921 and 1922 for the Egypt Exploration Society at Tell el-Amarna.

Günther Roeder (1881–1966)

The German Egyptologist Günther Roeder was born at Schwiebus, Germany, and was educated at the University of Jena in Germany. Like many others he went on to Berlin to study under the German Egyptologist Adolf Erman (1854–1937). In 1904 he received a Ph.D. from Friedrich-Wilhelm University in Germany. Not only was Roeder a meticulous scholar and archaeologist, but also he was committed to the importance of museums. At the Berlin Museum he classified objects in the Egyptian Department with exacting care and later transcribed inscriptions in the collections there.

In 1907 Roeder became a member of the Egyptian Antiquities Service under Maspero and worked at the temples of Debod, Kalabsheh, and Dakkeh copying reliefs and inscriptions. From 1915 to 1945 he was the Director of the Pelizaeus Museum in Hildesheim, Germany, publishing a catalogue of the collection in 1921. During this headship he visited the Egyptian Foundation of Queen Elizabeth of Belgium in 1926 and praised the Egyptian collection housed in the Sixteenth Century Brussels palace. For ten years beginning in 1929 Roeder excavated at Hermopolis, where he found numerous blocks which came from Tell el-Amarna. From 1940 to 1945 he also directed the Berlin Museum.

Oric Bates (1883–1918)

After his studies at Harvard University, the American archaeologist Oric Bates was given a post in the Egyptian Department of the Boston Museum of Fine Arts. In 1908–09 he went to Egypt and excavated in Nubia supported by the Egyptian government under Khedive Abbas II and the Harvard-Boston Expedition. In 1910 he was again in Nubia and the Sudan. In 1914 he became Curator of African Archaeology in the Peabody Museum at Harvard University.

Figure 5–9. W. M. Flinders Petrie

Flinders Petrie is focused as he takes a photograph of the excavation with his "biscuit box" camera under the cloth. Tell el 'Ajjul, Gaza, 1938.

Dows Dunham (1890–1984)

Dows Dunham was an American Egyptologist who travelled to Egypt before studying art history at Harvard University from 1909 to 1913. In 1913 he took a post working as chief assistant to George Reisner at Gizeh. In 1915 Dunham excavated at Gammai in Nubia. After a series of excavations, including Gebel Barkal, the Sudan, Sakkara, Dashur, and again at Gizeh, he returned to the United States and became a Curator in the Egyptian Department of the Boston Museum of Fine Arts until 1956, when he retired. Then he was committed to completing the publications of his former colleague and predecessor, George Reisner. Dunham achieved a number of honors and in 1979 was awarded a gold Medal for Distinguished Archaeological Achievement from the Archaeological Institute of America.

Photography Assists Archaeology

> *...nothing is equal to photography, because artistic license is impossible.*[6]
> ***—J. Stevens, 1868***

The reproduction of an archaeological image by means of a camera was one of the many valuable applications of photography in the Nineteenth and early Twentieth Centuries. One of its most important qualities was its accuracy. There was no chance for human error. The camera did not lie.

The value of photography as a technical tool for archaeology was soon realized. Perhaps photography proved its greatest value to archaeology and Egyptology in the documentation of architectural monuments. Photographs could show differences in masonry courses to reveal relative dates, or various changes made due to either restoration or deliberate destruction. Because the camera captured details with such honesty, accurate restorations of fallen temple columns were possible by referring to photographs which were taken prior to the damage. A photographic print of a monument reproduced the structure in such microscopic detail that even the depth and clearness of shadows were defined as were textures, coloration, and shapes. Photographs became a positive aid to archaeological research and the recording of sites.

Publications illustrated with photographs taken by archaeological project photographers and site directors abounded during the Nineteenth and early Twentieth Centuries. Among some of the earliest photographers who knew the importance of publishing their photographic work as an aid to scientific documentation and study were the French Egyptologist Emmanuel de Rouge (1811–1872), whose album of photographs was first published in 1863, and the images by the British astronomer Charles Piazzi Smyth (1819–1900) of the Gizeh pyramids published in 1864 and 1867. Smyth took some one hundred and sixty-six photographs at the pyramids and fifty stereoviews to advance scientific study.

Egyptologists and archaeologists depended more and more on the camera to document their excavations. Auguste Mariette marvelously illustrated his sumptuous book, *Voyage dans la Haute l'Égypte*, 1878, with eighty-three photographs taken by him of objects and important sites that he had excavated. In 1902, Flinders Petrie revealed his having drawn thirty-seven plates and taken the photographs for his publication documenting his excavations of the Temenos of Osiris at Abydos. However, archaeologists faced difficulties photographing sites and excavated material. At Petrie's excavations of the royal tombs at Abydos some two hundred photographs were taken by him, but he ran out of glass plates because a shipment from Britain had not arrived in time. In 1905, while excavating at Esneh, the British Egyptologist John Garstang wrote: "I regret very much that the photos enclosed are so bad, and that the bulk of them I had prepared for this report cannot be sent."[7] Garstang faced the usual frustrations of a photographer. He tried to keep the water cool enough to process the photographs in temperatures which was for some days 110° in the shade. The intense heat would cause film and paper to dissolve during the photographic process.

While in Egypt George Reisner made ample use of photography in systematically documenting excavated material from his sites. At Gizeh he made a thorough photographic record of clearing the burial chamber in the Tomb of Queen Hetep-heres, his most important find. Some eleven thousand six hundred negatives from his excavations are in the Phoebe Hearst Museum at the University of California at Berkeley. James Henry Breasted, made numerous photographic studies during his expeditions to Egypt and the Sudan. From 1905 to 1907 Breasted and two photographers took over one thousand photographs during the expeditions. His main interest was to copy and record as many monuments and inscriptions as he could while they were still legible, thereby enriching the work being accomplished by archaeologists. At Abu Simbel he and his crew spent forty days photographing and copying the inscriptions. Later he and his team photographed all the inscriptions recording the history of Nubia.

Figure 5–10. James Henry Breasted

Breasted takes a photograph from the top of Pyramid N8 during the University of Chicago Egyptian Expedition at Meroë, Nubia, 1905–1906.

Courtesy Museum Archives, Oriental Institute Museum, University of Chicago

The photographer for the famous Tomb of Tutankhamen was the British archaeologist Harry Burton (1879–1940). Burton excavated with Theodore Davis at Thebes and in 1914 became photographic recorder of excavations of the Metropolitan Museum of Art in New York.

Figure 5–11. Harry Burton

Burton steadies himself on a tall ladder while photographing at Thebes, circa 1925.

Courtesy of the Metropolitan Museum of Art, New York

Figure 5–12. Howard Carter

Lindsey Hall photographs Howard Carter photographing the Queen of the Belgians and royal party in the "well" at the Tomb of Tutankhamen in 1923.

Courtesy Lindsley Foote Hall Photograph Collection, Division of Special Collections & University Archives, University of Oregon Library System

Burton produced a complete record of the contents of the incomparable tomb from the time of its discovery to the many seasons it took to clear the tomb. He made invaluable photographs of Howard Carter, Lord Carnarvon, the British Egyptologist Arthur Mace, and others as they worked at emptying the chambers, wrapping and packing the treasures for their eventual transportation to the Egyptian Museum in Cairo. He made nearly one thousand negatives of the tomb and objects.

The American, Lindsley F. Hall (1883–1969), joined the Metropolitan Museum of Art's Egyptian expedition as a draughtsman. In 1922 Howard Carter borrowed him to draw plans of the main chamber of the tomb of Tutankhamen. While working on the tomb, Hall took numerous photographs of sights and activities at the tomb and other sites now preserved in the Special Collections and University Archives Library system in the University of Oregon at Portland.

Notes

[1] Petrie, *Seventy Years*, p. 36.

[2] Petrie, *Royal Tombs* I., p. 2.

[3] *JEA* 9 (1923), p. 115.

[4] *JEA* 9 (1923), p. 116.

[5] Capart, "Necrologie," p. 324.

[6] Henderson, "Photography", p. 158.

[7] Downes, *Excavations*, p. ix.

Credit

Figure 5–9 from Margaret S. Drower, *Flinders Petrie, a Life in Archaeology*, London: Victor Gallancz Ltd., 1985. Copyright Margaret S. Drower and The Estate of Flinders Petrie.

Selected bibliography

Archaeological Report. London: Egypt Exploration Fund, 1891–.

Breasted, James Henry, *The 1905–1907 Breasted Expeditions to Egypt and the Sudan: A Photographic Study. The Oriental Institute, Vol. 1–2*. Chicago: University of Chicago Press, 1975.

Capart, Jean, *"Necrologie" in Chronique de l'Égypte*, 1936.

Dawson, Warren R. and Eric P. Uphill, third revised edition by M. L. Bierbrier, *Who Was Who in Egyptology*. London: The Egypt Exploration Society, 1995.

Downes, Dorothy, *The Excavations at Esna, 1905–1906*. Warminster: Aris & Philllips Ltd., 1974.

Henderson, J., "Photography as an aid to the Study of Archaeology" in *The British Journal of Photography*, April 3, 1908, pp. 158–159.

Journal of Egyptian Archaeology. London: Egypt Exploration Society, 1914–.

Petrie, W. M. Flinders, *The Royal Tombs of the First Dynasty 1900*. Part I. London: Egypt Exploration Fund, 1900.

———, *Seventy Years in Archaeology*. London: Sampson Low, Marston & Co., Ltd., n.d.

Auguste Mariette at Sakkara. See Figure 5–1 on page 57.

Figure 6–1. Exterior View of The Boulaq Museum, circa 1871

The photograph was taken by Hippolyte Délié and Henri Béchard. In the foreground, the courtyard of the Boulaq Museum is the setting for a typical arrangement of objects to be photographed in natural daylight. In the background is the Nile River.

Courtesy Library of Congress

Figure 6–2. The So-Called Sheykh-el-Beled

Old Kingdom, Dynasty IV
Sepia toned silver print
Photographer: Émile Brugsch (?)
McClung Museum: A1: 621 Egypt 5S
Gift of Mr. and Mrs. Louis Bailey Audigier, 1934

This admirable wood statue, well-carved and standing about three feet eight inches high, has a very realistic appearance. Arabs thought the rotund figure looked like a village headman, ergo its name. The frontal position, forward stride, and steady gaze present a style typical of Old Kingdom sculpture. The arms have been pegged to the upper body and the once-missing feet were restored, possibly by the conservator Alexandre Barsanti (1858–1917). The eyes are of opaque white quartz set in copper to suggest lids, and rock crystal disks are the pupils. The statue was found at Sakkara, along with a wooden statue of the subject's wife, in the chapel of the mastaba tomb of a priest and high official, Ka-aper, who lived at Memphis around 2450 B.C. The statue was found during the course of Auguste Mariette's excavation. The once-painted masterpiece was exhibited for the first time at the Boulaq Museum, where it was placed on a pedestal in the Center Gallery and protected by a waist-high brass guardrail.

CHAPTER

6

The Creation of the Cairo Museum

The story of museums in Egypt probably begins in 1834 during the energetic rule of Mohammed Ali, when a collection of precious antiquities was preserved in a Cairo school and later in quarters at the Citadel, a part of the fortifications that circled Cairo. The minister of education was appointed director, and antiquities of various kinds were to have been catalogued by the French geographer and explorer Liant de Bellefonds (1799–1883). In any event, the artifacts were probably insecurely housed and in jeopardy, for somehow they vanished, either appropriated by thieves, tourists, and dealers, or given as gifts to notables and distinguished visitors—some perhaps even before they arrived at the Citadel. Such practices were common. When the Archduke Maximilian of Austria visited Cairo in 1855, he was presented an entire collection that went with him back to Vienna. Egypt was losing its cultural heritage. A few individuals knew something had to be done.

The determined salvaging of the archaeological treasures of Egypt began in earnest through the vision and energy of one such person, the indefatigable French Egyptologist Auguste Mariette (1821–1881). Mariette was a gigantic figure of his time in the cause of Egyptological science and the preservation of Egyptian antiquities. He justly has been called "the father of the Cairo Museum."

The Boulaq Museum

The Boulaq Museum, or Museum of Egyptian Antiquities, was the first museum of Egyptian antiquities in Egypt. It was founded in 1857 and opened in 1863, due to the self-imposed efforts of Mariette, who deeply felt the need to preserve the remains of all periods of the ancient culture of Egypt before they perished in situ or reached the hands of thieves, who then sold them to eager buyers.

In the beginning Mariette had to safely assemble the huge number of objects from his excavations wherever he could find storage space. Although a proper museum was his goal, he was greatly opposed by the ministers at Cairo, who, as followers of the Muslim faith, thought these antiquities represented the monumental relics of a former land of infidels. Nevertheless, in the end Mariette convinced the Viceroy Saïd (1854–1863) of the value of protecting Egypt's heritage. The ruler of Egypt decreed that a new museum be built and designated Mariette as its first director. Alas, however, the realization of a new museum was—not unexpectedly—to be much delayed.

Utilizing his powers of persuasion, Mariette obtained an old post-office building at Boulaq, the port of Cairo, as a temporary solution for the installation of his antiquities collection. The building was on the banks of the Nile River, near a large banyan tree, with a garden at the front. Among the antiquities flanking the entrance was a colossal seated statue of a king, which Mariette had found at Tanis, and three handsome sphinxes. Mariette set up a white marble statue to the left of the door and, adjacent, a rose-colored stone pedestal that had once borne a statue found in Middle Egypt of the handsome imperial Roman courtier Antinous, favored by the emperor Hadrian (A.D. 76–138).

Figure 6–3. Stela of King Thutmose III

New Kingdom, Dynasty XVIII
Sepia toned silver print
Photographer: unidentified
McClung Museum: A1: 221 18th Dyn. 83
Gift of Mr. and Mrs. Louis B. Audigier, 1934

The "Poetical Stela" was found by Auguste Mariette in the Temple of Amen-Re at Karnak and was another of the treasures first preserved in the Boulaq Museum. The intact black granite stela has twenty-six registers of beautifully inscribed hieroglyphs. The large top register shows two scenes of the king offering homage to the king of gods and god of the sky, Amen-Re, while the goddess of warfare(?), Neith, looks on. The god recounts the victories of his son, King Thutmose, and reminds him of the many great achievements and conquests achieved with the god's help. The text names one of the countries Thutmose conquered and battles he fought all the way to Mesopotamia. It was under the reign of Thutmose that Egypt recovered its lost prestige from the disastrous invasion of the Hyksos.

Figure 6–4. Prince Rahotep and Princess Nofret

Old Kingdom, Dynasty III
Sepia toned silver print
Photographer: unidentified
McClung Museum: A1: 221 3rd dyn. 5N 5R
Gift of Mr. and Mrs. Louis Bailey Audigier, 1934

The clear colors still preserved on the approximately four-feet-high painted limestone statues of the couple help to make the figures seem alive as they sit calmly on large, plain chairs. Their physical features are skillfully modeled, and their heads are striking in their realism, with eyes made in same manner as those of the Sheykh-el-Beled. The sculptures were found in 1880, by an assistant to Auguste Mariette, in the mastaba tomb of Rahotep at Medum. The tomb is near the unfinished Pyramid of Medum built later by the Dynasty IV Pharaoh Snefru, predecessor of King Khufu (Cheops).

Travellers must have been duly impressed even before they entered the Museum. In the small vestibule, where visitors were required to leave their canes, umbrellas, and parasols, they could purchase Mariette's "Notice of the Principal Monuments on Exhibit" (1864) and Maspero's "Visitor's Guide to the Boulaq Museum" (1883), which provided a particular order for visitors to follow, should they choose. Other publications by Mariette also available were photographs of objects on exhibit in the Museum, which sold for one franc each. Admission was free, but smoking was strictly forbidden in the galleries, and taking impressions or rubbings was prohibited without the permission of the director.

After passing into the Main Gallery visitors were amazed by the rich array of treasures surrounding them, including stone statues of deities, sarcophagi elaborately decorated with hieroglyphics and delicately carved images of deities, a torso of a dignitary excavated at Karnak, a royal portrait head made of black granite (possibly King Merneptah, thought by Mariette to be the pharaoh of the Exodus), an impressive naos, various important royal statues, and the famous black granite portrait head of King Taharka of Nubia. In an adjoining hall was the famous Decree of Canopus, or Tablet of Tanis, found at Tanis in the Delta and inscribed in hieroglyphics, demotic, and Greek. The decree was a duplicate of the famous Rosetta Stone and proved the decipherment of the Rosetta Stone by Jean Françoise Champollion in 1822 to be correct. Also on exhibit were a relief from the tomb of Harmhab, a campaign relief of Queen Hatshepsut, and fragments from the Temple of Seti I at Abydos. In other rooms were objects from Memphis and Gizeh, as well as the widely known lifelike Old Kingdom statue of the Sheykh-el-Beled, from Sakkara.

Mariette soon realized that the building was unsuited to his purposes, with its small rooms, thin walls, poor floors, and its lack of protection from the threat of greedy robbers. But the space proved inadequate and was soon filled with the additions of newly excavated material. Many objects had to be boxed up and put in outside storehouses so that much of the collection could be neither exhibited nor readily accessed.

Mariette was also plagued with environmental problems. Rising morning mists issued into the building from the Nile River, and condensation ran inside the exhibit cases containing mummies. Then tragedy struck with the great Nile flood of 1878, which greatly damaged the Museum. The collections were saved, but the exhibit cases were destroyed and the building walls badly cracked. Mariette struggled to save the Museum.

Figure 6–5. The Gizeh Palace, 1870–1880s

The photographer J. Pascal Sébah took this view of the north wing of the luxurious khedivial palace that became the Gizeh Museum.

Courtesy of Library of Congress.

The Gizeh Museum

Great disappointment and frustration hovered over the visionary Mariette from the lack of funding from the government, which delayed the promised new museum. However, the Egyptian Antiquities Service of the government was finally pressed into moving the endangered collection from Boulaq. In 1891, ten years after Mariette's death, the French Egyptologist Eugene Grebaut (1846–1915), then the Director-General of Museums and of the collections, had the Boulaq collection brought to the Gizeh Palace, opposite the Island of Roda.

The gorgeous structure had been built by Khedive Ismail (1863–1879) to house his *harim*, but in 1890 he gave it to the Antiquities Service. Through the earlier efforts of Mariette and then of Gaston Maspero in his later role as director of the Boulaq Museum and of the Egyptian Antiquities Service, the antiquities were to have new quarters. Another temporary measure to protect Egypt's national treasure had been undertaken.

But even in the opulent building with its hundreds of rooms, there were problems. To begin with, the palace was not well built. Precautionary steps, including fire prevention, had to be taken so that the collections would be safeguarded. Also, the objects were arranged rather unsystematically in the rooms, and the palace was on the west side of the Nile, farther from Cairo than the Boulaq and somewhat distant for tourists. It was much better to have a proper museum in the center of the city.

Thirteen years later, in 1903, the new Egyptian Museum in Cairo was inaugurated. The Gizeh Museum was then past history; Mariette must have been watching developments all the while.

Figure 6–6. Relief from the Tomb of Sabu

Old Kingdom, Dynasty VI
Sepia toned silver print
Photographer: Émile Brugsch
McClung Museum: A1: 521 Old King. C 3.2
Gift of Mr. and Mrs. Louis Bailey Audigier, 1934

The first register of the relief fragment depicts Sabu, the director of artworks for the king, seated on a cushioned chair, holding a staff and baton in his hands as attendants haul him forward with a long rope. In the second register he receives from a procession of women offerings of fruit, vegetables, fowl, cattle, and other animals. In the next two registers, cattle are being slaughtered, and Sabu enjoys a ride on his sailing vessel. In the bottom register he watches a scribe taking inventory as animals are driven toward him. This telling relief implies that the next world will be an even more abundant continuation of earthly life. The fragment, discovered by Auguste Mariette in Sabu's mastaba tomb at Sakkara, was first displayed in the Boulaq Museum on one side of the door to the Old Kingdom Room.

Figure 6–7. The Sarcophagus of Khufuankh

Old Kingdom, Dynasty IV
Sepia toned silver print
Photographer: Émile Brugsch
McClung Museum: A1: 521 4th dyn. C3.3
Gift of Mr. and Mrs. Louis Bailey Audigier, 1934

The well-executed rose granite coffin of an Egyptian nobleman is covered in perfect deeply incised hieroglyphs. Architectural reliefs on all sides of the bottom half represent the facades of a domestic house, or eternal house, of the deceased. The owner's name appears near the corner at the end of the sarcophagus. This fine coffin was first exhibited at the Boulaq Museum.

Figure 6–8. Princess Amenirdas I

Late Period, Dynasty XXV
Sepia toned silver print
Photographer: unidentified
McClung Museum: A1: 221 25th dyn. 5A
Gift of Mr. and Mrs. Louis Bailey Audigier, 1934

Amenirdas, a priestess at Thebes, was the "divine adoratrice of Amen-Re," the earthly bride of the god. The divine consort was the sister of King Piankhi, the Kushite ruler of much of Egypt during 700 B.C. In her role as an important religious figure, she could not marry, and her post was passed on by "adoption." Although of foreign origin, Amenirdas is portrayed with the poise and regal bearing given Egyptian royal statues. She holds a flail close to her body, wears a well-defined tripart wig and a feathered headdress surmounted by a circle of cobras, and clutches a folded cloth in the right hand. She stands on a pedestal of gray granite incised with her name and titles in hieroglyphics. The fine alabaster figure was found at Karnak in the ruins of a small chapel of a Ptolemaic temple.

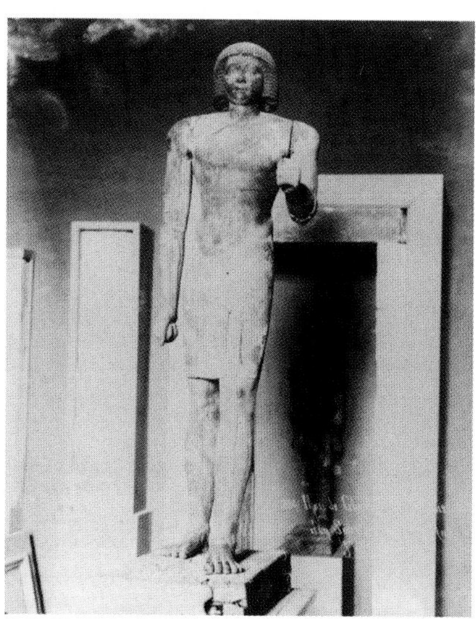

Figure 6–9. Statue of an Official

Old Kingdom, Dynasty V
Albumen print
Photographer: J. Pascal Sébah
McClung Museum: 1996.10.2
Gift of Friends of Egyptology, 1996

The marvelous example of Old Kingdom art represents an official who held the position of secretary in the Old Kingdom bureaucracy. The well-executed wooden figure wears a short curled wig and a kilt. The hand of the bent left arm held a staff, now missing, and the right hand once held a baton. He is shown on exhibit in the Gizeh Museum.

The Egyptian Museum

The new museum was designed in the Greco-Roman style by the French architect Marcel Dourgnon; construction started in 1897. In March 1903 the monuments at the Gizeh Museum were moved into place in the new building, and in July the transfer was complete. Nevertheless, there was the necessary refurbishing to do. Antiquities in cases and on pedestals had to be protected by glass, and damage to the walls and pillars caused by moving numerous large, heavy objects into place had to be repaired. An attempt also was made to bring order out of disorder by reclassifying the objects and rearranging them in the galleries. The chronology set out by the historian Manetho was used to provide relative dates for important people and monuments.

The gala opening of the largest collection of Egyptian antiquities in the world was on November 15, 1903. Above two large pillars flanking the main entrance were two reliefs by Ferdinand Faivre (1867), symbolizing Upper and Lower Egypt. Beneath these pillars visitors swept forward and entered into a dazzling display. In the gallery they were overwhelmed by four colossal granite statues set against the four pillars that supported the balcony under the great dome.

Although it was officially the "Museum of Egyptian Antiquities," it was usually referred to as the "Egyptian Museum", or "Cairo Museum" due to its location. Even its first director, Gaston Maspero, titled his 1903 catalogue of the collections (translated from the French by James and Anne Quibell) *Guide to the Cairo Museum*. Initially, the Museum was open every day but Friday during the winter season, but by 1927 it closed also on Mondays and official holidays. At the end of the building was the sales room, where visitors could buy authenticated antiquities, photographs, postcards, and publications. There was an admission charge of five P.T. (big Piastre), or five cents in American money! By 1927 it was up to ten cents, but only a penny during the summer! At the entrance was an attendant who spoke the principal European languages.

In 1926 objects from the splendid Tomb of Tutankhamen were put on exhibit on the first floor, causing quite a sensation. However, less than half the famous treasures were displayed since there were many still being restored and consolidated in the laboratory at Thebes. But as more of the tomb's contents were delivered to the Museum, adjustments were made in the galleries to show the new arrivals.

In the forecourt at one end of the garden is an imposing monument: The great Auguste Mariette-Pasha, founder of the Museum, died at Boulaq in 1881 and was buried in a marble sarcophagus in the courtyard of the Boulaq Museum. The sarcophagus was later moved, first to the Gizeh Museum, then, in 1902, to the Egyptian Museum, where it now rests in front of a handsome bronze statue of Mariette, unveiled in 1904.

Figure 6–10. The Egyptian Museum

Original postcard
Undertermined French publisher
Circa 1915
Anonymous Lender.

The Cairo street scene, with the Egyptian Museum in the background.

Figure 6–11. Mrs. Louis Bailey Audigier of Knoxville

Silver print
Photographer: probably Louis Bailey Audigier
Frank H. McClung Museum: A1: 927
Gift of Mr. and Mrs. Louis Bailey Audigier, 1934

Mrs. Audigier stands in front of the Egyptian Museum, next to a pyramidion that capped an obelisk erected at Karnak in Dynasty XVIII by Queen Hatshepsut.

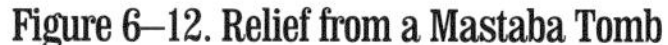

Figure 6–12. Relief from a Mastaba Tomb

Old Kingdom, Dynasty V
Albumen print
Photographer: Bonfils Family
McClung Museum: 1/696
Gift of Friends of Egyptology, 1995.

The image represents a copy made of a section of a wall relief in the exceptional mastaba tomb of Ptah-hotep at Sakkara, Upper Egypt. The reliefs from this tomb are among the finest and reach the high point of Old Kingdom artistic achievement. This section is from a larger cattle and poultry scene and shows two herders leading an ox for inspection before Ptah-hotep. One herder holds a beating stick aloft in his right hand and the other herder leads the bull on a tether rope and holds a butchered haunch (?) over his left shoulder.

Figure 6–13. Painting of Geese

Old Kingdom, Dynasty IV
Sepia toned silver print
Photographer: unidentified
McClung Museum: A1: 321 3rd–4th dyn. 9
Gift of Mr. and Mrs. Louis Bailey Audigier, 1934.

The charmingly detailed fresco wall painting of six Egyptian geese is from the twin mastaba tomb at Medum of King Snefru's Vizier Neferma'at and his wife Atet. The fresco is an entire view, demonstrating the artist's careful attention to naturalistic detail. At the right, a pair of red-breasted geese walk toward a grazing bean goose. In the Nineteenth Century, the Italian Egyptologist Luigi Vassalli (1812–1887) hacked the section from the tomb wall, damaging the surrounding area.

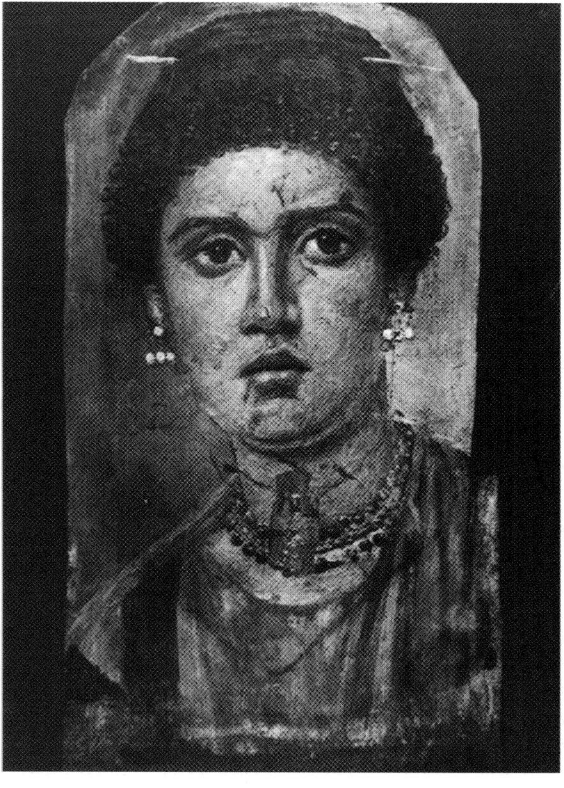

Figure 6–14. Two Portrait Paintings

Roman Period, A.D. 100
Sepia toned silver print
Photographer: unidentified
McClung Museum: A1: 521
Roman Per. C3.5; C3.4
Gift of Mr. and Mrs. Louis Bailey Audigier, 1934.

These realistic encaustic (pigment in a beeswax matrix fused to a surface by heat) paintings on wood are from the Fayum in Upper Egypt and are typical of the individualized images of the deceased made during the Greco-Roman period. Such shaped paintings were set in at the head of the coffin in a recessed space created for the portraits so that they appeared to be framed. In this way the dead could be better remembered by the living. The portraits were found in 1888 by Flinders Petrie at the cemetery at Hawara, in the Fayum.

Figure 6–15. Model of Soldiers

Middle Kingdom, Dynasty XII
Sepia toned silver print
Photographer: Unidentified
McClung Museum: A1: 621 12th dyn. 1
Gift of Mr. and Mrs. Louis Bailey Audigier, 1934.

The model army of painted wooden Egyptian and Nubian soldiers seems to advance in their display in the Gizeh Museum. At the left forty Nubians carry bows and arrows, and at the right forty Egyptians carry spears and ox-hide shields. The warriors were found at Assiut, entombed at the side of the important official Mesehti, Nomarch and military commander of Egypt.

Figure 6–16. Statue of King Thutmose III

New Kingdom, Dynasty XVIII
Sepia toned silver print
Photographer: probably Émile Brugsch
McClung Museum: A1: 221 18 5T
Gift of Mr. and Mrs. Louis Bailey Audigier, 1934.

The detail of the upper portion of the standing figure reflects the style of New Kingdom sculpture. The pharaoh wears the White Crown of Upper Egypt with a large cobra centered above his forehead, both of which reaffirm his position as the supreme ruler of Upper Egypt and his power as a mighty king. Of particular note are the eyebrows and cosmetic lines drawn out in delicate low relief. The finely sculpted work was found in 1903 by Georges Legrain (1865-1917) in a vast pit, among an extraordinary mass of seventeen thousand statues and figures piled up one upon another in the Temple of Amen at Karnak.

Figure 6–17. Combined Gods Sobek and Haroeris

Ptolemaic Period
Sepia toned silver print
Photographer: probably Émile Brugsch
McClung Museum: A1: 221 26th dyn. 4
Gift of Mr. and Mrs. Louis Bailey Audigier, 1934.

At the Temple of Kom Ombo in Upper Egypt, two chief deities were worshipped: the crocodile god, Sobek, and the falcon god, Haroeris. This limestone sculpture depicts a representation of the two gods united in the recumbent body of a crocodile with the head of a falcon. The Temple, in its beautiful hilltop setting above the Nile River, was cleared in 1893 by the French archaeologist, Jacques de Morgan (1857–1924), when he was Director-General of the Egyptian Antiquities Service.

Figure 6–18. Mummy of Rameses II

New Kingdom, Dynasty XIX
Sepia toned silver print
Photographer: probably Émile Brugsch
McClung Museum: A1 521 19th dyn. C 3.7
Gift of Mr. and Mrs. Louis Bailey Audigier, 1934

The mummy of the famous pharaoh is one of the best preserved. It was among the royal mummies found in a tomb shaft south of the Temple of Hatshepsut at Der el-Bahri. After Rameses II's tomb in the Valley of the Kings was plundered by robbers, the mummy was moved several times for safekeeping. Finally, priests of Dynasty XXII hid the mummy—along with those of other royals—so well that it wasn't rediscovered until 1881. In 1928 the mummies were removed from exhibit in the Egyptian Museum. To see them, one had to obtain a permit from the minister of education.

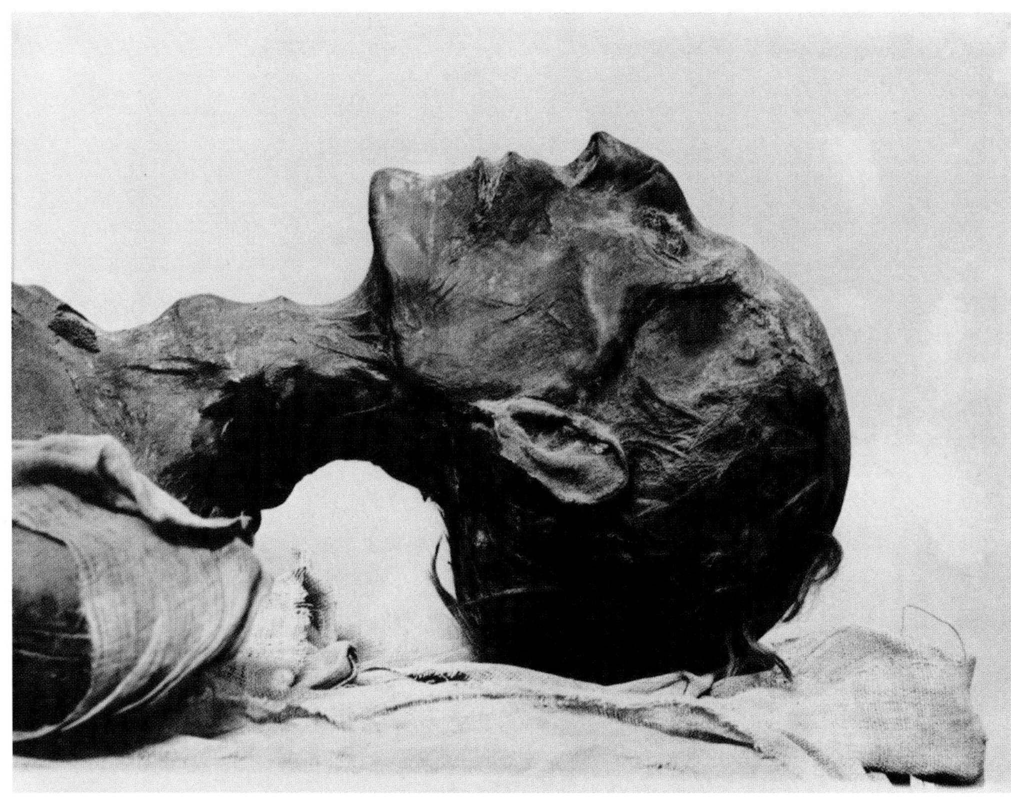

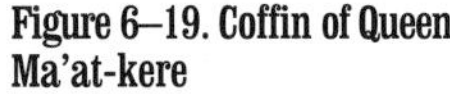

Figure 6–19. Coffin of Queen Ma'at-kere

Third Intermediate Period, Dynasty XXI
Sepia toned silver print
Photographer: Émile Brugsch
McClung Museum: A1: 521 19th dyn. C 3.9
Gift of Mr. and Mrs. Louis Bailey Audigier, 1934.

The upper section of gilded and painted inner coffin shows the queen, wife of high priest and "king" Paynozem I (Pinudjem I), wearing a large, elaborate feathered headdress that frames a face of noble expression. Her hands are crossed over a wide *wesekh*-collar on her chest, and the nicely modeled left hand holds a folded cloth. The coffin containing the queen's mummy, along with that of a pet baboon found lying against her shoulder, was among the cache of royal mummies discovered in 1881. The mummies were transported first to the Boulaq Museum and later to the Egyptian Museum in Cairo.

Selected Bibliography

Baedeker, Karl, *Egypt and the Sudan*, fourth edition. Leipzig 1898.

Borchardt, Ludwig, *Works of Art from the egyptian Museum at Cairo, with explanations by Ludwig Borchardt*, translated by G. A. Reisner. Cairo: Diemer, 1908.

Budge, E. Wallas, *The Nile. Notes for Travellers in Egypt and in the Egyptian Sudan*. London: T. Cook & Sons Ltd., 1912.

——, *Cook's Handbook for Egypt and the Sudan*. London: T. Cook & Sons Ltd., 1911.

Mariette-Bey, Auguste, *Album du Musée de Boulaq: comprenant quarante planches photographiees par MM Délié et Béchard avec in texte explicatif redige par Auguste Mariette-Bey*. Cairo: A. Moures & Cie, 1871.

Maspero, Gaston, *Guide du Visiteur au Musée de Boulaq*. Boulaq 1883.

——, *Guide to the Cairo Museum*, translated by J. E. and A. A. Quibell. Cairo: Printing Office of the French Institute of Oriental Archeology, 1910.

——, *Notice des principaux monuments exposes au Musée de Gizeh*, third edition. Cairo: Imprimerie nationale, 1892.

Murray, John, *A Handbook for Travellers in Egypt*. fifth edition. London: John Murray, 1875.

A Short Description of the Objects from the Tomb of Tutankhamun Now Exhibited in the Cairo Museum. Cairo: The Museum Authority, 1926.

CHAPTER 7

Dealers, Scoundrels and Fakers

Figure 7–1. Sales were lively at the tombs.

The 1895 illustration shows excited travelers buying "just-discovered" antiquities! But in many instances it was doubtful they were just found, or were genuine.

Courtesy Library of Congress.

From ancient times on Egypt has long been blessed with magnificent tombs and long cursed by cunning thieves. Egyptian relics have been the main attraction and greed the cause. There is seldom an excavator who discovers under the golden sands or deep in a rock face a dark tomb that has not been previously entered by tomb robbers and its contents picked over. Theft has had a long heritage.

Robbery and destruction of the Gizeh pyramids and cemeteries began in the Old Kingdom and continued until the Twentieth Century, when more positive protective methods were undertaken. The dynastic thefts and damages were not recorded, but early classical authors saw the monuments before the limestone facings of the pyramids had been removed. Later Arab historians wrote that they had long been damaged by theft. At Thebes tombs continued to be in constant danger in dynastic times, particularly from robbers living in the Theban village of Kurna near the temples at Medinet Habu. In Dynasty XX, during the Ramesside Period, the temple hierarchy and other officials, who were guardians of the tombs, were outraged as they often found them plundered, strewn with open coffins, pieces of mummies, jewelry, gold and silver, and other treasures gone. To protect their sacred royal dead and save what they could, the most revered mummies such as those of pharaohs and of the high priesthood were secretly removed and hidden in the Theban necropolis. Centuries passed, but it was not until 1881 during the rule of Khedive Tawfiq that Gaston Maspero as Director of the Egyptian Antiquities Service was to learn of the hiding place of one group of these mummies concealed in rock galleries at Der el-Bahri. Under the direction of Émile Brugsch, then an assistant conservator of the Boulaq Museum, more than ten mummies and coffins, including that of Seti I and Thutmose II, were transported to the Boulaq Museum. Other secret locations containing a number of important royal mummies and valuable tomb furnishings came to light later. A happy circumstance for the excavators of the Dynasty XVIII Tomb of Tutankhamen was finding the tomb intact, although it had been entered a few times before in the reign of Rameses VI.

The mummy-merchants are the population of the Theban ruins. Grave ghouls, they live upon dead bodies. [1]

—G. W. Curtis, 1851

Figure 7–2. Certificate of Antiquity and Blanchard's *Handbook.*

Object: book: Courtesy Hodges Library, University of Tennessee.
Object: card: McClung Museum: unnumbered Gift of Mr. and Mrs. Louis Bailey Audigier, 1934

The card of authentication was signed by the charming Mr. Blanchard, proprietor of a small, long-established and thriving antiquities shop at the corner of Shepheard's Hotel, Cairo. Many travellers, professional Egyptologists, and amateur collectors bought antiquities from him. Blanchard was indeed an experienced collector, particularly of scarabs and seals, some of which rivaled those excavated by the leading British Egyptologist Flinders Petrie. Blanchard was so convinced of the quality of his objects he published a book in 1909, *Handbook of Egyptian Gods and Mummy Amulets,* with forty-four photographic plates illustrating the quality of his collection. However, even Blanchard may have sold objects that were questionable.

Not only were the tombs violated by robbers seeking treasures, but they were frequently damaged by having been converted into local family dwellings along with the dust and smoke produced by the occupants. The same was true of temples with mud brick structures built on them or close by in a village-like atmosphere. In the case of tombs, a particularly discouraging result was the loss of the original contents of the tomb chamber and the context in which objects were placed. This created gaps in our knowledge about the daily life and cultural development of an extraordinary ancient people. Even in the mid-Nineteenth Century, when the Egyptian government undertook the supervision of the monuments in an attempt to protect them from plunder, they were not safe. Clever thieves continued their lucrative work. Eventually the stolen objects reached the outstretched hands of antiquities dealers or museum personnel and other officials attempting to build up their own or museum collections, further blurring the origins of the objects.

Fellahins (peasants) living in the villages at Gizeh, Sakkara, and in Kurna at Thebes were particularly active in the tombs supporting a lively traffic in illicit antiquities. Some were independent and carried their wares in the many pockets within their flowing *galabeyahs*. They won over many an innocent and unsuspecting buyer, standing graceful and straight in their white turbans and red slippers, with their winning smiles and friendly manners. Even for those visitors with great persistence, the fellahins displayed charming ways. Most, however, conspired with the controlling local dealers and others worked with dealers in Cairo, some of whom were Europeans such as Germans and Italians. Private individuals and government officials were involved as well, expediting the transactions. The lure was great.

There was no shortage of European and American buyers. A steady flow of antiquities maintained the profits, and the more experienced in the business knew to ask a high price. Concealment and safety measures were essential. In many cases sales were made at night under the cover of darkness. Potential customers, who were brave hearted, were guided through the dark into the deep, shadowy recesses of tombs where some objects were hidden. Adventurous travelers might go several hundred feet into the ground and further toward the tomb chamber, where mummy-merchants had been before them. At other times they were taken to a tomb during the day. Emerging from the hot darkness to the fresh air once again travelers were met by waiting dealers who spread their wares before them. All sorts of objects were offered for sale, including rings, necklaces, fragments of mummy cases, jewelry, and even the arms, feet, hands and heads of mummies.

> ***Statues, inscribed tablets, sculptured slabs from sepulchres and temples, indeed, the sliced-off walls of whole tombs, are among the well known fruits transported to Europe mostly within the last forty years.[2]***
>
> ***—A. Henry Rhind, 1862***

Archaeologists and the Tomb Robber

This plundering seriously impeded excavations. Concerns were voiced by archaeologists such as the eminent British Egyptologist Flinders Petrie, who felt it was essential to finish the excavations in one season in order to record his findings in a one-volume publication. Other information about the site could be published later. Petrie was eager to collect as much material as he could from what had been left or overlooked by tomb robbers. If they had entered the tombs before he had begun excavating, this was not only disappointing, but filled him with apprehension. Such threats were of constant concern and added to the normal stresses of the digs.

Petrie pointed out that not only had valuable metals and larger treasures been stolen or destroyed through the centuries, but these crimes were followed by the systematic destruction of monuments by fanatic, Christian religious sects as well. But perhaps worst of all were the activities of the dealers who sought anything of value to sell for a profit. Blind greed obsessed the cunning vendors who asked no questions about the object's source. Then there were the scoundrels who destroyed antiquities outright to make them rarer thus increasing profits.

The American Egyptologist George Reisner was just one of many archaeologists who lamented such vandalism. In his report in *History of the Giza Necropolis,* Reisner pointed out that generally the incidents of destruction, which started in the Old Kingdom, continued to be unrecorded through time as the acts were done by shadowy persons looking for valuable objects. An ongoing question that perplexed Reisner about another type of theft was how and when the fine white limestone casings were removed from the pyramids.

Egyptologists also criticized their colleagues for their collecting methods. One such person was the Scottish Egyptologist Alexander Henry Rhind (1833-1863), who excavated at Thebes and Kurna and used worthy archaeological methods for his time. In 1862 he was one of the first to justify his collecting practices by claiming "...that objects of this kind are best deposited in a public collection...where their presence is more likely to be useful, and security against loss or dispersion is ensured."[3] Rhind placed his objects in the national collection of the Royal Museum at Edinburgh, Scotland. However, he was greatly concerned about the methods used by others. He records Karl Richard Lepsius (1810-1884) as a particular offender whom he believed should have known better. From 1842 to 1845 this great German Egyptologist travelled to Egypt under the patronage of the Prussian Commission to collect numerous objects for the Berlin Museum. Rhind describes the reprehensible methods used by Lepsius. One such act was the toppling of a column at Seti I's

Figure 7–3. An Egyptian merchant laden down with tempting necklaces to catch the eye.

Original postcard
Photographer: Rudolf Lehnert
Lehnert & Landrock
Cairo, 1924
Anonymous Lender

tomb at Thebes to disengage a piece of relief from it and then leave the column in ruins. Rhind contrasts this by promoting the methods used by other Egyptologists who meticulously copied inscriptions and decorations, even by candlelight rather than damage the integrity of the monument. Although Lepsius stated that the choices he made were to benefit science and to increase public knowledge, Rhind found his reasoning unconscionable in view of his use of destructive methods and the influence such practices would have on upholding proper standards. Despite his respect for Lepsius' great contributions to scholarship, Rhind was greatly concerned about the impact of such methods on archaeology as a science. Rhind was also troubled about the effect on the stripping of monuments for any reason, thereby diminishing their grandeur and historic value.

A scaffolding of spars and oars was at once improvised and the men, delighted as children at play, were soon swarming all over the huge head....All they had to do was to remove any small lumps...and then tint the white patches with coffee....It took them three afternoons...we were sorry when it came to an end. [4]

—Amelia Edwards

After arriving at Abu Simbel in 1873, the British Egyptologist Amelia Edwards was alarmed to discover clumps of plaster remaining on one of the colossal, sandstone heads of Rameses II. These flakes were the remains from an earlier cast made for the British Museum a decade earlier by the British traveller Robert Hay (1799-1863), along with the British sculptor Joseph Bonomi (1796-1878), in their attempt to document the monument. To modify the unsightly blotches Edwards directed that coffee be used to tint the plaster.

Figure 7–4. "Scientific Researches"

An 1842 illustration shows coffins wantonly being removed from a tomb to enrich the collections of the British Museum under the guise of "Scientific Researches." An American scholar James Ewing Cooley was among those who questioned the benefit and social advantage to such reckless plunder other than to satisfy such personages as wealthy English lords.

An Old Story

The removal of antiquities from Egypt was not new. It was a long and complicated story and involved numerous nationalities, many provided convincing motives. The ancient Romans had boldly taken imposing obelisks from Egypt to enhance the imperial cities of Rome and Constantinople and to sanction the stolen obelisk as an important symbol of a Roman emperor's power. Many centuries later, in the Nineteenth Century, obelisks were transported from Egypt to London, Paris, and the United States, in part, it was said, to save them from eventual ruin and disappearance from neglect. More numerous, however, were the Egyptian mummies that were wantonly destroyed by the thousands and prepared for use as so-called potent medicine. Invasions of Egypt by the French and British provided much plunder for the Louvre Museum in Paris and the British Museum in London. Ambassadors and con-

sul-generals helped themselves to the contents of tombs and had fragments wrested from the walls of monuments to benefit themselves and museum collections. Guiltless looting became a national style for more and more treasures. On a lesser level, but nonetheless destructive, was the graffiti of egotistic travellers, who delighted in putting phrases, their initials, and names on so many monuments such as at Abu Simbel.

For centuries the interest generated by the mysterious and unresolved hieroglyphic writings sparked the craving for ancient Egyptian objects. Travellers returned home with great tales, and popular publications dramatized the exotic Egyptian experience. A major breakthrough came in 1798, when Napoleon Bonaparte sent his scientific commission to record Egypt and collect specimens and artifacts for the Louvre Museum in Paris. Not too long after the French philologist Jean Françoise Champollion (1790-1832), the decipherer of the hieroglyphic language, and the Italian Egyptologist Ippolito Rosellini (1800-1843) went to Egypt. Sponsored by the united French and Tuscan commissions, they studied and recorded the monuments and secured antiquities for the Louvre and for museums in Florence, Italy. A particular offense happened when they were working in Seti I's tomb in the Valley of the Kings at Thebes and cut out two slabs from a section of a doorway to carry away. However, it was at the time when such destructive methods were generally accepted. Even the French Egyptologist and preservationist Auguste Mariette, as Director-General of the Egyptian Antquities Service, helped to expedite objects to the Louvre Museum, albeit approved. Museums and private collections around the world attest to the countless number of objects, from monolithic statues to the smallest scarab, legally or illegally removed from Egypt during the Nineteenth and early Twentieth Centuries.

Figure 7–5. The Sphinx of a King

Polemaic Period, 332-30 B.C.
Albumen print
Photographer: Émile Brugsch
McClung Museum: A1 521 Ptol.Per. C3.8
Gift of Mr. and Mrs. Louis Bailey Audigier, 1934

The recumbent body of a lion has the head of a king, who wears the striped, royal *nemes* headdress. Around his chest is a stylized mane. When the statue was discovered as part of the Avenue of Sphinxes at the Serapeum in Memphis it had been long unprotected, which resulted in the graffiti on his body and outstretched legs. Many monuments were defaced by thoughtless individuals, who scratched their names or initials into stone statues and buildings. But this sphinx was rescued and went to Cairo's Egyptian Museum.

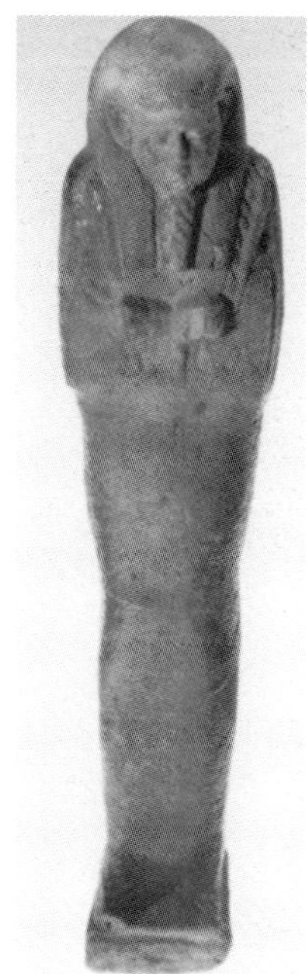

Figure 7–6. Fake *Shawabti*

Object: glazed ceramic
12.7 cm. high (5 inches)
McClung Museum: unnumbered

Small figurines called *Shawabtis* (answers) were placed in the tomb to magically serve the deceased as workers in the fields in the Afterworld. Some, however, never saw the inside of a tomb, as in this example. The color and uneven application of the glaze is questionable and incompatible with the shape and proportion of the figure. Such combinations are inconsistent compared to dated examples. The agricultural implements are unclear and do not connect to the hands. On the rear pillar is a jumbled hieroglyphic inscription.

Figure 7–7. Three Fake Scarabs

Object: painted plaster
9.4 ; 8.9; 7.7 cm. Long (3-11/16; 3-1/2; 3 inches)
McClung Museum: 513/A1; 515/A1; 516/A1
Gift of Mr. and Mrs. Louis Bailey Audigier, 1934

An attempt was made to replicate genuine scarabs. The faker has carved the scarabs out of white plaster and coated them with a matt color to imitate the dulled glaze often found on ancient objects and roughly carved a cartouche of Thutmose III on the underside! However, these examples are exceptions to the rule. Most falsified scarabs were extremely difficult to detect. Some were buried in dung mounds, removed, oiled and rubbed in dirt to make them appear dug up and old. Other forgers recut the hieroglyphs on the underside of genuine scarabs for more appeal, or recut a cartouche belonging to an important pharaoh to increase its sales appeal.

You buy anticas?" he said in a whisper, casting a sidelong glance of apprehension at a mounted policeman...[5]

—T. G. Wakeling, 1912

Fakers of Antiquities

In Egypt in the Nineteenth and early Twentieth Centuries there were fakers and then there were fakers. And oh how they flourished. Sometimes it was more advantageous to make your own antiquities than to rely on what you could find. But the huge number of ancient objects sold each year meant the number had to be matched in kind to have enough to sell. The most popular souvenirs of all were mummy parts. A mummy head, hand, or foot would do nicely and surely impress those back home in Europe or America. Even modern Egyptians were embalmed if the tombs failed to provide a much-needed mummy. Curiously, the Egyptian forger did not think he was dishonest in his deception and was only sorry if he were to be found out by the hands of unkind fate. A good bit of money had almost been his, but then was plucked from his grasp!

Artistic skill determined how much you could sell, too. As with any endeavor, a fake was done poorly or done well. Many a piece of stone was clumsily modeled into a scarab, or other amulet-shape, in an attempt to fool the unsuspecting. Hieroglyphic inscriptions were ineptly scratched on ancient jars to increase sales appeal and entice unwary buyers. There were fakes that were expertly falsified with great accuracy. Such clever frauds were devilish to detect. Then there was the question of written documentation, or pedigrees, for an object which did not always provide accurate proof of authenticity. Also, fakes were made and sold by sophisticated Europeans living in Egypt. Museums and private collections all over the world contain examples of forgeries including bronze figurines, alabaster vases, faience amulets, stone statue fragments, painted wall reliefs, and papyri. However, modern science has usually triumphed and remains on the alert.

In July 1912, a law by the Egyptian Government took effect whereby all finds of antiquities became state property. Dealers had to have a certain license, and objects could not be exported without a special permit, otherwise the objects would be confiscated by the government. All excavations undertaken required permission from the Director of the Egyptian Antiquities Department, and any objects found had to be reported. Unfortunately, the law only increased the production of forged objects and Egyptians concentrated on stepping up the production of fakes. One person would make faience vessels, another cut inscriptions in stone scarabs, some made stone vessels of all periods, and yet another would carve a huge stone head of a pharaoh by copying it from an existing portrait.

Notes

1 Curtis, *Nile Notes,* p. 303.

2 Rhind, *Thebes,* p. 256.

3 Rhind, *Thebes,* p. 90

4 Edwards, *A Thousand,* p. 308–309

5 Wakeling, *Forged,* p. 27

Selected Bibliography

Cooley, James Ewing, *The American in Egypt, with Rambles Through Arabia Petraea and the Holy Land.* New York: D. Appleton & Company, 1842.

Curtis, George W., *Nile Notes of a Howadji.* London: Harper & Brothers, 1851.

Edwards, Amelia B., *A Thousand Miles Up the Nile.* Glasgow/Manchester/New York: George Routledge and Sons, Ltd., 1891.

Gliddon, George R., *An Appeal to the Antiquaries of Europe on the Destruction of the Monuments of Egypt.* London: J. Madden, 1841.

Lepsius, Richard, *Letters from Egypt, Ethiopia, and the Peninsula of Sinai.* London: Henry G. Bohn, 1843.

Rhind, Alexander Henry, *Thebes Its Tombs and Their Tenants.* London: Longman, Green, Longman, and Roberts, 1862.

Wakeling, T. G., *Forged Egyptian Antiquities.* London: A. & C. Black, 1912.

Figure 7–8. Kneeling Figure

Object: alabaster
21 high x 15.2 wide x 10.8 cm. deep (8-1/4 x 6 x 4-1/4 inches)
Detroit Institute of Arts: X1989.3692
Old Collection, 1890s

The fake statuette has several telltale features. The stripes on the royal headdress are poorly incised, the shape incorrectly understood, and the kilt crudely defined. The eyes are too large, the mouth is too close to the nose, and the neck is stuffed into a stubby torso. These un-Egyptian characteristics identify the figure as a fake.

Figure 7-9. Royal Head

Object: cast plaster
23 high x 14.7 wide; 13.4 cm. deep (9 x 5-3/4; 5-1/4 inches)
Carnegie Museum of Natural History: Z-9-409

At first glance the head looks very much like an ancient studio model of a Dynasty XVIII head of a king, possibly Tutankhamen, from Tell el-Amarna. The clue that gives it away as a fake is not the plaster, for plaster was used in ancient Egyptian sculpture. The main clue is the piece itself—an almost identical head made of limestone is in the Berlin Museum, which was found during excavations in a sculptor's studio at Tell el-Amarna by the Deutsche Orient-Gesellschaft in 1912.

An illustration of the 1870s shows a European couple strolling through unpaved, Egyptian streets bustling with activity, donkey riders, and veiled women. See Figure 8–8 on page 91.

Courtesy Library of Congress

CHAPTER

Automobiles and camels! They enter and cross Cairo, side by side, just as the East meet West in the Ezbekiyah. [1]

—Archie Bell, 1916

Town and Desert Life

Cairo and Environs

The best months to visit Egypt were November through mid-March. Visitors could take the railway from Alexandria, a local ride of six hours for one hundred and thirty-three miles, passing time at stops along their way to the bustling capital, Cairo. Stops up the Nile afforded views of the scenic landscape, daily life, impressive and humble buildings, and sometimes included a festival. Awaiting visitors at Cairo's Central Station were motor coaches, carriages, and donkeys to transport them through a city ablaze with activity, strange noises, and exotic smells. Men in patterned *galabiyahs*, turbans of swathed cotton, or red tarbushes, flashed by. Women with their dark eyes accentuated by kohl gazed above their veils as they moved in billowy blue or black garments extending to their feet. Children, animals, and carts heaped with mysterious goods darted here and there. Fruit and water vendors, itinerant cooks, and open barber shops were seen selling their wares and attending their customers.

Figure 8–1. The Kasr en-Nil

Original postcard
Cairo, circa 1912
Anonymous Lender

The Kasr en-Nil, the iron or main bridge, spanned the Nile connecting Cairo to the west side and led to the road to the Gizeh pyramids.

After settling in the Shepheard's Hotel, the Hotel du Nil, or other lodging, one might take a turn around town by carriage, or by donkey along the narrow streets of the Oriental sections, pleasant ways to get about, even over the crowded Kasr el-Nil Bridge. However, walking was a bit precarious in the more populated areas of this very old center, which by 1911 had almost 655,000 inhabitants.

Figure 8–2. Shepheard's Hotel

Original postcard
Undetermined French publisher
Circa 1900
Anonymous Lender

Shepheard's Hotel, mostly booked by British and American travellers, was the most fashionable establishment in town, attracting Egyptologists and photographers as well

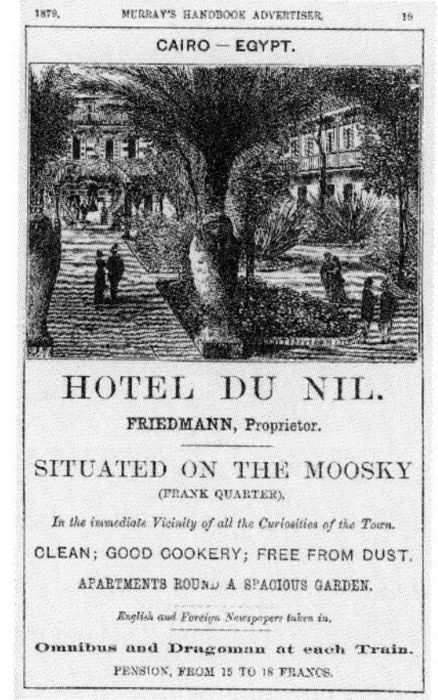

Figure 8–3. An advertisement for the Nile Hotel
Cairo, 1900

The oldest Muslim capital of Egypt was founded in 641 and called el-Fustat (the camp, or tent). The new capital, Cairo or el-Kaherah ("the victorious"), was established by the Fatimate general Gowher, builder of the Mosque of el-Azhar. In 973 it replaced the old city, el-Fustat, as the center. In the Twelfth Century the Sultan, Saladin (1137–1193), had the thick walls of Cairo rebuilt, and the Citadel, the dominating feature of the city made with stones taken from the small pyramids of Gizeh. The old palace of Saladin on the site was demolished in 1829, and in its place rose the Mosque of Mohammed Ali, completed after his death. From almost every quarter of Cairo one could see the magnificent mosque made almost entirely of alabaster with its lofty minarets and commanding presence above the city. Through the centuries Cairo expanded beyond the heavy walls, used during the French occupation for defense, and passed the city gates, one of which continued to admit persons wishing to walk along the historic walls. Mosques abounded and curious travellers visited some five hundred, many in a ruinous state but others intact. Mosques were a favorite for commercial photographers, who also used them as the backgrounds of their views. One European visitor was so enchanted by them she wrote "...we entered a vast court, sacred to all who have hearts, whether they be heathens, Mohammedans, or Christians, for the solace and peace which are to be found there."[2]

Figure 8–4. Ghezireh Palace Hotel
Original postcard
Raphael Tuck & Sons'
Printed in England, circa 1907
Anonymous Lender

An image of the Ghezireh Palace Hotel, a former vice-regal chateau erected by a German architect in 1863-1868 on the Island of Ghezireh, Cairo.

I was donkeying one morning through the bazaars of Cairo, looking up at the exquisitely elaborated overhanging lattices, wondering if the fences of paradise were not so rarely enwrought....[3]

—George W. Curtis 1851

Figure 8–5. The Nile Barrage
Original postcard
Cartosport Max H. Rudmann
Cairo, circa 1908-1912
Anonymous Lender

The Nile Barrage, twelve miles south of Cairo, was begun by Mohammed Ali in 1847. Its intended purpose was to restrain the Nile waters during its eight-month ebb and during the inundation to increase cultivable land in the Delta. The castle-like turrets made it architecturally grand and a fascination for those interested in hydraulic engineering.

In addition to the wondrous mosques was the exotic architecture of the old city, a fascination to travellers who followed the narrow ways that wound in and out of a jumble of dwellings, bazaars, and mosques. The houses were built so each story projected beyond the one below and thereby promised more coolness. Photographers as well were captivated and composed their images, including local inhabitants, before façades articulated with projecting windows in elaborate and delicate wooden fretwork and stained glass that glowed in bright colors. Some travellers were permitted to see the hidden interior courts decorated with inlaid marble and open fonts. About three hundred public fountains, many sumptuously ornamented in the Oriental style, graced the city. People strolling through the city could walk near the main hotels and through the Ezbekiyah, between Old Cairo and New Cairo, which was turned into a public garden by the efforts of Khedive Ismail. The garden with rare shady trees and abundant shrubs, cafés, Arab theater, a British soldiers' club and Military Band that played several time a week, was laid out in 1870 by the chief gardener to the City of Light, Paris, France. Various nearby booksellers offered foreign publications, stationery, photographic supplies, and D. Robertson and Company had a reading room with English and American newspapers. A free circulating public library was open during weekdays.

In 1875 one of the main covered Arab bazaars, the Khan el-Khalili built in 1292, was the most popular market for cloth, dresses, swords, silk, slippers, and embroidered materials. Dealers also offered other tempting Oriental objects such as handsome copper platters and fine carpets. Many so-called Oriental items, however, were made in Europe and could be purchased more cheaply there. Travellers were dependent on their guide or donkey-boy to take them to the proper shop for what was desired and to negotiate a bargain!

In contrast there were the scientific societies to join, schools for visiting educators, and several museums. The *Société Royale géographie d'Égypte,* founded in 1875, had a library and small ethnographical museum. The *Institut d'Égypte,* was established in 1859. The *Institut français d'archéologie Orientale* had libraries and students, and the *Deutsches Institut für ägyptische Altertumskunde* had an Egyptological library. These societies promoted the work of archaeological excavations and published the findings of Egyptologists. There were other organizations for interests in medicine, political economy, statistics and legislation, science, zoology, entomology, agriculture, and art. Before the Nineteenth Century education was primarily religious. One might hear the prayers being recited by Egyptian boys as they attended the local Koranic schools, where the sacred *Koran* was memorized. Although Egypt's ruler Mohammed Ali tried to modernize education, it was slow to take place. In 1875 the most important university in the Arab world to visit was el-Azhar. It provided both primary and secondary classes and the study of algebra, arithmetic, law, logic, philosophy, and Islamic theology. In 1928 there were English, French, and German, missionary schools and colleges, and Egyptian government schools and numerous local schools. Nevertheless, by the 1930s illiteracy was still over eighty percent.

Museums were another attraction. Americans and Europeans could marvel over precious specimens of Egyptian minerals, or the Eocene and Oligocene fossils discovered in the Libyan Desert by H. J. L. Beadwell and displayed in the Geological Museum. The Arabian Museum housed antiquities from ruined mosques and buildings in Cairo, including tombstones with cursive and ornamental Arabic scripts, excavated items from al-Fustat and a magnificent carnelian dish, nearly eighteen inches in diameter and four inches high, decorated with cut facets. In 1926 Cairo's Egyptian Library, established by Khedive Ismail in 1869, contained not only 126,000 exceptional volumes, but a "Show Room" as well. There exhibits included a wide range of rare items and early Arabic and ornamental Persian writings.

Figure 8–6. Panoramic View of Cairo

Color tinted silver print
Lichtenstern & Harari of Cairo
McClung Museum: A1: 161 C136 1C
Gift of Mr. and Mrs. Louis Bailey Audigier, 1934

The mosque of Mohammed Ali is seen at the upper right above the long wall of the Citadel, the seat of government and the official residence of Egypt's rulers until the mid-Nineteenth Century. Mohammed Ali, Pasha of Egypt, had the buildings on the summit of the Citadel swept away to allow for the construction of his great "alabaster mosque" which was completed in 1857. It was designed by the architect, Yusuf Bushnaq, and modelled after the Blue Mosque of Istanbul.

The important religious center rises high above Cairo on the horizon, supported by a spur of the Moqattam Hills. A haphazard jumble of hundred-year-old dwellings were built as close as possible to the mosques of the city.

Figure 8–7. Two Muslims at Prayer

Original postcard
Lichtenstern & Harari
Cairo, 1906
Anonymous Lender

The two Muslims at prayer was taken in a photography studio.

Figure 8–8. European Couple in Cairo

An 1875 illustration of a European couple amid the hustle and bustle of Cairo streets.

Figure 8–9. The Cairo Museum, Interior View

Original postcard
Lichtenstern & Harari
The Cairo Post Card Trust, Cairo, 1911
Anonymous Lender

Interior view of the Cairo Museum with the Old Kingdom statues of Prince Rahotep and Princess Nofret at far left.

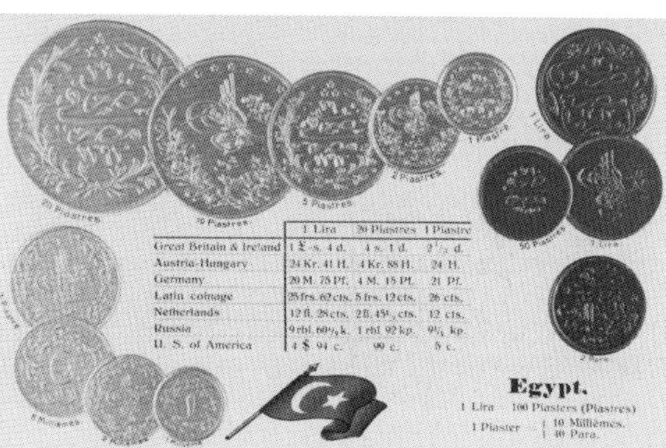

Figure 8–10. "Circular Notes"

Original postcard
M. H. Berlin Schbg.
Made in Germany, circa 1910
Gift of Mr. and Mrs. Louis Bailey Audigier, 1934

In 1911 European travellers, advised to carry "Circular Notes" issued by Thos. Cook & Son for greater security, exchanged their money for the Egyptian pound, which equaled one hundred Egyptian piastres.

But the museum most frequented by travellers was the Egyptian Museum of Cairo, located near the Kasr el-Nil Bridge. It housed the largest and most valuable collection of ancient Egyptian objects in the world, thanks to the vision of its founder Auguste Mariette and the additions made by later Egyptologists and directors, particularly Gaston Maspero. Visitors passed into the Great Gallery on the ground floor to wonder at colossal statues and handsomely decorated and finely carved sarcophagi of the earliest periods. The first rooms contained objects of the pyramid period of the Old Kingdom, many found at Gizeh. An imposing life-sized diorite statue to arrest attention was of Khafre (Khephren), protected by a falcon with its outspread wings about the seated pharaoh, found in his Valley Temple at Gizeh. Another masterpiece of the period was the standing figure of the Sheykh-el-Beled carved from wood, whose eyes made of quartz seemed to look straight ahead into eternity. In an adjacent room were the seated statues of Prince Rahotep and Princess Nofret. Their painted features still fresh with color could

...they are such safe, little, sure-footed creatures, and pick their steps so wonderfully over the rough roads.[4]

—M. S. Craig, 1909

Figure 8–11. Souvenir Card

Original shop card
Manmes, Lyon, France
Circa 1900
Gift of Mr. and Mrs. Louis Bailey Audigier, 1934

A Souvenir card from a fashionable shop in Cairo that sold genuine Panama hats as well as straw and felt hats for ladies, gentlemen, and children. The reverse side has a foreign money conversion table.

Figure 8–12. Cairo Street Scene

Silver print
Photographer: unidentified
McClung Museum: A1: 161 C136 3C
Gift of Mr. and Mrs. Louis Bailey Audigier, 1934

Posing for the photographer is a "donkey-boy" standing next to his constant companion, his faithful, bridled and saddled donkey. A passing traveller might desire to gallop or trot around Cairo, while the donkey-boy prodded his animal with a stick to make it step lively.

be seen through the glassed, wooden exhibit case. In an adjacent case was the famous standing copper statue of the pharaoh Pepi I of Dynasty VI and his son, discovered by James Quibell at Hieraconpolis in 1897-1898. The royal mummies found in 1881 and those found in 1898 by Victor Loret were on display in a special room. But a permit from the Minister of Education was required for those wishing to view them. However, museum-goers of 1929 could freely marvel at half of the treasures from the Tomb of Tutankhamen discovery of 1922 and other earlier excavated items such as those from the Tomb of Queen Hetepheres found in 1905, and the gold Treasure of Dashur found by Jacques de Morgan in 1894-1895. Other galleries and floors contained masterworks dating from all periods, including the Greco-Roman and displayed Coptic antiquities of the Fifth to Seventh Centuries. At least one thoughtful author advised visitors "to go to the museum, look at one single statue and leave everything else until the return from the Nile trip." [5]

Figure 8–13. Mosque el-Azhar

Silver print
Photographer: Zangaki
McClung Museum: A1: 161 C136 2 EA
Gift of Mr. and Mrs. Louis Bailey Audigier, 1934

The Mosque of el-Azhar, or "the resplendent," was completed in 972 and became in 988 a university. By 1911 it was the largest in the Muslim world, teaching some seven thousand to nine thousand students free of charge. Young men are seen reading the precepts of *The Koran*, the holy book of the Muslim faith.

Village and Desert Life

Not too far from Cairo on the way to the Gizeh pyramids one entered the world of lush green fields and homes of village life, unchanged since pharaonic times. The houses were covered in straw and corn stalks, or made of mud bricks arched in a half-barrel shape. Outside under the cloudless blue sky, tall date palms, and further up the river the shorter dum palms, offered some shade from the relentless heat of the sun. Occasional gardens with lemons, oranges, and figs were seen. Inside families and their animals lived together on earthen floors thick with dust and dirt flies all around. A simple mud bench served as a bed, or perhaps the villager would sleep in a corner of the flat roof. Observed in the court was a small beehive-shaped mound of mud used as a stove, with a small wooden door and inside a space. Photographers liked to capture on film the nearby *sakiyeh* as it lifted buckets of water, or the shaduf from the canal or Nile, to supply water for irrigating the crops. In the distance peasants could be seen tilling the fields with their ploughs, unchanged since ancient times, drawn by oxen or other animals. Or they could be seen working with an age-old hoe, or in grain cutting time swinging a sickle like those illustrated in ancient tomb paintings. Many crops were grown including wheat, maize, barley, beans, lentils, greens, various vegetables, sugar cane, and cotton known for its silky gloss. Village life appeared hard, dusty, and simple, but the villagers cheerful and friendly.

On the skyline were the mighty pyramids of Gizeh seen from the tram-way, the quickest and almost dust-free method of transportation along the carriage road from Cairo to the site. After insistent begging from a mob of boys, a choice would be made either to trot on a donkey or bob on a camel to the plateau for a complete tour. In 1905 it cost twenty pilasters and a little *bakshish*, but the services of an experienced dragoman would cost more. There was the breathless climb to the top of the Great Pyramid, the pyramids of Khafre and Menkure only attempted by a few of the

Figure 8–14. A Coffee Shop in Cairo

Silver print
Photographer: unidentified
McClung Museum: A1: 161 C136 8C
Gift of Mr. and Mrs. Louis Bailey Audigier, 1934

Men gather at an Arab cafe to chat, drink, and smoke a water pipe, or *nargileh*. Women were not permitted.

Figure 8–15. A Peasant Village

Albumen print
Photographer: Edition Photoglob
McClung Museum: 28/655
Gift of Marcia S. Young, 1992

A typical fellahin village with houses made of mud brick and shaded by lofty palm trees was built on high ground. No land was wasted. Dwellings are compact and minimized so the fields had the largest cultivatable space. The village was all to them.

Figure 8–16. The *Sakiyeh*

Silver print
Photographer: Zangaki
McClung Museum: A1: 161 C136 1C
Gift of Mr. and Mrs. Louis Bailey Audigier, 1934

A common sight was the *sakiyeh*, or large wheel, being turned by a camel. The animal activated a system of cog wheels that turned a series of attached water-pots to raise water from a deep well. As each vessel slowly reached the top of each cycle the water emptied into a trough that caught the water, which emptied and fed the irrigation channels.

stalwartly curious, being easier to ascend and enter. A visit to the dusty and dirt-filled interior of the Great Pyramid necessitated a candle to navigate the one hundred and fifty-five feet long, steep and slippery way to the Great Hall, where it was said that one could not insert a needle or a hair between the stones. The King's Chamber was a bare room its walls desecrated by names of visitors carved or written on the stone; the plain stone sarcophagus had a broken lid and was empty. A strong smell of bats permeated the air. Also part of the tour was to have a photograph taken with the pyramids and the inscrutable Sphinx in the background. Although the area was cleared of sand a few times in the Nineteenth Century, by 1905 the paws of the Sphinx and the New Kingdom pharaoh Thutmose IV's "Dream Stela" were again covered over.

Figure 8–17. Young Water Sellers

Albumen print
Photographer: Zangaki
McClung Museum: A1: 161 C136
Gift of Mr. and Mrs. Louis Bailey Audigier, 1934

A group of female water carriers use pottery jugs which cool the warm water taken from the Nile River. Other sellers filled goatskins for drinking purposes even in Cairo, although the city waterworks kept the houses and public fountains well supplied. Some water was sweetly flavored with orange-blossom, liquorice, or raisins.

Figure 8–18. A Beduin Sheykh

Color tinted silver print
Photographer: unidentified
McClung Museum: A1: 157 P179
Gift of Mr. and Mrs. Louis Bailey Audigier, 1934

Beduin groups were nomadic, pastoral, camel breeders who travelled from Arabia to Egypt. Although this photograph is of a Sheykh, a chief of a tribe, from Syria, he represents a type that often came to Egypt. He wears a stripped *kaffeh* and typical cuffed hat of his culture group.

Figure 8–19. Desert Dwellers

Color tinted silver print
Photographer: unidentified
McClung Museum: A1: 161 E28
Gift of Mr. and Mrs. Louis Bailey Audigier, 1934

A Beduin man and a young boy are members of nomadic Arabs who settled in the Nile Valley. They stand in front of an easily portable desert hut, essential in their endless search for grazing areas for their sheep and camels. The two culture groups of Beduin that widely dispersed in the desert valleys were the Bisharin and Ababda. In 1927 there were twenty seven thousand Beduins in Egypt. To photograph them patience, a sympathetic relationship with them, and an understanding of their way of life was needed.

Figure 8–20. The Pyramid Boys

Silver print
Photographer: Zangaki
McClung Museum: A1: 161
C136 1P
Gift of Mr. and Mrs. Louis
Bailey Audigier, 1934

A group of young hopefuls wait on the road for travellers to engage them for a tour of the pyramids to gain a little *bakshish* ("gift" of coins). The tree-lined way was the main route between Cairo and Gizeh.

Figure 8–21. The Guide K. M. Topous

Albumen print
Photographer: unidentified
McClung Museum: 1997.5.3
Gift of the Friends of Egyptology, 1997

The dragoman, Topous, cuts a dramatic figure in one of his elaborately embroidered and bejeweled costumes, composed of various dress elements of Turkish origin. Such splendid finery and his ability to speak several languages no doubt attracted many travellers to engage his services.

Figure 8–22. Travellers Climb the Great Pyramid

Albumen print
Photographer: Zangaki
McClung Museum: 3/696
Gift of Ms. Marcia Young, 1992

Ladies of the 1890s, in their cumbersome dresses, with leg-o-mutton sleeves and wide-brimmed hats, are pulled up the Great Pyramid at Gizeh. One woman needs the assistance of a hand around her waist. Will they make it to the top, a challenge of some four hundred and fifty feet? (The ancient height was four hundred and eighty-one feet.)

Figure 8–23. At the Pyramids, 1929

McClung Museum: 222/94
Gift of Judge and Mrs. John W. Green, 1959

Judge and Mrs. John W. Green of Knoxville pose on camels with the pyramid of King Khafre in the background. It must have been a cold day in January or February as they seem quite bundled up. The photograph was printed (and touched up) later on board the *Empress of Australia*, while they were on a Round-the-World cruise. This suggests their own camera was used.

Dahabiyehs and Hotels

There were those who preferred hotels and those who wanted the more exotic experience of seeing Egypt independently and leisurely in a comfortable sailing ship called the dahabiyeh. The boat, costing more than the faster steamer, could navigate very shallow water and be moored close to the Nile banks. But in unfair winds it had to be towed upstream, causing delays, unless it was fitted for steam. Between 1850 and 1870 some travellers spent the winter months living on them and drifted along making desired stops at monuments on either side of the Nile. The smallest included two cabins and a bath, and the largest contained eight single-bed cabins and additional rooms for dining, etc. According to Murray's *A Hand-book for Travellers in Egypt, 1875*, a voyage from Cairo to Assuan and back could take upwards of six to eight weeks under the best weather conditions. A good dragoman would be engaged to buy fine food and hire the crew, servants, cook, guides, and donkeys for

Figure 8–24. The Mena House Hotel

Original postcard
Raphael Tuck & sons'
Made in England, circa 1907
Gift of Mr. and Mrs. Louis Bailey Audigier, 1934

The Mena House Hotel could be reached by the electric tram-way. Located on the edge of the Libyan Desert close to the pyramids of Gizeh, it offered luxury and convenience.

Figure 8–25. The Luxor Hotel at Luxor

Albumen print
Photographer: Edition Photoglob
McClung Museum: 22/655
Gift of Marcia S. Young, 1992

The Luxor Hotel, some four hundred and fifty miles south of Cairo, was located in a spacious park surrounded by greenery and ancient Egyptian statues that stood at either side of the garden. Extensive excavations were carried out on both sides of the Nile affording the most recent information about new discoveries to visitors as they chatted on the terrace.

visiting the monuments and to handle all other necessities. For a trouble-free voyage a dependable dragoman was paid well, or he would be seen as having inferior status and perform badly. However beautiful and luxurious a voyage might be, travellers were urged to take one or two rat-traps, and for the fly plague on the river "fly-paper" was recommended! Tolerance of live animals aboard for subsequent dinners was a must.

Sometimes Egyptologists found the *dahabiyeh* a convenience while excavating. Flinders Petrie engaged a far more modest "boat with a cabin twelve feet long and four and a half to seven feet wide; just enough for two to sleep on the side benches, and hang a box-lid by strings to serve as a table by day."[6] Photographers used small *dahabiyehs* which carried all necessary equipment and served as a photographic lab as well. Such boats were seen moored at the banks of nearby monuments while the photographer or archaeologist was at work.

For those in a hurry, or lacked money to stay longer, river steamers and railways were available for a trip up the Nile. In 1886 Thos. Cook & Son began booking travellers on tourist and express steamers as well as a rail and steamer combination. By 1911 a tax had been levied by the Khedive Abbas II on travellers to the monuments and temples for the purpose of their preservation and upkeep.

Figure 8–26. The Savoy Hotel

Original postcard / Cairo, circa 1910 / Gift of Mr. and Mrs. Louis Bailey Audigier, 1934

Figure 8–27. The Cararact Hotel at Assuan

Original postcard / Cairo, circa 1918 / Anonymous Lender

The Cararact Hotel at Assuan was another luxurious resort at the First Cataract, built on the rosy granite cliffs of the East Bank of the Nile across from Elephantine Island. During the night visitors could hear the squeaking and droning sound of the waterwheels on the Island.

> *But sort of a torpor crawls over one in a dahabeah. You feel, as you lie on the divan, and float slowly along...as if it were the passage to some other world....*[7]
>
> ***—Florence Nightingale, 1849-1850***

Figure 8–28. A *Dahabiyeh*

Albumen print
Photographer: Zangaki
McClung Museum: 1999.2.1
Gift of the Friends of Egyptology, 1999

A trip up the Nile might be taken on a comfortable houseboat called the *dahabiyeh*. The one shown here was called "Timsaah," a regal yacht used by the American Consul in Egypt. Felukas, used as freight boats, can be seen along the embankment in the background.

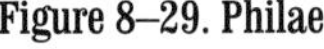

Figure 8–29. Philae

Original postcard
Lichtenstern & Harari
Cairo, 1913
Gift of Mr. and Mrs. Louis Bailey Audigier, 1934

Boats floated on the high waters that flooded the temples at Philae.

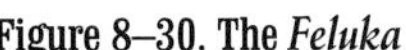

Figure 8–30. The *Feluka*

Albumen print
Photographer: Edition Photoglob
McClung Museum: 27/655
Gift of Marcia S. Young, 1992

The humble but effective *feluka* (boat) used to transport cargo spreads its sails near the high limestone cliff on the East Bank in Middle Egypt. The cliffs in this region are the closest to the river in the Nile Valley.

Mohammed improved the agriculture of Egypt by introducing the cotton plant, and by restoring the canals and embankments,...[8]
—Baedeker, 1902

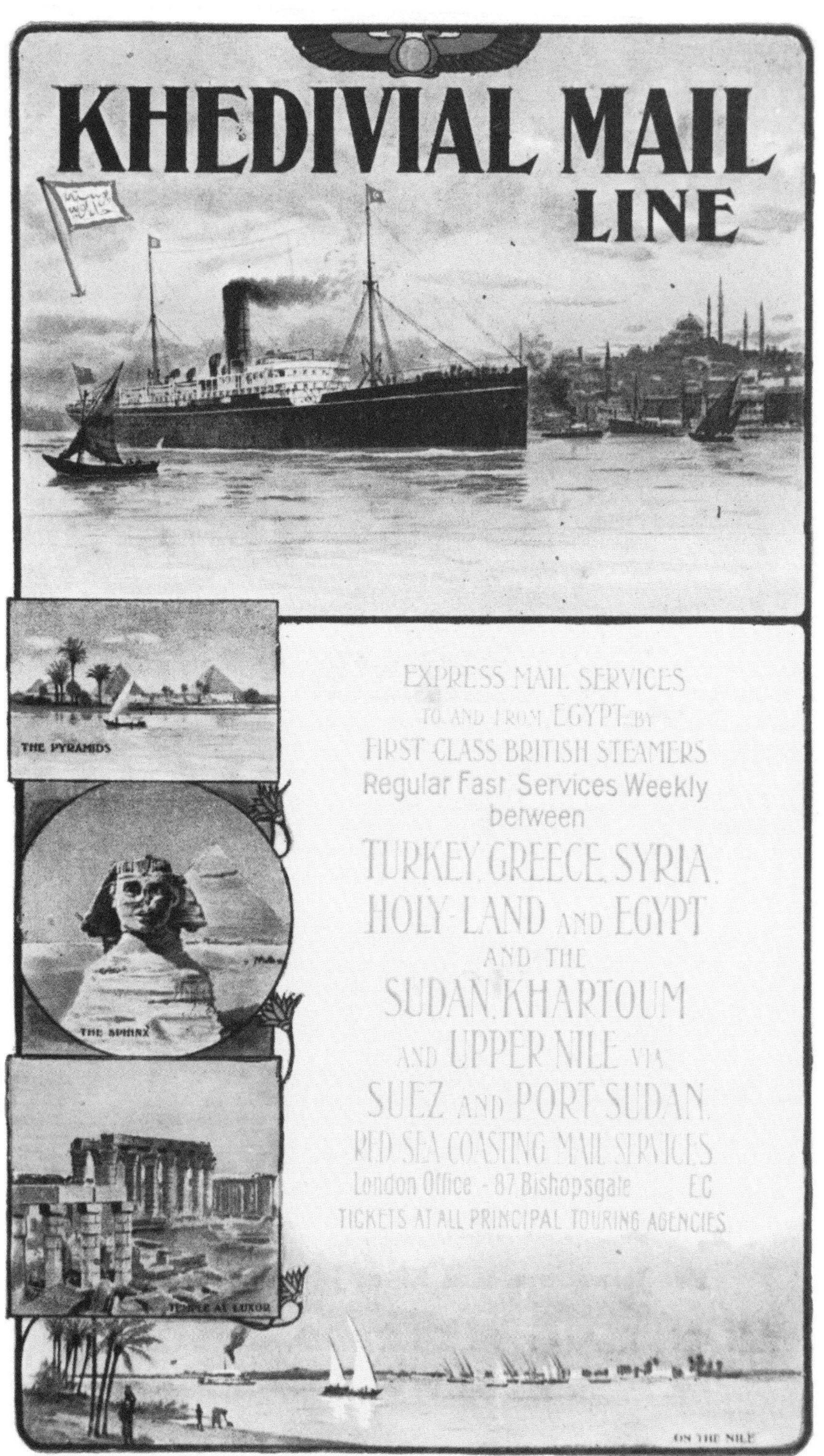

Figure 8–31. The Khedivial Mail Line

Original postcard
Circa 1913
Gift of Mr. and Mrs. Louis Bailey Audigier, 1934

Travellers could take the Khedivial Mail Line from Constantinople and embark at Alexandria. Numerous steamship lines operated from London, New York, Naples, Venice, and other cities. One could also travel by land via railway and ferry-boat.

Sultans, Pashas, Khedives and Viceroys

Travellers to Egypt in the period between 1850 and 1930 stepped off the ship at Alexandria to begin an exotic new experience. There were those who were aware not only of the monuments and museums, but also of the important historical and tumultuous political developments that shaped the country they were about to encounter. Prior to their arrival some would have read books and other publications or consulted with friends about Egypt. Guide books, such as the trusty, small, red covered *Baedeker's Egypt,* were the constant companions of many travellers. Its pages, devoted to these topics, served as references for a better understanding of the strange world now surrounding the travellers. They could wonder, too, about the opulent rulers of Egypt and how they came to be.

During its long history Egypt frequently came under foreign domination, including Hyksos, Libyan, Nubian, Assyrian, Greek-Macedonian, and Roman. The invaders of later centuries introduced feudalism, caused economic problems, and powerful external and internal factions waxed and waned. The Muslim conquest in 641 introduced major changes after the Khalif, the supreme ruler of Islam, sent his armies on to conquer Egypt. As a province of the great Empire of the Khalifs the religion of Islam took hold, and very quickly Egypt became one of the centers of the Islamic world. Arabic became the main language. Much later, in 1517, the military forces of the Ottoman Turks swept over Egypt and the country became a province of Turkey. The modern history of Egypt had begun.

European countries, too, wanted to control the land of the pharaohs. At the end of the Eighteenth Dynasty foreigners in Egypt were thrown into the midst of a military campaign by the French under the command of Napoleon Bonaparte. Napoleon had set his sights on Egypt in order to sever British trade lines with India. From his landing in Alexandria in July 1798 to August 1799 Egypt was in turmoil, particularly at Gizeh, as Napoleon confronted the rebellious, politically influential Mamelukes in the Battle of the Pyramids. His victory, however, was short lived. The British, aided by the Ottoman sultan, attacked the French at Abuqîr Bay at Alexandria. Napoleon lost and was forced to withdraw from Egypt by the Anglo-Turkish forces, leaving his troops behind. But by 1801 the French were completely gone. Although Napoleon had good intentions in his attempt to improve conditions in Egypt, instead destabilization resulted. His legacy was the establishment of a French Institute in Cairo, the discovery of the famed Rosetta stone, and the commission which made possible the enormous scientific contributions that fanned the flame of Egyptology. In 1809 the monumental volumes of the *La Description de l'Égypte* began to be published. They contain the brilliant work of a scientific team of one hundred and sixty-five scholars sent to Egypt by Napoleon. The volumes had a profound influence on untold numbers of Egyptologists and photographers, including the Frenchman Maxime du Camp, who studied them before he travelled to Egypt in 1849, with his travelling companion the French novelist Gustave Flaubert, to photograph the monuments of the Nile Valley.

In 1805 an important new era began. Mohammed Ali became Pasha (governor) of Egypt, and with him the modernization of Egypt was launched. But Ottoman military campaigns involving other Mediterranean nations continued to cause unrest and expense. In 1882 the British invaded Egypt following the bombardment of Alexandria and began to govern the country with increased and lasting influence. Like Napoleon the British wanted a stepping-stone to India, symbol of Britain as a world power. In 1914 the Egypt became a British protectorate until 1922, when it was granted a limited independence, and Sultan Fuad assumed the royal title King Fuad I of Egypt under the influence and investments of Great Britain. The presence and participation of Britain and France as well other European countries were major influences on various developments, both good and bad, in the fields of Egyptology and photography in Egypt.

Figure 8–32. Palace of the Khedives in Cairo

Original postcard
Undetermined French publisher
Anonymous Lender

Figure 8–33. Mohammed Ali Pasha

Mohammed Ali Pasha founded a dynasty that ruled modern Egypt. His military campaigns were legendary as were his reforms, which opened paths to the modernization of Egypt.

EGYPTIAN RULERS: Mohammed Ali Pasha (1805-1848)

In 1805, the first Egyptian leader of importance achieved power as "Pasha." Rising out of military victories and his defeat of the Mamelukes, Mohammed Ali became the founder of a royal line, a dynasty which lasted until 1952 and the abdication of the last ruler of the dynasty. Under Mohammed's leadership Egypt became more independent from Ottoman rule, and under his wise direction the first Egyptian education reforms and modernization of Egypt began. However, at the end of his reign the average peasant was still working harder and was no richer. Nor did Egypt adopt European ways to any extent; rather it seems Europeans adopted Egyptian modes in food, exotic dress, and housing styles.

Viceroy Abbas I (1848-1854)

Mohammed Ali's grandson, Abbas I, succeeded him and changed much of his grandfather's ground-breaking modernization and westernized programs. He ruled as Viceroy for the Ottoman government in Constantinople. Abbas was an inept ruler who may have been strangled to death in 1854.

Figure 8–34. Khedive Ismail

Khedive Ismail II had a keen business sense and an instinctive ability in judging men. In power during the construction of the Suez Canal, he helped in this immense contribution to the world.

Figure 8–35. Khedive Tawfiq

After Khedive Tawfig succeeded his father, Ismail, the British and French more firmly reestablished dual control of the Egyptian economy and administration. His tenure was troubled by popular resentments against Europeans and the threats by a nationalist movement.

HIS HIGHNESS ABBAS II.,
Khedive of Egypt.

Figure 8–36. Khedive Abbas II

The reign of Khedive Abbas II saw in 1898 the British victory over the thirteen-year Mahdist government in the Sudan. In 1905 Abbas issued a Khedivial decree which established the special position of Britain in Egypt.

Viceroy Said (1854-1863)

Abbas I was followed by Mohammed Ali's son, Viceroy Said (1854-1863), who granted the first Suez Canal concession and continued modernization policies set forth by his father. In 1855 the Alexandria-Cairo railroad was completed and a Nile steamship service and telegraph system granted concessions. He enlarged canals to improve irrigation and communication by water and was an avid supporter of archaeological excavations of ancient Egyptian sites. In 1857 the first important museum, the Museum of Egyptian Antiquities at Boulaq, was established.

Khedive Ismail (1863-1879)

Ismail Pasha, grandson of Mohammed Ali, carried on the sweeping modernization policies of Mohammed Ali and in 1867 was given the princely title of Khedive. That same year the Egyptian postal service opened, and in 1869 he inaugurated the Suez Canal. In 1873, during his rule, the Sultan of Turkey acknowledged the autonomy of Egypt and applied the law of heritage to his family.

Although well meaning, Ismail sent Egypt into a financial tailspin. Unfortunately, poor advice and over ambition, with costly expansionist inroads into Africa, were activities which led to bankruptcy and the subsequent international control of Egypt's finances.

Khedive Tawfiq (1879-1892)

Khedive Tawfiq succeeded his father after Ismail was deposed. Under his rule a dual British-French control of the economy was reestablished. But Tawfiq fell under the control of British, Ottoman, European, and Egyptian political factions.

Khedive Abbas II (1892-1914)

Under Tawfiq's son, Khedive Abbas II, France gave up claims in Egypt. Britain decreed its financial independence and revenue control. In 1914 an attempted assassination was made on Abbas and he was removed as Khedive.

Sultan Kamil (1914-1917)

Abbas II's uncle, Kamil, took charge after being proclaimed Sultan as World War I began and reigned during the war years. In 1914 Egypt declared war on Germany and her allies, but with British support Turkish and German attacks were repulsed. Kamil died in 1917.

King Fuad (1917-1936)

Fuad, brother of Kamil, became Sultan and ruled through a period of much political unrest. Fuad strove toward absolute rule, reformed authority and opposed Parliamentary power. In 1923 he became the first constitutional monarch of Egypt. His main contribution was the establishment of the Egyptian state university at Cairo in 1925.

TURKISH RULE DURING WORLD WAR I
Sultan Mohammed Khan V (1909-1918)

After thirty-three years of mismanagement under the despotic rule of his predecessor, Mohammed V took over as Sultan of Turkey and reigned for twenty years. In 1914 Turkey declared war against Egypt and her allies, but failed to win, and in 1918 an armistice was made with Turkey. The name "Khan" is a title of respect in Mohammedan countries derived from a Mongolian term equal to "sovereign."

Figure 8–37. Sultan Mohammed Khan V

Original postcard
The Cairo Post Card Trust
Cairo, 1913
Gift of Mr. and Mrs. Louis Bailey Audigier, 1934

Notes

1 Bell, *Spell,* p. 257.

2 Murray, *A Handbook,* p. 131.

3 Curtis, *Nile Notes,* p. 33.

4 Craig, *Dairy,* p. 39.

5 Dunning, *To-day on the Nile,* p. 14.

6 Petrie, *Seventy Years,* p. 74.

7 Nightingale, *Letters from Egypt,* p. 48.

8 Baedeker, *Egypt,* p. xcix.

Selected Bibliography

Ayrout, Henry Habib, *The Egyptian Peasant,* Boston: Beacon Press, 1963.

Baedeker, Karl, *Egypt. Handbook for travellers. Leipzig 1902.*

Bell, Archie, *The Spell of Egypt*. Boston: The Page Company, 1916.

Craig, M.S., *Diary of a Trip to Egypt*. Paisley: Printed by A. Gardner, 1909.

Curtis, George W., *Nile Notes of a Howadji*. New York: Harper & Brothers, 1851.

Dunning, H. W., *To-day on the Nile*. New York: James Pott & Company, 1905.

King, Joan Wucher, *Historical Dictionary of Egypt*. African Historical Dictionaries, No. 36. New Jersey: The Scarecrow Press, 1984.

Murray, John A., *Handbook for Travellers in Egypt*. Fifth edition. London: John Murray, 1875.

Nightingale, Florence, Anthony Sattin ed., *Letters from Egypt: A Journey on the Nile, 1849-1850.* New York: Weidenfeld and Nicolson, 1987.

Petrie, Flinders, *Seventy Years in Archaelogy*. London: Sampson Low, Marston & Co., Ltd., n.d..

Tawfiq, M., *A Short History of Islam and Islamic Egypt*. Cairo: Tsoumas Press, 1968.

Figure 9–1. Jewelry of Princess Khnumet

Middle Kingdom, Dynasty XII
Sepia toned silver print
Photographer: Émile Brugsch
McClung Museum: A1: 521 12th dyn. 7
Gift of Mr. and Mrs. Louis Bailey Audigier, 1934

Beginning in the mid-Nineteenth Century, Egyptologists such as Mariette, Brugsch, Petrie Theodor Davis and others made important finds of precious jewelry. In 1895 Jacques de Morgan found the exquisite treasure of Princess Khnumet at Dashur.

Among the jewelry pieces were two gold diadems. One circlet (left) is composed of rosettes and lyre-shaped pieces, with eight uprights, that are inlaid in lapis lazuli, red jasper and green feldspar. Another delicate diadem (right) is interlaced in finely made wires of gold interspersed with tiny star-shaped flowers caught together by six Maltese cross forms. An aigrette as a spray of golden leaves (center) was also found.

Such ornaments were too fragile to actually wear and were fashioned for the burial. Émile Brugsch recorded the treasure in his studio at the Gizeh Museum.

CHAPTER

Photographic Studios and Sellers

As would be expected, various Cairo hotels attracted a number of well-established photographic firms. Photographers found it profitable to open shops nearby. Customers could also go to other sellers located in the Place Faghalla, Rue du Tribunal, Rosetti Garden, Ezbekiyah Garden, and elsewhere. The bookseller D. Robertson and Company in the Ezbekiyah near Shepheard's Hotel sold photographs by Francis Frith. Tourists could find very fine prints of Egyptian landscapes, temples, and other monuments by the photographer J. Pascal Sébah available at his studio near the French consulate in the Ezbekiyah or at A. Kauffmann, bookseller to the Khedive, in the Muski. There were photographs by the Bonfils family taken in their studio in Lebanon, too. Photographs by Émile Brugsch of objects in the Boulaq Museum could be bought at that museum, and at a later date at the Egyptian Museum. There was no shortage of customers.

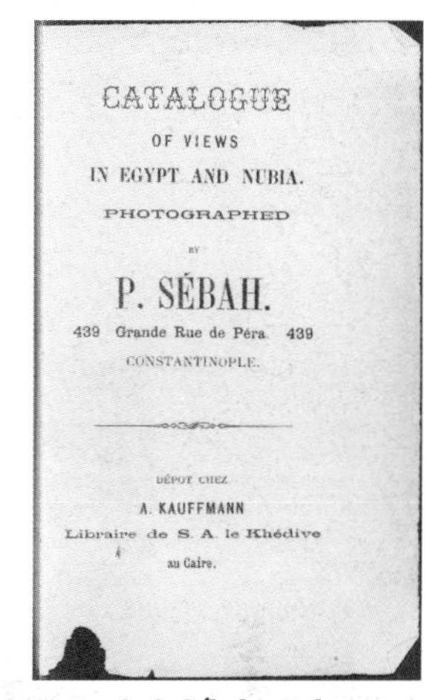

CATALOGUE
OF VIEWS
IN EGYPT AND NUBIA.
PHOTOGRAPHED
BY
P. SÉBAH.
439 Grande Rue de Péra 439
CONSTANTINOPLE.

DÉPOT CHEZ
A. KAUFFMANN
Libraire de S. A. le Khédive
au Caire.

Figure 9–2. Sébah catalogue
Courtesy Library of Congress

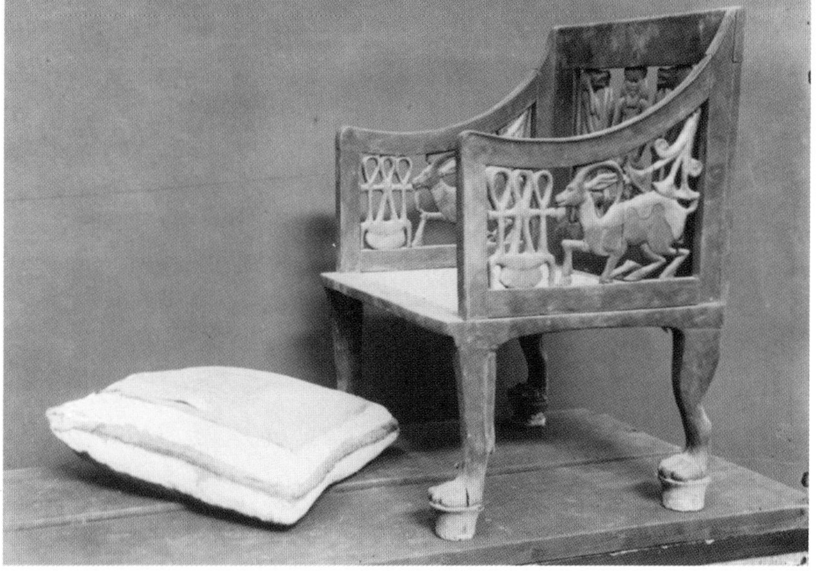

Figure 9–3. Chair of Tuiu
New Kingdom, Dynasty XVIII
Sepia toned silver print
Photographer: Émile Brugsch
McClung Museum: A1: 621 Egypt 18th dyn. 5
Gift of Mrs. and Mrs. Louis Bailey Audigier, 1934

The handsome, wooden chair is decorated with gilt. The animal-shaped legs end in lions claws, the center back has a figure of a smiling, frontal view of Bisu flanked by side views of the goddess Touweret. On the matching, openwork side arms is an almost kneeling ibex, and before the animal are two *ankh*-signs with an Isis-knot in the middle. The unique chair cushion is made of white and pink linen and filled with pigeon feathers.

The chair was with funerary objects found in the tomb of Yuia and his wife Tuiu, parents-in-law of King Amenhotep III. The tomb was among the discoveries of the American business man and excavator Theodore M. Davis (1837-1915) in the Valley of the Kings in 1915. A special room was named for him at the Cairo Museum called the Theodore Davis Room, where the chair was exhibited. The photograph represents a typical studio view taken by Brugsch.

Figure 9–4. Bracelets of Ramesses II
New Kingdom, Dynasty XIX
Sepia toned silver print
Photographer: Émile Brugsch
McClung Museum: A1: 521 19th dyn. 7
Gift of Mr. and Mrs. Louis Bailey Audigier, 1934

The two, heavy-looking, gold bracelets bear the cartouche of King Rameses II and were not intentionally made as jewelry for the dead. They actually belonged to the pharaoh and, no doubt, were worn by him. Each bracelet is finely decorated by filigree work and two geese with a lapis lazuli body and one tail and were found in 1906 at the ancient site of Bubastis in the ruins of the Temple of Bastet. The photograph is another example of studio work by Brugsch.

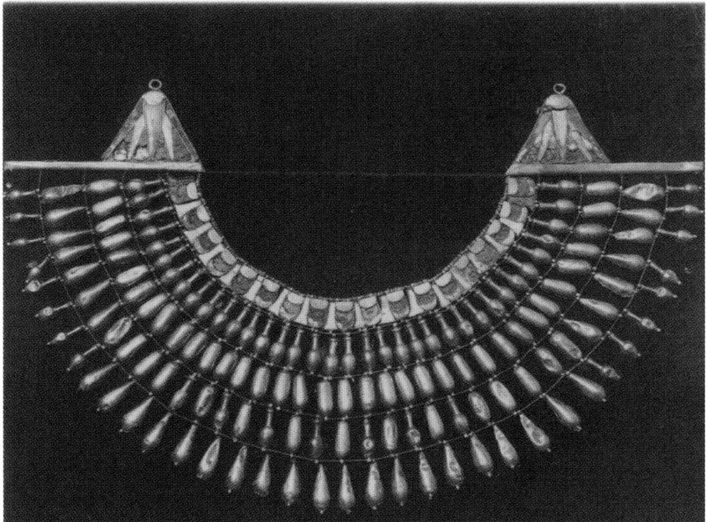

Figure 9–5. Collar of King Smenkhkare (?)

New Kingdom, Dynasty XVIII
Sepia toned silver print
Photographer: Émile Brugsch
McClung Museum: A1: 521 18th dyn. C3.10
Gift of Mrs. and Mrs. Louis Bailey Audigier, 1934

The fine art of the gold worker is illustrated in the broad collar made of gold and electrum. It is composed of drop beads, date-shapes, *nefer*-signs, inlaid colored glass, and decorative lotus blossom terminals. The collar was found in the sarcophagus on the mummy of a king in the valley of the Kings by Theodore M. Davis and the British Egyptologist Edward Ayrton (1882-1914), in 1907.

Figure 9–6. Two Brides

Albumen print
Photographer: Bonfils Family
McClung Museum: A1: 158 D155 95
Gift of Mr. and Mrs. Louis Bailey Audigier, 1934

The elaborately decorated silk cloth covers two Muslim brides from Syria of the upper class. The cloth is pinned at the chest. Under the silk cloth the bride wears a head cap with a flat crown. The cloth on the woman at the left has a printed imitation of a head scarf with tassels.

The photograph was taken in the Bonfils studio.

Figure 9–7. Young Woman

Albumen print
Photographer: Bonfils Family
McClung Museum: A1: 158 D155 A5
Gift of Mr. And Mrs. Louis Bailey Audigier, 1934

The young woman is dressed in a festive costume of Lebanon. The pose was staged in the studio of the photographer, probably in Bonfils' studio in Beirut, Lebanon.

Figure 9–8. An Engaged Woman

Albumen print
Photographer: Bonfils Family
McClung Museum: A1: 158 D155 A5
Gift of Mr. and Mrs. Louis Bailey Audigier, 1934

The young woman sits calmly dressed in a wedding costume as she poses in the studio of the photographer. She is pictured as a betrothed Druse maiden from Mt. Lebanon. The High-ranking woman wears a *tantur,* a headdress with a tall, silvered copper cylinder which supports a veil. Worn by Druze women in Lebanon and Syria, it faded from fashion in the 1880s.

Figure 9–9. Beduin Women and Children

Color tinted silver print
Photographer: unidentified
McClung Museum: A1: 157 A658
Gift of Mr. and Mrs. Louis Bailey Audigier, 1934

Staged in the studio, the two Beduin women stand in their simple black clothing, which absorbs as much as twenty-five degrees additional heat compared to the air temperature. However, the dark dress makes the women stand out against the yellow desert sands. Such women usually went about without veils. Children were commonly carried on their shoulders as there were no baby carriages in the modest villages where they lived. The woman on the left is fortunate. She wears a pair of sturdy shoes.

Appendices to Scholars, Scoundrels, and the Sphinx

...the art of photography is progressing with rapid strides, and though still but a child in years, it is doubtless destined to play an important part in the future history of civilization.[1]

—Francis Frith 1860

The Lens of the Artist

At the time archaeology was developing into a science so was photography. As excavations and the activities involved in the removal of ancient Egyptian treasures were flourishing along the Nile, so were commercial and excavation photographers. They documented many aspects of the antiquities that were subsequently removed from their original sites, vanished due to erosion, or were plundered. Important photographic records were taken and studied by scholars as well as by travellers interested in the subject. These images could be carried and studied in places far from Egypt.

Early Cameras

The advent of the photographic camera in 1839 came to its full development in the later Nineteenth Century. It was in the 1850s that its importance began to be recognized. Cameras have come a long way since the time when the optical and technical quality of the photograph was of utmost importance and a scientific struggle to perfect. Although early cameras were somewhat cumbersome, they were carefully built. Most were made by craftsmen who assembled and skillfully fitted each camera with mahogany bodies reinforced by brass. The glass plates, the "film," were carried in wood or metal plate holders; prints sized 10" x 12" and 12" x 16" were common. Smaller cameras were also developed for smaller images such as those used by the British excavator C. Piazzi Smyth in 1865 inside the Great Pyramid.

However, most photographers favored the larger plate cameras of the box type due to their ability to capture more detail. Photographers looked through a glass plate at the rear of the camera covered by a black cloth and adjusted the focus with the collapsible leather bellows, which sealed out light. They also could use dangerous, explosive flash powder to illuminate a subject even in the field. In most cases natural daylight proved best, which also gave enough light for interiors of buildings. Business boomed until the small, mass-produced, hand-held Brownie box camera, or the Kodak snapshot cameras, were introduced in 1888, and became popular.

Figure A–1. Wet Collodion Process

Photographers used the wet-collodion process in the field, as suggested in this illustration of the 1880s.

Figure A–2. Early Camera

An image of one of William Fox Talbot's early cameras. Traces of his sensitized paper can be seen adhering to the back panel, circa 1840.

The Inventors

The development of the photographic process was the work of many creative persons. Without their commitment and determination images of Egypt would have been quite different. Several such individuals made major contributions. Early pioneers set the stage for the improvements of later cameras and the workable, pre-sensitized photographic paper.

Johann Heinrich Schulze (1687-1744)

Before 1700 it was the camera obscura and the magic lantern that provided the means to copy a scene. By 1725 advances on the light sensitivity of silver salts were being made by the German chemist Johann Heinrich Schulze. Schulze, who was also a natural philosopher. He found that light darkened a chalk solution with silver nitrate. Although they were not permanent, he produced contact copies from stencils. From these beginnings modern photography was born.

Joseph-Nicéphore Niépce (1765-1833)

In 1826 Joseph-Nicéphore Niépce, a wealthy Frenchman and experimenter, used as early as 1816 a camera with a lens and bellows. He sought a camera-made image that would also serve as a printing plate and alternative substances that would provide a direct positive. In 1826 Niépce produced the world's first photograph from nature, a scene taken of a landscape view from the window of his home. He called his process *heliography,* a form of photography. He used a polished pewter plate coated with bitumen of Judea to capture the scene.

Louis J. M. Daguerre (1787-1851)

Great strides were made as a result of the short partnership Niépce had with Louis J. M. Daguerre. In 1839 French artist and inventor Daguerre created the *daguerreotype* camera and made this turning point public. The invention caused quite a stir, much general excitement, and a surge of business in the photography trade. However, exposures took twenty to thirty minutes in bright sunshine, the photographic equipment was bulky, and more importantly it produced only one original, whereby no copies could be produced. Also, the copper plate, the "film," had to be held at a certain angle to catch the image. Engravings and paintings had to be copied from a daguerreotype in order to replicate the scene. Nevertheless it was an important milestone.

William Henry Fox Talbot (1800-1877)

It was left to an aristocratic Englishman, William Henry Fox Talbot, to open the era of a negative-positive system of photographing images. Talbot experimented with the action of light on chemically coated paper and strove to fix these images by chemical means to the paper. His work made it possible to produce numerous positive prints from original negatives in the camera. Talbot accomplished this in a process he called *talbotype,* or *calotype,* and patented it in 1840.

In 1843, Talbot established the first printing company where professional photographs were mass-produced. Although the printed image lacked detail and sharpness it was popular with tourists because of its light weight. Already, in 1846, prints taken of hieroglyphs were published in a booklet by Talbot entitled "The Talbotype Applied to Hieroglyphics."

Frederick Scott Archer (1813-1857)

An advancement followed called the *wet-collodion process,* which caused the eventual demise of daguerreotype and talbotype photography. When the quickly processed wet-collodion glass plate was presented in 1851 by Frederick Scott Archer, an English professional photographer, portrait studio photographers were elated. However, landscape and monument photographers were not. Even with the new process, they were still burdened by the weight of the photographic field equipment including lugging the camera, a supply of glass plates, tripod, several lenses, dishes, scales and weights, glass measures and funnels, a rinsing water pail, a portable dark room such as a tent, and a box full of bottled chemicals with which to coat, sensitize, develop, and fix the glass negatives. This was toted in a wheelbarrow, or small cart, or some of it kept in a moored boat. An improvement came, when paper was pre-sensitized.

Claude Félix Abel Niépce de Saint Victor (1805-1870)

In the late 1840s, Claude Félix Abel Niépce de Saint Victor, a French calvary office and inventor, developed the *albumen-on-glass* process, a modification of the bitumen-on-pewter-plate process of his cousin Nicéphore Niépce. Niépce de Saint-Victor produced a glass plate coated with an extract of egg white containing potassium iodide. When the plate was dry it was sensitized by an acid solution of silver nitrate. After exposure, which took five to fifteen minutes depending on the view, it was developed with gallic acid. The end result reproduced architectural images with minute detail. This process was also used for making glass lantern slides.

Photographic Processes Represented In the Exhibition

Salt Print

Before the advent of the albumen print in the 1850s, early photographs were commonly made on good sheets of salted paper where images were embedded in the paper fibers. Such positive prints were mostly made by the action of light on paper impregnated with sodium chloride, or common table salt, and gelatin in water. Before finally being used the salted paper was put in a solution of silver nitrate and acids in the dark to sensitize it and dried. The paper was then exposed under a similarly prepared negative ("film") in the daylight. The result was a positive image that was toned in a chemical bath, fixed in hypo, washed in water and dried. A deep, warm, brown-toned image resulted. However the prints were often on the light side without much contrast. It was to take another advance of the coating of the paper with egg white, which held more of the silver, to bring forth better detail.

Albumen Print

The most common type of photographic print in the Nineteenth Century was the *albumen print*. A photographic image was no longer embedded in the paper fibers, but was now suspended on the paper surface. The process, introduced in 1850 by the French amateur photographer **Louis Désirée Blanquart-Evrard (1802-1872)**, involved coating thin paper with an extract of egg white, a substance that made the surface glossy and smooth. A company in Dresden, Germany used as many as 60,000 eggs each day to coat their paper! The next step included sensitizing the paper with a sodium nitrate solution, then exposing it under a glass negative, usually a collodion-on-glass negative, in the daylight. The result, which appeared from the action of light on the sensitized paper, was a positive albumen print.

At first photographers had sensitized their own paper, but by the early 1870s such ready-sensitized albumen paper was commercially available much like photographic paper today. The paper was also used for photographs for *carte de visite* and stereoviews. This pre-sensitized paper was used until the early 1900s. This was a faster technique for developing prints than previous methods. Mass produced photographs were on their way.

Collodion-on-Glass

The *collodion-on-glass* process was the most common negative technique until around the 1880s. Before the photograph was taken the glass plates were coated with collodion, a tacky substance causing light-sensitive silver salts to attach themselves. The glass plates were then exposed to light in a camera, which took five to fifteen minutes depending on the view. Next the glass plate negative image was developed in chemical baths. No further chemical development was necessary. Most negatives were produced by the "wet-plate negative" process. This meant the plates had to be prepared just before exposure and then quickly developed afterward, while the plates were still wet. For this reason photographers had to carry all of their equipment and chemicals with them while photographing sites along the Nile.

The albumen print was a great improvement as it produced more tonal variations and detail. However the time element was still a concern, particularly for portraiture.

Silver Prints

The introduction of the *gelatin-on-glass* negative process destroyed the popularity of albumen prints. In the process, paper was covered with a gelatin emulsion containing silver, which produced a gelatin silver paper. The paper varied in thickness from thin to thick with a glossy surface. Also produced was a paper coated with silver bromide suspended in gelatin called silver bromide paper. It came in a variety of thickness, color tones, and textures. Although the paper was much easier to handle, it lacked the tonal qualities of albumen paper.

Platinum Prints

The *platinum print* was developed commercially in the 1870s. The paper has a matte surface and produces subtle tones. The photographic image is not suspended on the paper surface, but embedded in its fibers. In this process paper is sensitized with iron salts and exposed in contact with a negative until a pale form results. When the paper is developed the iron salts are replaced with platinum, which creates a more defined image and the most stable of metal-based prints. Prints are also made with a mixture of platinum and palladium. This material is less expensive as it conserves the amount of the more costly platinum to make a print. Eventually the cheaper *palladium prints* eclipsed the platinums.

Other photographic Images

Postcards

Since their beginning in the 1890s they were the most popular printed photographic items bought in Egypt and elsewhere. Picture postcards possessed a good depth of field, were colored, and were of the most visited sites and places in Egypt. The cards were inexpensive, educational keepsakes, and a perfect medium of communication for travellers.

Stereoviews

Stereoscopic photography began in earnest in the 1850s. The advantage of the photographic double image was its ability to capture forms at various distances in the eyes of a viewer that made a scene appear three dimensional in a stereoviewer. A common medium for stereoviews was the albumen print, generally favored for its warm tones.

A stereoview is composed of two almost twin photographic images. The two prints are taken with a special camera, with two lenses that are an eye-width apart, and the negatives are exposed at the same time. Some are printed on heavy card stock, and some are taken on paper such as the albumen print and attached to heavy card stock. When one looks into a stereoviewer the image appears in three dimension. The image has a depth of field and an impression of reality. Stereoviews were popular from the 1850s through the 1920s.

Figure A–3. Statue of King Khafre, Dynasty IV, in Egyptian Museum, Cairo.

Original stereoview
Underwood & Underwood Publishers, 1908
McClung Museum: 1998.10.4.10
Gift of Friends of Egyptology, 1998

Figure A–4. Temple of Luxor Entrance

Original glass lantern slide, circa 1900
Courtesy Special Collections, The University of Tennessee

Lantern Slides

In 1850 transparent positive albumen-coated glass plates were patented as lantern slides. Later wet-collodion and dry plates were used. The image on the glass plate was projected onto a suitable surface by a projector, or " magic lantern." Lantern slides were commercially produced and widely used by lecturers, for home entertainment, scientific study, or educational purposes. Compared to photographs on paper they could be shown to a larger audience.

Note

[1]Frith, "Egypt and Palestine," p 32.

Selected Bibliography

Baldwin, Gordon, *Looking at Photographs. A Guide to Technical Terms.* Malibu/London: J. Paul Getty Museum in association with the British Museum Press, 1991.

Darrah, William C., *The World of Stereographs.* Gettysburg: W. C. Darrah, 1977.

Frith, Francis, "Egypt and Palestine" in *The British Journal of Photography*, February 1, 1960.

Mannheim, L.A., Principal Technical Editor, *Focal Encyclopedia of Photography*. New York: McGraw-Hill Book Company, 1969.

Photography from 1839 to Today: George Eastman House, Rochester, NY. Koln: Benedikt Taschen Verlag , 1999.

Welling, William, *Collectors' Guide to Nineteenth-Century Photographs.* New York: Macmillan Publishing Co., Inc., New York and London: Collier Macmillan Publishers, 1976.

Appendix B
Additional Bibliography

Andrieu, Jules, *Catalogue Historique et Descriptif des Vues Stéréoscopiques de Palestine, de Syrie et d'Égypte.* Paris: self published, 1869.

Bedford, Francis, *Photographic Pictures of Egypt the Holy Land and Syria, Constantinople, the Mediterranean, Athens, etc., by Francis Bedford, During a Tour in the East, in Which, by Command He Accompanied His Royal Highness the Prince of Wales.* London 1863.

Bird, Michael, *Samuel Shepheard of Cairo.* London: Michael Joseph, 1957.

Bonfils, Félix, *Catalogue des vues photographiques de l'Orient: Égypte..., photographiees et éditees par Bonfils Félix.* Alais: A. Brugeirolle et Compagnie, 1876.

Cammas, Henri & André Lefevre, *La Vallée du Nil: Impressions and Photographies.* Paris: Hachette, 1862.

Du Camp, Maxime, *Égypte, Nubie, Palestine et Syrie.* Paris: Gide et Baudry, 1852.

Fagan, Brian, *The Rape of the Nile: tomb robbers, tourists, and archaeologists in Egypt.*New York: Scribner, 1975.

Flaubert, Gustave, Francis Steegmuller (trans. & ed.), *Flaubert in Egypt: a Sensibility on Tour.* Chicago: Academy Chicago, 1987.

Frith, Francis, *Egypt and Palestine Photographed and Described,* Vols I-II. London: J.S. White, 1857.

———, *Egypt, Nubia and Ethiopia Illustrated.* London: Elder Smith, 1862.

———, *Lower Egypt and Ethiopia.* London: W. Mackenzie, 1862

———, *Upper Egypt and Ethiopia.* London:W. Mackenzie, 1862.

Gavin, Carney E. S., "Bonfils and the Early Photography of the Near East" in *Harvard Library Bulletin,* Vol. XXVI, no. 4, October 1978.

Gordon, Lady Duff, *Letters from Egypt.* New York/ Washington: Frederick A. Praeger, 1969.

Greene, John Bulkley, *Le Nil-Monuments-Paysages-Explorations photographiques.* Lille: Blanquart-Evrard, 1854.

Horeau, Hector, *Panorama d'Égypte et de Nubie.* Paris 1941.

Jammes, André and Marie-Therese Jammes, "Egypt in Flaubert's Time: the First Photographers, 1839–1860" in *Aperture* 78 (1977).

Marden, Philip S., *Egyptian Days.* Boston; New York: Houghton Mifflin Company, 1912.

Onne, Eyal, *The Photographic Heritage of the Holy Land 1839-1914.* Manchester: Manchester Polytechnic, 1980.

Osman, Colin, *Egypt Caught in Time.* Cairo: The American University in Cario Press, 1999.

Perez, Nissan N., *Focus East. Early Photography in the Near East (1839-1885).* New York: Harry N. Abrams, In., Publishers, in association with the Domino Press, Jerusalem, and the Israel Museum, Jerusalem, 1988.

Prime, William C., *Boat Life in Egypt and Nubia.* New York: Harper & Brothers, 1897.

Rouge, Emmanuel, *Album photographique de la mission remplie en Égypte par le Vte. E. de Rouge...1863, 1864.* Paris: L. Samson, 1865.

Schaaf, Larry, "Charles Piazzi Smyth's 1865 Conquest of the Great Pyramid" in *History of Photography,* Vol. 3, no. 4, October 1979.

Smyth, Charles Piazzi, *A Poor Man's Photography of the Great Pyramid.* London: Henry Greenwood, 1870.

———, *Descriptive Album of Photographs of the Great Pyramid.* Manchester: Pollitt, 1879.

Talbot, William Henry Fox, "The Talbotype Applied to Hieroglyphs" (booklet). London 1846.

Teynard, Félix, *Égypte et Nubie, Sites et Monuments les Plus Intéressants pour l'Étude de l'Art et de l'Histoire.* Paris: Goupil & Cie., 1858.

Thomas, Nancy, *et al, The American Discovery of Egypt.* Los Angeles: Los Angeles County Museum of Art, 1995.

Thomas, Ritchie, "Some 19th Century Photographs in Syria, Palestine and Egypt" in *History of Photography 3,* January 1979.

Thompson, Joseph Parrish, *Photographic views of Egypt, past and present.* Boston: J.P. Jewett and Company, 1854.

Vaczek, Louis and Gail Buckland, *Travelers in Ancient Lands.* Boston: New York Graphic Society, 1981.

Van Haaften, Julia and Jon Manchip White, *Egypt and the Holy Land in Historic Photographs, 77 Views by Francis Frith.* New York: Dover, 1980.

Warner, Charles D., *My Winter On the Nile.* Boston: Houghton, Mifflin and Company, 1891.

Wortham, John D., *The Genesis of British Egyptology, 1549–1906.* Norman: University of Oklahoma Press, 1971.

Title List of Original Photographs

Catalogue Number	Title/Description	Size in inches (width x height)	Figure No.	Page No.
Facing Title Page:				
3/655:	"Sphinx Armachis No.11 Phot. Art. G. Lekegian & Co."	10-1/4 x 7-3/4	1	ii
Age of Discovery:				
1/655:	"Edition Photoglob 5025. Alexandrie la Colonne Pompée."	8 x 10-1/2	3-2	14
1996.10.1:	"No. 39- Obélisque d'Héliopolis à Matariah P. Sebah, Phot."	10-3/8 x 13-3/4	3-3	15
A1: 161 C136 9P:	"Caire. Pyramide de Guizeh."	10-3/4 x 7-1/2	3-4	15
A1: 121 C136 8P:	"Zangaki N. 411 Pyramide de Guizeh"	11 x 8	3-5	16
A1: 121 C136 1P:	"Zangaki N. 448 Sphinx de Pyramides"	11-7/8 x 7-7/8	3-6	16
1996.9.4:	"Ramses II" and "Statue de Sesostris a Sakara ... Caire No. 717 H. Arnoux"	10-3/4 x 8-1/4	3-8	17
4/655:	"Sakkarah (Pyramide) No. 20 Photog. Art. G Lekegian & Co."	10-3/4 x 8-1/4	3-9	17
1996.10.3:	"No. 137 Saqqarah, Tombeau de Ti H. Béchard"	14-3/4 x 10-1/2	3-10	18
1/697:	"Interieur du tombeau de Ti à Zakarah 525 J.P. Sebah"	10-1/2 x 8-1/4	3-11	18
1996.10.7:	"A. Beato 48" [in print] and "Façade of Temple at Abydos" [in ink on mount]	14-5/8 x 10-3/8	3-13	20
1996.10.5:	"Zangaki No. 616 Triomphant Seti les ablimes de la Roqxute"	9 x 11	3-14	21
1996.9.5:	"Zangaki No. 619 Abydos Interieur du temple"	10-3/4 x 8-5/8	3-15	21
1997.5.6 :	"Frith No. 10 1857" [in print]; "PORTICO OF THE TEMPLE OF DENDERA" [printed on mount]	9 x 6-1/4	3-18	22
1996.10.8:	"733 Dendérah temple (pris du Sud Ouest) J P. Sebah"	10-5/8 x 8-3/8	3-19	23
1996.10.9:	"Zangaki No. 728 Isis (Dendérah)"	8-1/2 x 10-1/8	3-20	23
5/698:	"No. 1012 Dendérah Phot. Art. G. Lekegian & Co."	8-1/4 x 10-3/4	3-21	23
1997.5.11:	"Thèbes Tombeaux des Rois J. P. Sebah"	10-5/8 x 8-3/8	3-24	25
1996.10.12:	"Publishers Photo Services, Inc." and "608 Egypt. At King Tuts Tomb, in the Valley of the tombs of the Kings, where twenty dynasties are buried." [printed on border]	9-1/4 x 7-1/2	3-25	25
10/655:	"Edition Photoglob 5528. Thèbes les C..."	10-1/2 x 8-1/4	3-26	26
1996.10.11:	"Zangaki N. 951 Thèbes Tableau dans le tombe de roi N 15"	8-5/8 x 11	3-27	26
6/697:	"A. Beato" [in print]; "271 Tombeau Nakht" [in pencil on back]	8 x 10-1/4	3-28	26
11/655:	"1038 (Thèbes) Deir-el-Bahari. Chambre de la vache. Porte de Thotmès II. Phot. Art..."	11 x 7-1/2	3-29	27
A1: 221 18th dyn. 9:	No caption	7 x 9-1/2	3-31	28
1997.5.7:	"A. Beato" [backwards in print]; "1045 Medinet-Habu Les prisonniers de Ramses" [in pencil on back]	7-3/4 x 9-3/4	3-34	29
1996.10.18:	"121. Medinet-Abou Galerie de la Deuxieme Cour H. Béchard"	10-1/2 x 14-3/4	3-35	29
1996.10.16:	"Bonfils 57"[in print]; "57 Royal Pavillion of Rameses III., and Temple of Medinet-Abu." and "Egypte." and "Bonfils. Phot. Beyrouth Syrie" and "Charles Taber & Co. New Bedford, Mass." [printed on mount]	10-7/8 x 8-3/4	3-37	30
1996.10.14:	"75 Thèbes Ramesseion (vue generale) J.P. Sebah"	10-5/8 x 8-1/4	3-38	30
3/697:	"Peridis No. 1108 Thèbes Ramseon"	11 x 9-1/2	3-39	31
1996.10.15:	"No 109 Thèbes, Temple de Ramaseum, Intérieur de la Salle Hypostile H. Béchard"	10-1/2 x 14-7/8	3-40	31
16/655:	"(Karnak) Piliers de Thoutmès III. Papyrus et Lotus. 1102 Photog. Artistique G. Lekegian & Co."	8-3/4 x 11	3-42	32
1996.10.19:	"Publishers Photo Service, Inc. 541. Egypt. Karnak. The entrance Pylon of the Karnak Temple."[printed on border]; "39147" [in print]	9-1/4 x 7-1/2	3-43	32
19/655:	"Edit. Schroeder & Cie Zurich 5489. Karnak Pylone de Horemheb et les Colos...."	10-1/4 x 8-1/4	3-44	33
20/655:	"Luxor. Ramesses II 1072 Photogr. Artistique G. Lekegian & Co."	8-3/4 x 10-3/4	3-46	34

Catalogue Number	Title/Description	Size in inches (width x height)	Figure No.	Page No.
1997.5.14:	"Zangaki No. 956 Luksor Stastue de la femme de Ramses"	8-1/2 x 10-7/8	3-47	34
1997.5.12:	"Frith" [in print]; "ENTRANCE TO THE GREAT TEMPLE-Luxor." [printed on mount]	6-1/4 x 8-1/2	3-48	35
1997.5.13:	"Zangaki No. 975 Louxor ensemble des colonnades"	10-5/8 x 8-1/4	3-49	35
1997.5.15:	"Frith No. 42 1857" [in print]; "Frith. Photo. 1857;"and "CLEOPATRA'S TEMPLE AT ERMENT" [printed on mount]	6-1/4 x 9	3-50	36
1999.2.2:	"Zangaki No. 1018 Esneh Colones du temple"	10-3/8 x 8-1/8	3-51	36
1996.10.23:	"860 Edfou le Sanctuaire J P Sebah"	10-5/8 x 8-1/4	3-52	37
A1: 161 C136 2E:	"Zangaki No. 1039 Edfou le couronnement"	8 x 10-7/8	3-53	37
1996.10.22:	No caption; "No. 54 Edfou Le Pronaos" and "Beato" [in pencil on back]	11-1/8 x 8	3-54	37
1997.5.16:	"Edfou" [on board] and "Vue generale du temple" [in ink on mount]	11-7/8 x 9-1/4	3-55	37
1997.5.19:	"Frith" [in print]; "KOUM OMBO- From the North East" [printed on mount]	8-3/8 x 6	3-56	38
1996.9.8:	No caption; "63 Kom Ombo Le Courennement de Ptolomee" [in pencil on back]	10-3/8 x 8	3-57	38
A1: 161 A849 1A:	"Peridis No. 1135 Assouan"	11 x 8-1/2	3-58	39
A1: 161 A849 1A:	"7. A. MARQUEZ Asswan"	10-1/4 x 7-3/4	3-59	39
A1: 161 A849 1A:	"Assouan. Première Cataracte Lichtenstern et Harari, Cairo."	9 x 6-3/4	3-60	40
2/698:	"880. Phylae: vue generale des temples J. P. Sebah"	10-3/8 x 8-1/2	3-61	40
25/655:	"Zangaki No. 1074 Phylae ..."	11 x 8-1/2	3-62	41
3/698:	"Phylae (colonnades) J. P. Sebah 897"	11 x 8-1/4	3-63	41
A1: 161 P578 1P:	"No. 33 (Registered) PHYLAE, THE INUNDATED ISLAND Lichtenstern & Harari, Cairo."	9 x 6-3/4	3-64	41
1997.5.21:	No caption; "Inscription giving the same decree as the Rosetta, but only in Hieroglyphic and Coptic. Philae." [in ink on mount]	8-1/4 x 9-3/4	3-65	42
1996.10.28:	"No. 105. Temple de Debod. Nubie P. Sebah Phot."	14-5/8 x 10-3/8	3-68	43
1996.10.29:	"934: Nubie: Kalabcheh portique du temple J P Sebah"	10-5/8 x 8-1/4	3-69	43
1997.5.22:	"Frith" [in print]; "THE TEMPLE OF KALABSHE, Nubia" [printed on mount]	8-3/4 x 6-1/8	3-70	44
1997.5.25:	"Frith No. 11 1857" [in print]; "Frith. Photo. 1857 THE TEMPLE OF MAHARRAKA, Nubia" [printed on mount]	8-5/8 x 6-1/8	3-71	44
1996.10.27:	"949 Abu Simbel. Statues ramesses II. (Nubie 949)" and " J. P. Sebah"	10-5/8 x 8-1/4	3-74	46
1997.5.24:	No caption; "Beato" [in pencil on back]	10-1/4 x 8	3-75	46
1997.5.23:	"A. Beato" [in print]	10-1/4 x 8	3-76	46

Funds Are Established

A1: 161 C136 1P	Mr. and Mrs. Louis Bailey Audigier	8-3/4 x 6-1/2	4-15	56

The Creation of the Cairo Museum:

A1: 621 Egypt 5S:	No caption	3-1/2 x 9-1/2	6-2	72
A1: 221 18th dyn. 83:	No caption	7 x 9-1/2	6-3	74
A1: 221 3rd dyn. 5N5R:	No caption	7 x 9-1/2	6-4	74
A1: 521 Old King. C3.2:	No caption	7 x 9-1/2	6-6	75
A1: 521 4th dyn. C3.3:	No caption	9-1/4 x 7	6-7	76
A1: 221 25th dyn. 5A:	No caption	3-1/2 x 9-1/2	6-8	76
1996.10.2:	"204 (Mus: de Ghiseh____ d'un Secretaire... Ank...J.P. Sebah"	8-1/2 x 10-5/8	6-9	76
927/A1:	No caption	3-1/2 x 5-3/4	6-11	77
1/696:	"Bonfils 1 203 Vache trouvée á Sakara dans le tombeau d'Ephto Stoptep"	11 x 8-1/2	6-12	78
A1: 321 3-4th dyn. 9:	No caption	9-1/4 x 3-1/2	6-13	78
A1: 521 Roman Period C3.4:	No caption	7 x 9-1/4	6-14	78
A1: 521 Roman Period C3.5:	No caption	7 x 9-1/4	6-14	78
A1: 621 12th dyn. 1:	No caption	9-1/2 x 3-1/2	6-15	79
A1: 221 18 5T:	No caption	7 x 9-1/2	6-16	79

Catalogue Number	Title/Description	Size in inches (width x height)	Figure No.	Page No.
A1: 221 26th dyn. 4:	No caption	9-1/2 x 3-3/8	6-17	79
A1: 521 19th dyn. C3.7:	No caption	9 x 7	6-18	80
A1: 521 19th dyn. C3.9:	No caption	7 x 9-1/2	6-19	80

Dealers Scoundrels and Fakers:

A1: 521 Ptol.Per. C3.8:	No caption	9-1/2 x 7	7-5	85

Town and Desert Life:

A1: 161 C136 1C:	"LE CAIRE Tombeaux des Mammlouks Lichtenstern & Harari, Cairo"	9 x 6-3/4	8-6	91
A1: 161 C136 3C:	"Caire. Mosquée Kait-Bey	8 x 10-3/4	8-12	92
A1: 161 C136 2EA:	"Zangaki No. 1618 Interieur Mosquee El Azhar"	11 x 8-1/2	8-13	93
A1: 161 C136 8C:	"Caire. Café arabe	10-1/2 x 8-1/4	8-14	93
28/655:	"Edition Photoglob 5215. Environs de Bedouin"	10-3/4 x 8	8-15	93
A1: 161 C136 1C:	"Zangaki No. 547 Sakihe tournée par une chameau"	10-3/4 x 8-1/4	8-16	94
A1: 161 C136:	"Zangaki No. 708 Haute-Egypte Jeunes filles vendeuses d'eau"	8 x 11	8-17	94
A1: 157 P179:	"15,126. P.Z.-CHEIK BÉDOUINE DE PALMYRE."	6-1/2 x 9	8-18	94
A1: 161 E28:	"No. 31 (Registered) BICHARIS HUT Lichtenstern & Harari, Cairo."	9 x 6-3/4	8-19	94
A1: 161 C136 1P:	"Zangaki No. 410 La retoure des Pyramides"	11 x 8-1/4	8-20	95
1997.5.3:	"K.M. Topous Speaks several languages c/o address P. O. Box. No. 9 Cairo"	8-1/4 x 10-3/4	8-21	95
3/696:	"Zangaki No. 435 Ascension de la grande Pyramide"	8-3/4 x 11-1/4	8-22	95
22/655:	"EDIT. PHOTOGLOB 5493. Luxor-Hotel"	8 x 10-3/4	8-25	96
1999.2.1:	"Zangaki 214 Dahabie sur le Nil Egypte"	10-3/4 x 8-1/4	8-28	97
27/655:	"Edition Photoglob 5632 Ge...."	10-3/4 x 8	8-30	97

Photographic Studios and Sellers:

A1: 521 12th dyn.. 7:	No caption	9-1/2 x 3-1/2	9-1	102
A1: 621 18th dyn. 5:	No caption	9-1/2 x 7	9-3	103
A1: 521 19th dyn. 7:	No caption	9-1/2 x 3-3/8	9-4	103
A1: 521 18th dyn. C3.10:	No caption	9-1/2 x 7	9-4	104
A1: 158 D155 95:	"672 Femmes musulmanes syriennes, costume de ville Bonfils"	8-1/4 x 10-3/4	9-5	104
A1: 158 D155 A5:	"685 Jeune fille du Liban en costume de féte Bonfils"	8-1/4 x 10-3/4	9-6	105
A1: 158 D155 A5:	"679 Jeune fille du liban coiffée du tentour Bonfils"	8-1/4 x 10-3/4	9-8	105
A1: 157 A658:	"15,127. P. Z.- BEDOUINES"	6-1/2 x 9	9-9	106

Index

Page numbers in *italics* indicate figures.